THIS

Love

WE

SHARE

THIS
Love
WE
SHARE

Daily Devotional Teachings to Bring
Wholeness to Your Marriage

HARRY & EMILY GRIFFITH

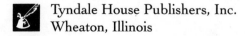 Tyndale House Publishers, Inc.
Wheaton, Illinois

Unless otherwise indicated, Scripture quotations contained herein are taken from the *Holy Bible,* Revised Standard Version, copyright © 1946, 1952, 1971 by the Division of Christian Education of the National Council of the Churches of Christ in the United States of America, and are used by permission. All rights reserved.

Scripture quotations marked NIV are taken from the the *Holy Bible,* New International Version®. Copyright © 1973, 1978, 1984 by International Bible Society. Used by permission of Zondervan Publishing House. All rights reserved. The "NIV" and "New International Version" trademarks are registered in the United States Patent and Trademark Office by International Bible Society. Use of either trademark requires permission of International Bible Society.

Scripture quotations marked TEV are taken from the *Good News Bible,* Today's English Version, copyright © 1966, 1971, 1976 by American Bible Society, and are used by permission.

Library of Congress Cataloging-in-Publication Data

Griffith, Harry C.
    This love we share : daily devotions to bring wholeness to your marriage / Harry and Emily Griffith.
      p.   cm.
    Includes index.
    ISBN 0-8423-7161-3 (softcover)
    1. Married people—Prayer-books and devotions—English.
2. Devotional calendars.   3. Marriage—Religious aspects—
Christianity—Meditations.   I. Griffith, Emily, date   .
II. Title.
BV4596.M3G75   1995
242'.644—dc20   95-4700

Printed in the United States of America

00 99 98 97 96 95
7   6   5   4   3   2   1

INTRODUCTION

No union on earth, other than our relationship with God himself, equals marriage in importance or potential. It is a relationship ordained by God, a covenant in which God himself is a partner. Therefore, as a man and woman seek to bring wholeness to their marriage and family life, they do so in full recognition of their responsibility not only to one another but also to God. For those who understand the essential nature of this commitment, daily teachings on marriage, presented from a scriptural point of view, can lead to wholeness in the relationship.

This Love We Share provides a year of biblically based teachings about marriage. Because the material is not dated for a particular year, it may be undertaken at any time and used year after year. Designed for married couples to read together, this book is equally beneficial for individual use when schedules conflict. Husband and wife may choose to have their own copies anyway so that each spouse may read the day's material at a convenient time. The index helps couples find where certain topics are covered in this book.

This Love We Share is also ideal for marriage support groups or couples' Bible studies. Such groups will find the "Today's Thought" section most helpful in sparking weekly discussion among study members.

Some teachings in this book are primarily spiritual in nature; others are primarily practical. The primarily spiritual teachings, however, all relate directly to marriage and family; the primarily practical teachings are approached from a scriptural point of view.

Because we live at a time when the world constantly assaults marriage and family values, Christian couples need all the help they can get in building strong foundations and strengthening their marriages. *This Love We Share* will assist couples as they build upon their relational foundation, no matter how long they've been married. Even with our society's staggering divorce statistics, evidence remains that the overwhelming majority of Christian marriages will survive if the couples pray together, read Scripture daily, and are regular in worship. *This Love We Share* provides substantial help in meeting this challenge.

The 365 devotional teachings of this book come from almost forty years of married life and also from the teachings of others (we've mentioned names when appropriate), marriage-enrichment sessions, books, and articles. Additionally, we've incorporated suggestions from friends whose marriages have been especially good examples for us.

To all who have helped us in our many years of marriage and in compiling this book, we express our deep gratitude.

Harry and Emily Griffith

January

If we hope for what we do not see, we wait for it with patience.
Romans 8:25

Upon entering a marriage-enrichment program, a husband wrote a love letter to his wife, expressing the feelings and thoughts he had as he began this particular venture in faith. In the following excerpts, he shares his hopes and dreams. They are ones we can see fulfilled in our own marriage if we patiently wait for them and work together as a team.

I hope to gain a better marriage, but I have specific hopes that reach much further than that general statement. I hope to learn to be more sensitive to you and your needs. I hope to be able to communicate better. I hope to learn how to share with you the things we should share in a way that is helpful to you as well as to me.

I want to learn how to make our marriage more of the covenant it is intended to be. I want us to be on the same spiritual wavelength. I want us to be able to pray together for those concerns we jointly share. I want us to be more of a "team" without losing our individuality that makes life interesting. ❦

*T*ODAY'S THOUGHT: *What hopes do you have as you begin this venture of faith?*

Love

Pour out your heart before him. Psalm 62:8

The Psalms are the great reservoir of feelings in the Bible. Time and again, the psalmists speak from the heart. Whether we are uplifted in joy or in the depths of despair, we can find a psalm to speak to our particular feelings. And feelings are an integral part of life together as a married couple.

Our feelings say much about who we are. Many times we substitute "I am" for "I feel": "I am happy" means "I feel happy." Feelings come from the core of our being and, as someone once said, "Feelings are neither right nor wrong, they just are."

A prime requirement of a happy marriage is to accept the feelings of our spouse. When we question our loved one's feelings, we are denying who he or she is. Although we may wish our spouse didn't feel a certain way about a situation or person, we had best not say, "You shouldn't feel that way." There's no faster way to stifle effective communication. On the other hand, getting to the root of the feeling and helping our spouse work through that feeling can be very constructive. ❦

*T*ODAY'S THOUGHT: *How do you feel?*

Love

Judge not, that you be not judged. Matthew 7:1

In married life, it's important to distinguish between *feelings* and *thoughts*. A *feeling* is a response to a stimulus. A *thought* is a product of mental activity. If a sentence makes the same sense by substituting "I think" for "I feel," the person has expressed a judgment, not a feeling. If I say to my spouse, "I feel you are in the wrong on this," I really am reaching a judgment about my spouse and not expressing a feeling.

As husband and wife, we must be careful we don't take liberties with our freedom to express feelings. However, in order to have effective communication within marriage, it's important for us to be able to express our feelings in an unchallenged manner. Men, in particular, need to be encouraged to express their feelings. As we grow in marriage, let's try not to get thoughts and feelings confused with one another. ❦

*T*ODAY'S THOUGHT: *Are you willing to try to catch yourself today erroneously substituting* think *for* feel, *and vice versa?*

Love

Let no one deceive you with empty words. Ephesians 5:6

It's time for a motive check. Before we share our feelings with our spouse, we need to make sure we don't have a selfish purpose in mind. Sometimes when we say, "I feel rejected," what we really mean is, "You are rejecting me." There is a more profound (and more fair!) way to say the same thing: "I feel unlovable."

Sharing also doesn't mean we can *use* a feeling. We can punish our spouse by saying, "Don't do that; you know how it makes me feel!" But we don't attain successful communication by punishing; rather, we grow closer through genuine sharing.

Finally, we need to avoid the trap of putting a "because" after expressing our feeling. When we say "because . . . ," we dump garbage and turn a feeling into a judgment.

God does not rejoice in deception via "empty words." But he claps his hands in joy when we legitimize our feelings by sharing them with our loved ones, thus leading to better understanding. ❦

*T*ODAY'S THOUGHT: *Have a "practice session" with one another on how to express feelings effectively.*

JANUARY 5 *Love*

You of little faith, why are you so afraid? Matthew 8:26 NIV

We are told not to be afraid many times in Scripture. Yet, even in our love relationship, we exhibit our lack of faith through fear of being open and vulnerable with one another. These feelings are typical of the adjustments every husband and wife face.

We disguise our fear behind a variety of masks. Many are public personas we think we take off at home. An example would be a businessperson who wears an "I'm competent, don't mess with me" mask. Just think of the problems it would create if that person forgot to take the mask off before arriving home!

Sometimes we do forget to take our masks off. The important thing is to be aware of our masks and the ways they can prevent effective family communication. As we learn to take our masks off, we will become less fearful toward our spouse and more vulnerable, so that intimacy may grow. 🌿

*T*ODAY'S THOUGHT: *What masks do you wear?*

Love

Try me and know my thoughts! Psalm 139:23

As we learned yesterday, removing our masks helps us to be less fearful. But it also allows us to share ourself more intimately with one another. In order to feel truly loved and accepted, we must reveal our true selves. For better or worse, our spouse is married to us; why not reveal who we really are?

It is in encountering ourselves that we best understand our motivations and prejudices and see what influences our thinking and actions. God knows us just as we are; we can't fool him. Don't we owe it to our spouse to discover and uncover ourselves to him or her too?

A starting point is determining our core mask: the basic mask we wear from time to time. If we can identify that mask, we will learn a great deal about ourselves, and our life together as a couple will be enhanced. ❦

*T*ODAY'S THOUGHT: *What is your core mask?*

JANUARY 7 *Love*

Thou . . . art acquainted with all my ways. Psalm 139:3

As we evaluate ourself so we might be real to our spouse, let us not be overly judgmental. We are fearfully and wonderfully made. As someone put it, "God don't make no junk." While being realistic in assessing our motivations, trying to understand ourselves, and removing our masks, we also need to thank God for who we are and the gifts he has given us.

God not only doesn't make junk, he performs maintenance on what he has made. He will take care of us, even allowing things to happen for our growth. Although we aren't happy when hard times come, in the long run those situations will work together for our good (Romans 8:28). Let us, with our spouse, affirm the graciousness of God in our lives. Let us rejoice in the good we can see in ourself, in one another, and in our marriage. ❦

TODAY'S THOUGHT: *What is the best thing about being you?*

Love

And they become one flesh. Genesis 2:24

It is God's plan that, in marriage, two become one. Often, however, what appear to be happy marriages really consist of two "married singles" living together. Neither has a full view of marriage; they simply do their own thing within the framework of marriage. The two don't become one; they remain two.

Married singleness exists to some extent in all marriages. It is important for each spouse to have "space" to be the special individual God has created him or her to be. We should not be absorbed into the personality of our spouse.

But there's great danger if husband and wife are so absorbed in work, hobbies, and other pursuits not involving their spouse that the marriage becomes secondary to their primary interests. If this is happening to you, note this danger signal and immediately deal with it. Fully share with one another what happens at work. And, to the extent possible, discover hobbies and interests you can pursue together. 🌱

*T*ODAY'S THOUGHT: *In what ways might you be in danger of being a "married single"?*

Love

Rather, speaking the truth in love . . .   Ephesians 4:15

Times come in every marriage when there is no alternative to a good fight. After exhausting all other avenues, it becomes the only way to speak the truth in love. But Christians need appropriate guidelines for such times, in order to keep their marriages God-honoring.

We've found the following principles helpful in our marriage: First, realize there are times when only constructive fighting can clear the air, and that the fight is worth it. Next, be fair. Don't hit below the belt — or put the belt around your own neck. Stick to the subject until you discover the real problem. Don't repeat past history; limit yourself to nothing more than forty-eight hours ago. Don't call each other names; that's character assassination and can do irreparable harm.

Finish the fight. If you don't carry it to its natural conclusion, the whole thing can be a disaster. Finally, hold hands while fighting. ❧

*T*ODAY'S THOUGHT: *Have you and your spouse had a fight recently? Do you think these guidelines would have helped?*

Do not be conformed to this world.   Romans 12:2

Long before we were married—in fact since babyhood—the world has been busily at work, trying to conform us to its idea of marriage. Television especially shapes people's views about marriage (and its alternatives), mostly in unchristian ways. As a result, most couples don't come close to reaching their marriage potential. They have been so conditioned by what the world expects of marriage (and its easy acceptance of divorce) that they're not conscious of what's really possible in their own marriage. As someone wisely said, "They have gone to sleep too close to the edge of the bed."

Thank God that, as Christians, we know there is a better way. By centering our marriage on Christ and learning what we can from godly teachers on the subject, we can refuse to be conformed to the world's idea of marriage and, instead, work toward the full potential God has for us. ❦

*T*ODAY'S THOUGHT: *In what ways have you resisted the ways of the world in your marriage?*

Love

Therefore you also must be ready; for the Son of man is coming at an hour you do not expect. Matthew 24:44

Matthew 24:44, which sounds like an ominous warning, is really an incentive for joyous and expectant living. If we lived each day as though it would be our last one on earth, wouldn't we have a different attitude? Rather than muddling through the day thinking mostly about ourself, wouldn't we be effusive with love and gratitude and forgiveness toward all those around us, especially our spouse?

Consider today to be your final opportunity to let your spouse truly know your love. Say "I love you," instead of angry, critical words; "I forgive you," instead of condemning, resentful words.

Jesus is our Lord, and we know he's coming back. We just don't know when. But if we are prepared, knowing when he'll return really doesn't matter. One way to be prepared is to be in a right relationship within our marriage. Today is the day to confess, repent, forgive, and love as Christ loves us. ❦

*T*ODAY'S THOUGHT: *What would you do differently if you knew today was your last day on earth?*

JANUARY *12* *Love*

If anyone would come after me, he must deny himself.
Matthew 16:24 NIV

Perhaps the greatest gift we have as Christians is that we have been set free from ourself. Christ has not been sacrificed for us merely so we might love ourself, but that we might be freed from self-obsession. That freedom allows us to focus our attention away from ourself and toward the will of God.

God has things for us to do that will inconvenience us, force us to change some of our life patterns, and involve us in the lives of others. It is in breaking free of the domination of our selfish motives that we find freedom indeed.

One of the places where we need to refocus is within our marriage and family. Where is it more important for us to deny our selfish leanings than in this relationship? At home we have the supreme opportunity to sacrifice time, attention, understanding, and effort for the benefit of the ones we love. 🍎

*T*ODAY'S THOUGHT: *What sacrifice of self would God have you make today for your marriage and family?*

Love

May the Lord make your love increase and overflow for each other and for everyone else. 1 Thessalonians 3:12 NIV

If our love for one another within marriage is everything it should be, that love will overflow for the benefit of others. When we have friends who have been happily married longer than we have, their example of love can overflow onto us.

There is a wonderful plaque that says, "The greatest gift a father can give his children is to love their mother." You can reverse the words *father* and *mother* too. Either way, the love that flows within our coupleness overflows to the benefit of our children.

As vital as our marriage is to one another, it goes further than family. The love within our relationship should be such that it overflows onto others with whom we come into contact. As Christians, our lives—our marriages—are examples (witnesses) to others. ❦

*T*ODAY'S THOUGHT: *What sort of overflow is your marriage producing?*

Love

It is my prayer that your love may abound more and more, with knowledge and all discernment. Philippians 1:9

Real love requires growth and maturity. We enter marriage with a lot of unrealistic expectations and illusions about who our spouse really is. If we never grow from that point, our marriage will be shallow and unrewarding.

In Philippians 1:9 Paul is telling us practical knowledge and sensitivity are necessary components of Christian love. Love is not just sentiment; it is rooted in knowledge and understanding.

What does this say to married couples? We need conscious ways of growing in our understanding of one another. That can mean courses on marriage, sensitivity, and communication, or reading books together like this one. In times of marital crisis, it can mean counseling. But, most of all, it means committing time and effort to the relationship itself. If we function closely enough in times of harmony and disharmony, we will have ample opportunity to grow! ❦

*T*ODAY'S THOUGHT: *What, specifically, could you do right now to grow in knowledge and understanding of one another?*

That you may be filled with the knowledge of his [God's] will in all spiritual wisdom and understanding. Colossians 1:9

It's essential for married couples to do all they can to know and understand each other and their relationship. As Christians who are married, we also know it is vital to seek God's will as best we can in those matters affecting our life together (and what matters would not affect our life together?).

There is not space here to go into methods of discerning God's will. Suffice it to say that Bible study, prayer, worship, and fellowship within our community of faith are avenues for us to grow in our understanding of God's will in the life situations we face. The important thing is we must commit ourself to seeking God's will rather than simply going our own way.

The apostle Paul spells out the results of such commitment in the verses that follow Colossians 1:9: We will "lead a life worthy of the Lord, fully pleasing to him, bearing fruit in every good work and increasing in the knowledge of God." We will be "strengthened with all power . . . for all endurance and patience with joy." What more could we ask? 🍂

*T*ODAY'S THOUGHT: *What should you do to better discern God's will in your life?*

Love

In all our distress and persecution we were encouraged about you because of your faith. 1 Thessalonians 3:7 NIV

All around us, family values are being destroyed, couples are living together without the commitment of marriage, and many marriages are ending in divorce. As we stand against those trends, we are clearly in a position of distress and persecution.

In times of darkness and distress, there are two temptations: (1) to blame others for our problems, growing bitter and cynical, and (2) to lapse into self-indulgence as a way to escape the pressures of difficult circumstances. In times of trial, Christians need one another more than ever.

In 1 Thessalonians 3:7ff., the apostle Paul prays that the hearts of those Christians to whom he writes will be strengthened, and he touches upon the miracle of grace that is available to them. As we face uncertain times, God does not expect us to face our problems alone and in our own strength. He promises to supply our needs (Philippians 4:19). But he also wants us to stand together, that he may use us to help stem the tide of ungodly living by showing others a better way. ❦

*T*ODAY'S THOUGHT: *How can you work more effectively together, as a couple, in order to "show others a better way"?*

Love

Consider how many are my foes. Psalm 25:19

Sometimes we feel overwhelmed by the obstacles that lie before us. We are besieged by health problems, financial problems, or relational difficulties.

We may feel defeated because other couples seem to "have it all together," and we do not. (Remember: We have a tendency to compare our inside with other people's outside!) Whatever the reason for our distress, the writer of Psalm 25 assures us that our feelings, situations, sins, and shortcomings are not unique; others have such feelings, as well.

Whatever or whoever our "foes" are, this psalm suggests two essential realities for dealing with them: our own responsibilities and God's faithfulness. In the midst of our pain, we need to be patient, humble, and teachable, looking to God for guidance. Equally important, we need to recall God's compassion and forgiveness in the past and his future promises for those who follow his path. This psalm can help us grow through, as well as go through, the inevitable valleys of life. ❧

*T*ODAY'S THOUGHT: *What foes do you need to deal with today?*

Love

We beseech and exhort you in the Lord Jesus, that as you learned from us how you ought to live and to please God, just as you are doing, you do so more and more. 1 Thessalonians 4:1

How do we please God? With a God-centered life.

We live in an age when self-fulfillment seems to be god. But self-fulfillment is not the focus of the New Covenant into which Christ has called us. We do not live in order to obtain the maximum pleasure for ourself; we are servants of God and of one another.

Paul then points out, in verses 3-8, that sexual purity is of vital importance to Christian married couples. Because we are to love God and our fellow human beings, sexual immorality is out. Violating one's marriage vows wrongs not only one's spouse but the Christian community at large. There is no room for rationalization or justification for sexual activity outside of marriage. Living a holy life (verse 7) means rejecting immorality and living to please God. ❦

*T*ODAY'S THOUGHT: *What can you do to strengthen holy living between your Christian sisters and brothers?*

JANUARY 19

Love

Be renewed in the spirit of your minds. Ephesians 4:23

Our attitudes create our feelings. Good attitudes produce good feelings. In Ephesians 4:17-24, the apostle Paul talks about the new nature we experience when we turn our life over to God.

If we believe our time is in God's hands, we will exhibit a patience and a peace in life that wouldn't otherwise be possible. If, on the other hand, we have a negative attitude, such as believing that what we are doing is more important than what our spouse or other family members may be doing, we'll create an explosion. The feelings of self-importance, impatience, and frustration that proceed from such an attitude will destroy our peace.

In order to pursue home harmony, we need to reconsider our old attitudes. Bad attitudes can be sources of real trouble in our coupleness. Just as our old nature is renewed by Christ, our old attitudes may need renewal, as well. ❧

*T*ODAY'S THOUGHT: *Do you have any bad attitudes? If so, how can you deal with them for the benefit of your marriage?*

Love

Love one another as I have loved you. John 15:12

When we met the person who is now our spouse and "fell in love," we felt very deeply about that person. We were a jumble of feelings as we worked through the process of dating, engagement, wedding plans, and the marriage itself.

But when the newness of passion wears off, we begin to notice faults in our spouse that weren't obvious before. Conflicts arise because we think quite differently. The "feeling" of love may begin to wear thin. We need to remember that, in the long run, love is a decision, not a feeling. It is a gift we bestow on our spouse as we enter the sacrament of marriage. Even when feelings of love are no longer the controlling factor of our relationship, we are committed to give the gift of love to our spouse. ❦

*T*ODAY'S THOUGHT: *In what ways can you love your spouse today?*

Love

Rejoice in your hope, be patient in tribulation, be constant in prayer. Romans 12:12

All of us enter marriage with hope and joy. We're glad to be facing an enticing future with a spouse who loves us and can share our dreams.

But tribulation comes into all lives and into all marriages. Someone has said that crises are not the death of love, but the proof of it. If we are patient in tribulation, we can learn from the tragedies that face us. (Often, tragedies, when viewed after the "heat of the moment," don't even look like crises anymore.) The unhappy events of life test our marriage. But they also can strengthen it, giving us an even stronger foundation on which to grow.

What gets us through our crises is not only the relationship we have with one another, but the relationship we have with a loving God who is right there with us in the midst of all the pain. Don't forget Paul's advice in times of tribulation: "Be constant in prayer." ❦

*T*ODAY'S THOUGHT: *Has your marriage weathered a crisis recently? If so, what did you learn?*

Love

To all God's beloved . . . , who are called to be saints. Romans 1:7

This verse from the beginning of Romans is typical of the way in which the apostle Paul addressed the Christians to whom he wrote. Regardless of the harsh things he might be getting ready to say, he wanted it to be clear he was writing a love letter to God's people.

Likewise, we can read Scripture as a love letter from God to us. The New Testament reflects the lifestyle of love that Jesus and the early Christians followed. A college professor who was an avowed atheist once told his students that he had read the Bible many times and found no value in it at all. One Christian student had the courage to tell him that the Bible is a love letter from God to his people—and that the professor's problem was that he had been reading someone else's mail!

The reading and study of Scripture can come alive for us if we see it as God's love letter to us. Few things can strengthen our marriage better than increasing our knowledge of God through his written Word. The more effectively we read it, the more it will influence our life together. ❦

*T*ODAY'S THOUGHT: *What are you doing individually, as a couple, and as a family to study Scripture regularly (preferably daily)?*

Pray then like this: Our Father . . . Matthew 6:9

John Powell, in his book *He Touched Me,* points out we should approach prayer as communication in a relationship of love, "a speaking and a listening in truth and in trust." Raw honesty is the essential element in the prayer relationship. Powell says that is what locates a person before God.

We are not really offering ourself until we do so within this context of vulnerability. Love demands presence, not presents. Too often our gifts are peace offerings, bribes, or attempted remedies for guilt.

The willingness to be totally vulnerable is the biggest gift a person can bring to a relationship. It is only when we are willing to put our true selves on the line, to be taken for better or for worse, to be accepted or rejected, that true relationship happens—with God, or with our spouse. ❦

*T*ODAY'S THOUGHT: *How open are you willing to be to God? to your spouse?*

Love

But your hearts must be fully committed. 1 Kings 8:61 NIV

When a couple commits to permanent, unconditional love in the sacrament of marriage, that commitment means certain other experiences and activities are no longer possible for that couple. In choosing our spouse as a life partner, we eliminate all others as possible spouses.

Every commitment is like every moment of life: There is birth and death. There is choice, but that choice also involves surrender. One thing is chosen, and, as a result, something else can never be.

In order to love, we pay a price. To love another unconditionally is a lifetime investment. We are putting ourself, all we have, all we are, all we ever will be, on the line, and there is no turning back. Be thankful that our Lord goes with us on the way! ❦

TODAY'S THOUGHT: *Do you show your spouse unconditional love? If so, in what ways?*

JANUARY *25* *Love*

As each has received a gift, employ it for one another, as good stewards of God's varied grace. 1 Peter 4:10

The famed psychiatrist Viktor Frankl said, "True self-esteem and a true sense of identity can be found only in the reflected appraisal of those whom we have loved." St. Francis of Assisi put it this way: "It is in giving that we receive."

It is through the gift of affirmation we know we are loved. If we do not see ourselves as valued by others, we will have no sense of personal value. We gain self-confidence when someone believes in us.

As we give the gift of love to another, we find something of deep, lasting value in our own life. And because the gift of love is from God, we also sense we have been good stewards of that gift when we lavish it generously on our loved ones. Yet, by paradox, we will not receive if we give only to get something in return. The genuine gift of love is an unselfish gift. ❧

*T*ODAY'S THOUGHT: *In this imperfect world, how can you give the perfect gift of love?*

As an example of suffering and patience. James 5:10

Every married couple faces little irritations, such as one spouse squeezing the toothpaste tube in the middle rather than from the bottom or leaving the toilet seat up. These are typical adjustments that every married couple will face.

But is *adjustment* (that is, changing our expectations) the answer? Every marriage will ultimately face major confrontations, so why endure the trivial ones that can be corrected by common courtesy?

Now is the time to learn how to make reasonable compromises within the relationship. Agree to start squeezing the tube at the bottom; remember to put the toilet seat down. After all, "Love is patient and kind" (1 Corinthians 13:4). ❦

*T*ODAY'S THOUGHT: *What minor irritants do you need to negotiate as a couple so that they don't build up lasting resentments?*

Love

For where two or three are gathered in my name, there am I in the midst of them. Matthew 18:20

No prayer group offers as much potential for being in the Lord's will as a couple praying together—or, better still, a family praying together. These are the ideal "two or three gathered." But we don't have to limit our consciousness of the Lord to those times when we intentionally pray together. We can be conscious of his presence in all our discussions and disagreements, in everything we do together. We can decide to act as though Jesus were sitting right there with us (and he is!).

When some couples pray or sit down for a meal, they set an extra place for Jesus. Others end the day by sharing with each other their closest moment to Christ during that day. As we become more conscious of the Lord's presence, our life together is enhanced. ❦

*T*ODAY'S THOUGHT: *What steps can you take to become more conscious of God's presence in your life?*

JANUARY 28 *Love*

He who abides in love abides in God. 1 John 4:16

If we are to abide in love, we need to love ourself. Scripture tells us: "You shall love your neighbor as yourself" (Matthew 22:39). Unfortunately, many people today have bad self-images; they do not love themselves. As someone put it, "The trouble is, we *do* love our neighbors as ourself—poorly!"

There's nothing more important in our love relationship than helping our spouse love himself or herself. John Powell, in his book *The Secret of Staying in Love*, said it this way: "My greatest contribution to your life will be to help you love yourself, to think better and more gently of yourself, to accept your own limitations more peacefully in the perspective of your whole person, which is uniquely valuable."

To give our loved one all he or she might need is beyond us, but we do have an obligation to know what those needs are and to meet them to the best of our ability. Powell sums up this thought by saying, "I will try to read your heart, not your lips." ❧

TODAY'S THOUGHT: *What can you do today to help your spouse love herself/himself?*

Love

You patiently endure the same sufferings that we suffer.
2 Corinthians 1:6

Author Keith Miller has said, "Advice we listen to; pain we obey." Despite what we may sometimes think, pain in and of itself is not an evil to be avoided, but a teacher from which we have a lot to learn. It gets our attention, showing us we had better do something about a matter of importance.

Often pain instructs us, telling us to change our attitudes, habits, or lifestyle. It encourages us to stop acting or thinking one way and start acting or thinking another. If we try to escape from our pain, we are led into addictive behavior, seeking to kill the pain rather than healing it.

God did not promise us a rose garden. In fact, he promised us pain (see, for instance, Luke 21:16-17). As we entered the marriage relationship, we pledged ourself to one another "for richer for poorer, for better for worse, in sickness and in health." We can either try to escape pain until it manifests itself in unhealthy ways, or we can work through pain to healing and wholeness. The choice is up to us. ❦

*T*ODAY'S THOUGHT: *Are you avoiding pain in your life? If so, take time this week to discuss it with each other.*

But be doers of the word, and not hearers only. James 1:22

It's easy to talk about the promises of God and the blessings of being a Christian while failing to face the sacrifices that are inherent in the Christian journey. As someone has said of the Christian faith, "It talks easy but it walks hard."

As Christians, we are called to compassion, sensitivity, concern, and love for others. We are especially called to love our spouse and our children. We can talk forever, but if our actions don't match, our talk is like "a noisy gong or a clanging cymbal" (1 Corinthians 13:1). The way we are to act has been modeled for us by Jesus Christ.

A natural part of Christian growth is an ever-increasing concern for others. People become very important to us. Our prayers are filled with others' pain and suffering. We begin to major in the minor problems of our spouse and children. Love is at the core of the Christian life, and we are called to express that love in action for the benefit of others. ❦

*T*ODAY'S THOUGHT: *How can you be "love in action" to your spouse today?*

JANUARY *31*

Love

Do not be conformed to this world but be transformed by the renewal of your mind. Romans 12:2

The mind, the source of our will and emotions, is the battlefield of life and is therefore frequently addressed in Scripture (see Ephesians 4:22-24; Philippians 4:8; Colossians 3:2). We have as much to unlearn as we have to learn.

It's easy to get caught up in the world's value system because peer pressure affects people of all ages. Every day we are pounded with a variety of worldly propaganda: advertisements, television programs, and conversation.

God seeks to transform our minds so that we may see things, instead, from *his* point of view. To be transformed by the renewing of our minds requires our participation and often includes the painful process of dying to self—something that cannot be done by simply rearranging the externals of our life. However, the good news is that God is with us in the effort. He is in the transforming business. 🐦

*T*ODAY'S THOUGHT: *In what ways are you pressured to conform to some worldly standard? What would help you take the pathway most pleasing to God?*

February

LOVE

Do not be overcome by evil, but overcome evil with good.
Romans 12:21

The Bible gives us wonderful guidelines for living. In Romans 12 Paul tells us that people are given various gifts to use for the benefit of all (verses 4-9) and that we are to mutually depend on one another. Paul then addresses how God's people are to live and serve amid the sea of pressures and problems that confront us, both individually and as a family. Because human nature hasn't changed in almost two thousand years, the principles Paul outlines are fully applicable to Christians today.

Although negative factors do enter our marriage and family relationships, we can overcome evil with good. We can take the "high road": Be genuine in love, honor our loved ones more than ourself, be aglow with the Holy Spirit, rejoice in the hope that is in us, be patient in times of trial, and be constant in prayer. By following Paul's instructions, we will find happiness in the home and be able to thwart the negative influences around us. We can then face life knowing that "he who is in you is greater than he who is in the world" (1 John 4:4). ❦

*T*ODAY'S THOUGHT: *What can you do to promote a positive attitude in your home?*

LOVE

I said, "I will confess my transgressions to the Lord"; then thou didst forgive the guilt of my sin. Psalm 32:5

Confession is an essential part of reconciliation with God, ourself, and our loved ones. It is an opportunity for spiritual housecleaning that requires self-examination, honesty, and personal accountability. If we experience only corporate confession at worship services, we limit considerably the gift God has for us.

Fortunately, God can guide us through the usually uncomfortable, often painful, process of self-examination, where we discover the roots of our sins that inevitably cause us to hurt ourselves—and those closest to us. When we confess those sins (1 John 1:9), God welcomes us with compassion, acceptance, and forgiveness. What begins as an act of obedience results in freedom and a new experience of the grace of God.

A sensitivity to recognizing our sinful behavior and a willingness to confess are at the heart of a happy marriage. Our relationship with our spouse should be the closest relationship we have in this life, and therefore the primary testing ground for displaying a penitent spirit. Not only should we keep short accounts with God (i.e., regularly acknowledging our sins and asking forgiveness), but with our spouse as well. 🌱

*T*ODAY'S THOUGHT: *Do you need to ask your spouse for forgiveness in any area? If so, give it prayerful consideration.*

Come away by yourselves to a lonely place, and rest a while.
Mark 6:31

When an African bishop visited a denominational headquarters in New York City, the clergyman who was escorting him figured out the best way to get from where they were to where they needed to go. He told the bishop they would have to rush. When they breathlessly arrived at their destination some time later, the clergyman grinned and said, "By doing it my way, we have just saved seven minutes." The bishop replied, "What will we do with the seven minutes?"

It's easy to fill our lives with things to do. Often, they seem to be important, yet they deprive us of the peace of mind, the quiet contentment, and the serene atmosphere that we need in the marriage relationship and in the home. When we are too busy to have time to really be with our loved one, when there is neither quantity nor quality of time for our children, we are too busy.

Just as Jesus encouraged his disciples to see the importance of times of solitude for reflection, prayer, and spiritual refreshment, we also need quiet times with the Lord and with each other. Retreat leaders invite retreatants to "waste time with God." Similarly, we need to "waste time" with our loved ones. ❧

*T*ODAY'S THOUGHT: *To what extent do you need to slow down? What will you do about it?*

LOVE

Always seek to do good to one another and to all.
1 Thessalonians 5:15

In 1 Thessalonians 5, Paul gives instructions about how Christians are to act toward one another in the local congregation. Much of what he says to the household of faith applies also to the individual household: the importance of having respect for authority, of children having respect for parents. By the same token, those who are in authority are not to take advantage of those under them, but are to be good examples. What a responsibility that places on those of us who are parents!

After Paul encourages us to be at peace with one another, he then says, "Admonish the idle, encourage the fainthearted, help the weak, be patient with them all" (verse 14). Those are good household rules too. Families need to share the load. Children can and should perform duties to help them learn early in life about responsibilities (and parents should be consistent in "admonish[ing] the idle" when they fail to take the garbage out, pick up their toys, or wash the dishes).

On the other hand, we also need to encourage the fainthearted. Each of us gets discouraged from time to time and needs cheerful, confident, loving support. Most of all, we need the glue that holds the family together: patience. ❦

TODAY'S THOUGHT: *What is spiritually out of order in your household? What will you do about it?*

He who brings trouble on his family will inherit only wind.
Proverbs 11:29 NIV

The patterns of family life we learn from our parents — good and bad — tend to follow us into our own marriage.

Troublesome patterns are often hard to break because they are part of our foundation. Sometimes they've been part of our parents' lives for so long that they have been elevated to the position of traditions, operating subtly, even unconsciously, in our lives.

These negative patterns can be of a religious nature: not attending worship regularly, not studying the Bible and praying, or failing to honor God in other ways. They may be personal: a spirit of sarcasm and always putting each other down. They can involve physical or emotional abuse. But the essential thing is to become aware of these patterns and to find ways to break them before they become a detriment to your family. ❦

*T*ODAY'S THOUGHT: *Have you brought any negative patterns into your family? If so, identify them. Then brainstorm ways to break those patterns.*

LOVE

It is better to take refuge in the Lord than to trust in man.
Psalm 118:8 NIV

How do we feel when our spouse says, "Let's talk about it," and we don't believe that our loved one really wants to take the matter seriously? "Let's talk about it" is meaningless unless, based on past experience, we know that it can lead to change. Really dealing with an issue takes time and great emotional energy; we don't want to invest that unless we believe it will produce helpful results.

Why talk about it if talk is all that will happen? First, so we know we have been heard. Second, to secure resolution from the discussion. If neither of these happen, talking is an exercise in futility.

To break the "let's talk about it; no, I don't want to talk about it" deadlock, we must begin to build a level of trust with one another that conveys that we *do* want to hear what the other has to say, and that we are willing to change as a result. When that begins to happen, "Let's talk about it" will become a positive, challenging experience. 🍂

*T*ODAY'S THOUGHT: *Which of you is most likely to say, "Let's talk about it"? How does that make the other feel?*

LOVE

Greater love has no man than this, that a man lay down his life for his friends. John 15:13

We have no doubt how much God loves us because of what Jesus was willing to do for us. His action in submitting to death on the cross speaks more eloquently to us than his words ever could.

Our actions also speak much more loudly than our words in showing how much we love our spouse. If a man, for instance, spends his time concentrating on his work, sports, or television, his wife will conclude, quite logically, that he loves those things more than he loves her. Author Keith Miller has said that we can tell what we really love by realizing what we first think about when we wake up.

Many of us need to look seriously at our actions from our spouse's point of view. If our actions show we love something more than our spouse, we need to begin to demonstrate that we love our spouse more. And that can be accomplished much more effectively with actions than with words. ❦

*T*ODAY'S THOUGHT: *Do you think your spouse could logically conclude that something is more important to you than him/her? If so, what is that thing or person? What can you begin doing to show you love your spouse more?*

Outdo one another in showing honor. Romans 12:10

Writer and family expert Gary Smalley says that, if we really love our spouse, we will honor him or her. *Honor* is an important word in the Bible. After God speaks of the ways in which we are to honor him (the Ten Commandments), his first command concerning our responsibilities to other human beings is to honor our father and mother. *Honor* carries with it such concepts as prizing highly (Proverbs 4:8), caring for (Psalm 91:15), and showing respect for (Leviticus 19:3).

There is no way we can better show our gratitude to a person or let that person know how highly he or she is regarded than to bestow some appropriate honor.

If we truly honor our loved one, our emotions, our attitudes, and our actions will follow. We will see our spouse as a very precious person whom God has made. And we will be honored because that special person chose us—for a lifetime! ❧

*T*ODAY'S THOUGHT: *What one continuous thing can you do to let your spouse know how much you honor him/her?*

LOVE

I hear a rebuke that dishonors me. Job 20:3 NIV

Nothing is as damaging to someone's self-confidence as being devalued by the person who is supposed to value him/her the most highly. And when this happens between marriage partners, the results are devastating.

A "rebuke that dishonors" doesn't happen when we have minor disagreements, in which we simply show we feel differently about a matter than our spouse. Sometimes we can become so overly sensitive to feelings that we just keep our mouths shut when something needs to be said. However, reacting in such a way isn't helpful in the long term.
So what is the "rebuke that dishonors"? It is name-calling and hitting below the belt. It is not taking a position because of what we believe, but rather to ridicule the beliefs of our spouse. It is attacking what we perceive to be a character weakness in our spouse in order to win an argument or to feel better about ourself. A dishonorable rebuke is destructive; it severely injures the marriage and provides a horrible example for children. Even in times of disagreement, we must be careful that our words to our spouse are honorable. ❦

*T*ODAY'S THOUGHT: *Do you have a tendency to dishonor your spouse? If so, in what area(s)? Write down steps you can take this week to make your words and actions honorable.*

LOVE

Wife, how do you know whether you will save your husband?
Husband, how do you know whether you will save your wife?
1 Corinthians 7:16

When we talk about differences between men and women, we are almost always generalizing, because there are exceptions. But if we base our conclusions on studies done by experts on male/female communication, we might wonder how (other than the sheer grace of God) we get along in our marriages as well as we do!

According to author Gary Smalley, men tend toward fact discovery, while women are more interested in feelings. Thus, it is no surprise that studies show women speak more than twice as many words a day as men do. Men soon run out of facts; women have an unlimited range of things to say about feelings.

In marriage, we must not dwell on problems but on possible solutions. Once we understand the differences that exist between males and females on such matters, we are much better equipped to seek solutions. ❧

*T*ODAY'S THOUGHT: *How can you better*
communicate in your marriage?

Nevertheless, each one should retain the place in life that the Lord assigned to him. 1 Corinthians 7:17 NIV

Studies show that another general difference between men and women is that men tend to seek solutions, while women are more interested in showing sympathy. Thus, in a crisis, a husband's reaction may be to get something done, while the wife may want to administer comfort.

Likewise, men tend to be more objective while women are more personal. A man can more easily separate himself from circumstances and surroundings, while the woman finds her identity there. The man is into accomplishments; the woman, relationships.

In marriage, and in all aspects of life, there is a great need for the balance that the differences between men and women bring. If we allow those differences to complement one another, rather than compete with one another, we can come to wonderful solutions while ministering genuine love and concern. ❦

*T*ODAY'S THOUGHT: *In what recent situation did your differences work together for the greatest good?*

LOVE

The married man is anxious about worldly affairs.
1 Corinthians 7:33

Another interesting difference between men and women is that men tend to generalize while women detail. That is why women remember "the little things" that seem so unimportant to the man and get upset when their husbands seem unobservant. To the woman, the man doesn't seem to care; to the man, the woman seems obsessed.

The reason for this difference is that women are, as noted earlier, more feeling oriented. Because we tend to remember more those things we feel than those things we simply think, women experience more fully what is going on around them and retain it longer than men do.

Understanding these differences doesn't mean the husband is excused for ignoring details, or the wife is excused for not making conclusions from the details. But as we become more conscious of, and strive toward, the opposite side of our nature, we will attain a greater sense of wholeness individually, and as a married couple. Understanding gender differences is key to improving the marriage relationship. 🍂

*T*ODAY'S THOUGHT: *What steps can you take to better see things from your spouse's point of view?*

LOVE

However, let each one of you love his wife as himself, and let the wife see that she respects her husband. Ephesians 5:33

How would you grade your marriage? Would you give yourself an *A*, or is a *C* the best it could score? Ideally, we all want our marriage to rate as high as possible. But sometimes we don't take the time to think about how we are really doing.

So grade your marriage, as objectively as you can. Do it separately, then compare the scores. Try not to focus too much on any difference in the grades (studies show that women tend to grade lower than men). Approach this "test" positively, using it as encouragement to make your marriage better.

Then discuss the following questions together:

1. What grade do you want to attain as a couple?
2. How much of yourself are you willing to commit toward accomplishing that goal?
3. What specific thing or things do you need to do to reach that goal? 🍏

*T*ODAY'S THOUGHT: *Do it!*

He who finds a wife finds what is good and receives favor from the Lord. Proverbs 18:22 NIV

Perhaps it should not amaze us that today's statistics reflect truths spelled out so many years ago in Scripture. Studies show that the better our spousal relationship, the longer we will live. We shouldn't seek to improve the relationship just to live longer, but that statistic does tell us something about health, happiness, and wholeness.

When the marriage relationship is healthy, two truly become one (Matthew 19:5). When we marry we are, in a sense, born anew. We become something different from what we were; with our spouse we are much more than we were individually.

There are several reasons for this: the built-in love and support we have in marriage; the life sharing that enhances our relationship; the raising of children. And, perhaps, more than anything else, we experience changes in each of us that occur as we work to live in harmony. These changes lead us toward wholeness. 🍎

*T*ODAY'S THOUGHT: *What changes in you, as a result of your marriage, have made you healthier?*

LOVE

Remember me for this, O my God, and do not blot out what I have so faithfully done. Nehemiah 13:14 NIV

Nehemiah was a man of action. He had made some hard decisions and taken some definitive action. Now he asks God to bless what he has done. According to studies, decision making is shown to be a stronger characteristic for men than for women. Women, on the other hand, are typically shown to be more intuitive. Sometimes they have difficulty making decisions because they are so aware of and sensitive to people and situations.

The wife should rejoice if her husband is a decision maker. And the husband should rejoice if his wife is intuitive and sensitive. What a wonderful balance we can be to one another! When a decision needs to be made, it doesn't have to be made hastily, without due consideration for the feelings of those involved. By working together, the married couple can balance their strengths to have the best result for all concerned. ❧

*T*ODAY'S THOUGHT: *What decision-making process do you use? What can you do to make this process more balanced?*

Then I said to them, "You see the trouble we are in, how Jerusalem lies in ruins. . . . Come, let us build the wall of Jerusalem." Nehemiah 2:17

Nehemiah was not only a man who made decisions, but a man who knew how to make and execute plans. Prior to the above quoted verse, Nehemiah had deliberately reviewed what he needed to know in order to form his plan. Then, at the appropriate moment, he announced it. Later, he wisely followed it through.

The ability to plan and then follow through is another strong characteristic of the typical male. This is good news in marriage, because if a man is convinced something needs to be done, and he understands how to do it, he generally will be motivated to pursue that plan.

A problem can occur, however, if the man is too functional in his thinking. If he is motivated toward a quick solution, he may go about the plan superficially; he may follow the letter of the plan but not the spirit. Here, the wife's sensitive side should be able to spot the problem and gently suggest the corrective. Once again, the characteristics of each spouse in marriage are meant to provide balance to the relationship. ❦

*T*ODAY'S THOUGHT: *How can you more effectively pursue plans together?*

LOVE

That you, being rooted and grounded in love. Ephesians 3:17

From time to time, many of us go to the nursery to buy plants for our home or yard. As we wander between the lush rows of flowers, perhaps we are reminded of the infinite variety and beauty of God's world.

Typically, as we decide which plant we want to purchase, we must then examine the ones available to determine which are worth purchasing. At that point, we find that some are wobbly in the soil. Others are green and bushy but have no flowers or buds. Some are laden with flowers but have no buds for future blooms. Still others are leggy and poor in color. It takes patience and determination to find just the right plant.

Are we wobbly in our marriage or in our faith, or are we firmly rooted? Do we look good on Sunday morning in church but know we are only shallow spiritually because we are not growing in Bible study, prayer, and our relationship? God wants us to be healthy in all relationships, rooted and grounded in love and capable of bearing good fruit. ❧

*T*ODAY'S THOUGHT: *How stable is your root system?*

But Peter . . . lifted up his voice and addressed them, "Men of Judea." Acts 2:14

Sometimes our marriage is like a fire. At times it burns brightly; at other times the glow seems to be dying. If we are on the edge of burning out, we need something highly inflammable to spark us back to life.

Perhaps that is why the Lord called us together, as a couple, and as a Christian community: because we need one another. Just as we add a twig or pinecone to the embers of a dying fire to make the fire dance to life, God uses us to renew each other's spark, to give us the fresh desire to go on. God's Spirit came as a flame on Pentecost, resting on the 120 who took that flame out to three thousand others in one day; and Peter, who had been brought low in the humiliation of denying Jesus, suddenly preached with supernatural power.

There is a message here for those of us who are married. We must support each other. But if both of us are suffering "burnout," we must call on the body of Christ for help and spiritual support. Our fellow Christians can be our "pinecones" to help us spring to life again. ❦

*T*ODAY'S THOUGHT: *What condition is your "fire" in?*

LOVE

Abide in me, and I in you. As the branch cannot bear fruit by itself, unless it abides in the vine, neither can you, unless you abide in me. John 15:4

Many couples set aside Saturday to do house and yard chores. Then comes a Saturday that is heavy with slow-falling rain. Although we have many projects planned, we suddenly find ourselves housebound and lazy.

What a good time to remember that God has commanded us to have days of rest, to be like the soil, drenched in his love, soaking in him, submitting to his Spirit! We need to take these days as opportunities to renew our sense of who we are in him and in each other.

Such times provide us with the chance to find out more about who our loved one is, and how things are in his/her life. We may astonish each other with our answers, revealing never-before-shared feelings and emotions. What a precious time to listen, laugh, cry, and hold hands as we pray for each other's dreams and hurts. When we do this, we are renewed in God and in each other and find ourselves abiding more closely together, in him. ❦

*T*ODAY'S THOUGHT: *When was the last time you shared a rainy day together at home? What will you do next time?*

LOVE

God is our refuge and strength, a very present help in trouble.
Psalm 46:1

Today's English Version of the Bible translates this verse: "always ready to help in times of trouble." A cat lover wrote this in her journal: "My cat is expecting her kittens at any time. As I write this, she is crouched on the page and I am craning my neck to write around her. She won't step away from me. I spent a sleepless night on her account; she just couldn't get close enough. She wants to be certain that I will be with her in her time of trouble."

Couples who have experienced the birth of their first child can identify with that feeling. Although the majority of childbirths turn out perfectly OK, it is quite normal for there to be fear and a crying out to the Lord. As one person put it, "Praying gets real."

As we grow older together, we become increasingly conscious of the security we have in God. He is a very present help in trouble. In marriage, we sometimes let each other down. We are insensitive to our spouse's needs. But even when we fail, God does not. 🐾

*T*ODAY'S THOUGHT: *When have you been conscious of God's "very present help"?*

Do you not know that your body is a temple of the Holy Spirit within you? 1 Corinthians 6:19

The most valuable thing Christians have, or ever could have, is God's presence, through the Holy Spirit, within us. The implications of that fact are astounding.

Consider how we would feel if our church were desecrated, its sacred symbols of worship defaced, the furnishings destroyed. We'd probably feel personally violated, but we'd also be in shock about the affront to God that such an action would evidence.

If we are conscious that our own bodies are temples of the Holy Spirit, what about the desecration of them? If we were unfaithful to our spouse, it would be the vilest act of desecration we could commit; it would violate our spouse, God, and ourself. In more subtle ways we desecrate the temple of the Holy Spirit when we overeat or underexercise our bodies and when we don't provide our mind and spirit with healthy spiritual growth. In order to grow more effectively in all relationships, including our marriage, we need to be conscious every day that God is dwelling within us. ❦

TODAY'S THOUGHT: *What do you need to do to get and keep your temple in better shape?*

LOVE

Because I live, you will live also. John 14:19

As Christians, we have Jesus living within us, and this should substantially affect the way we live. Christianity is much more than an ethical system. Rules of living can be changed from one generation to another by adjusting them to "what everyone is doing." However, Christians look to the Holy Spirit for guidance and for power.

When we squelch the Holy Spirit's work in our lives, our behavior becomes a reflection of our inner confusion, self-centeredness, and lust. By the grace of God, through the indwelling Spirit, we can deal with our confusion, self-focus, and temptations. Not only can we identify objectively between right and wrong rather than subjectively being drawn into the world's value system, we have the power to choose what is right.

Our Lord wants us to have life and to have it in abundance (John 10:10), but he is the one who knows what is best for us. How important this concept is for the family! Consciousness of God's presence is at the center of the well-functioning Christian home. As Bishop Donald Hultstrand has said, "Our inner life, out of which emanates our outer life, is the ocean of God's own inexhaustible life." ❦

*T*ODAY'S THOUGHT: *How does your family remember and rely upon God's living presence?*

He only is my rock and my salvation. Psalm 62:2

We think of the word *salvation* in relation to God's great saving act in Jesus Christ. Because of Jesus, those of us who accept him as Lord and Savior of our lives are "saved"—assured of eternal life with God.

A friend recently made the point that salvation, in that sense, is like life insurance. We pay the premium one time, and it is good forever.

There is, however, the matter of health insurance. God is calling us, individually and in our marriage, to more than a relationship with him in the hereafter; he wants us to grow into wholeness. That "health insurance" is something we have to purchase each day, and the marriage covenant is an important part of that insurance. As we learn to live for one another, we grow in wholeness. ❧

TODAY'S THOUGHT: *How are you doing with your "health insurance"? If you need to change your "policy," take steps today.*

LOVE

You shall love your neighbor as yourself. Leviticus 19:18

A friend who counsels Christians whose marriages are in trouble says that often one of the marriage partners tells him, "I just don't love my spouse anymore." In response, our friend points out that the Bible says, "Husbands, love your wives" (Colossians 3:19). "I know the Bible tells me to love her," the person responds, "but I just don't feel any love for her anymore."

Our friend then says, "If I asked you who, in the broadest sense of the word, is your closest neighbor, what would you say?" "Well, I guess, my wife," is the usual reply. "In that case," our friend continues, "Matthew 19:19 says you are to love your neighbor as yourself."

"But you just don't understand," the man will then say. "She may be my wife and my 'neighbor,' but she is also my worst enemy." At that point, our friend says, "Yes, but the Bible says in Matthew 5:44 that we are to love our enemies. You see, the thing you are missing is that you think love is all about feelings, but it isn't; it's about behavior. Feelings come and go. If we had to rely on feelings to sustain our marriages, they would always fail. But you have made a covenant of holy matrimony that requires a certain behavior on your part. And, by the grace of God, the wonderful thing is that, if we are behaving toward our spouse the way we agreed to do when we were married, the feelings of love return." ❦

*T*ODAY'S THOUGHT: *Are any of your behaviors endangering your marriage covenant? If so, in what ways?*

Love is. . . . 1 Corinthians 13:4

Paul's wonderful treatise in 1 Corinthians 13 is the key to what true love is all about.

To live within the covenant of marriage in the way God wants us to do, we must look to Jesus as our model. If we want to know what love really is, and how Jesus is our example of love, we need only substitute the word *Jesus* for the word *love* every time it appears in 1 Corinthians 13.

Doing this tells us that Jesus is patient and kind, that he isn't arrogant or rude, nor does he insist on his own way. He is not irritable or resentful; he rejoices in what is right; he bears all things and endures all things. These are great truths, but perhaps the greatest truth of all is at the start of verse 8: "Love never ends." Feelings change, but love (Jesus) never ends. The opportunity, by the grace of God, to show genuine love (what Jesus would do) to our spouse remains as long as we both shall live. ❦

*T*ODAY'S THOUGHT: *Read 1 Corinthians 13, substituting Jesus' name for the word* love *each time it appears.*

Love is patient. 1 Corinthians 13:4

What is love, and what isn't love? Verses 4 through 7 spell out specific characteristics, beginning with the fact that love is patient. Almost all subsequent definitions simply reinforce the importance of patience as an attribute of love.

The word *patient* means "bearing pains or trials calmly or without complaint; manifesting forbearance under provocation or strain; steadfast despite opposition, difficulty, or adversity." Paul, then, isn't far off when he speaks of love as being neither arrogant nor rude, not insisting on its own way, not being irritable or resentful, bearing all things, etc. He is saying that, if we truly want to manifest love, we must be patient!

Is there any better glue to hold a marriage together than patience? It is in this most intimate of relationships that we must exercise the maximum amount of forbearance and restraint, yielding our rights for the greater good, being slow to anger, not being arrogant, irritable, rude, or resentful. Showing patience toward our spouse is loving him or her. ❧

*T*ODAY'S THOUGHT: *What is your "patience score" in marriage?*

LOVE

The God of heaven will make us prosper, and we his servants will arise and build. Nehemiah 2:20

These words of Nehemiah, as he led the people in rebuilding Jerusalem's wall, are words we can take to heart as we seek to strengthen our marriage by "arising and building" whatever facet of our relationship is in need of renovation.

Nehemiah's story is fascinating because he used wisdom, an understanding of human nature, and prayer to plan and execute his plan. Most of all, he only wanted to do what God wanted him to do.

If we also are willing to spend time with God in prayer, he will show us the particular thing or things he wants us to do for one another today. He may just want us to go to our spouse and say, "Please make me a list of the things you would like me to do for you today." As we seek his will, he will give us sensitivity, wisdom, and a plan. God longs to build our marriage into something even more prosperous! 🍎

*T*ODAY'S THOUGHT: *Are you willing to seek God's guidance concerning his priorities for your marriage today? If you are, do so. If not, why not?*

LOVE

Now Adam knew Eve his wife, and she conceived and bore Cain.
Genesis 4:1

The NIV says, "Adam lay with his wife Eve." The polite way of putting it today would be, "He slept with his wife."

Prior to marriage, and in the early years of marriage, sexual activity is often the primary focus. At some point, most couples realize there is much more to marriage than sex. However, in any successful marriage, sexual relations remain an important factor.

Many of us enter marriage relatively ignorant about sex, even if we have dabbled in it prior to marriage. Childhood friends shared with us their fantasy-ridden ignorance, and we accepted much of it as fact. Although our parents probably tried to tell us a few things, they may have been too embarrassed to say much. If we had sex education in school, it was perhaps too clinical and hard to remember. Please remember that it's never too late to learn how sexual relations within marriage can be better. There are many helpful books on human sexuality written by Christians. Is it time for you to read one? ❦

*T*ODAY'S THOUGHT: *Many Christians are too embarrassed to go to a library or bookstore to get a book on human sexuality. Are you letting pride stand in the way of better sexual relations with your spouse?*

LOVE

So faith comes from what is heard, and what is heard comes by the preaching of Christ. Romans 10:17

Within a marriage, one of the best ways we can reflect the love of God is by consistently showing our spouse that we care. This builds our faith in one another as well as our faith in Christ. Caring for each other is an important way in which we "preach Christ."

A man who recently celebrated his fiftieth wedding anniversary has a special way of showing his wife he cares. Over the years, his work has required him to travel frequently. Whenever he has to be away, he writes his wife a love letter. "Sometimes I don't mail it though," he said. "I just give it to her when I get home. I tell her how much I love her and how much she means to me. I want her to know that I am committed to her for life."

A friend asked, "You write to her every time you go away?"

The man replied, "Yes, and I've been doing it for thirty-two years. I only wish I had done it the first eighteen years too." ❧

*T*ODAY'S THOUGHT: *Whether you are the one who sometimes travels or the one who stays at home, write your spouse a love letter the next time you are apart.*

March

*L*OVE

I will establish my covenant with you.   Genesis 6:18

A *contract* is an agreement between two or more human beings; a *covenant,* in the sense that Christians mean it, is an agreement in which God is a party. God has made several covenants with his people, and holy matrimony is a covenantal relationship. Marriage is not entered into solely by the man and the woman; God is also a party to it.

At a time when many marriages end in divorce, Christian husbands and wives are called not only to recognize the covenantal nature of their relationship but to help others understand marriage in this way. If we see marriage as just a contract, it is something we can dissolve simply by mutual consent. Contracts can always be terminated if the parties so desire. But if we acknowledge that God is also a partner in the covenant, escape from the relationship is another thing altogether.

What is God's position concerning marriage? "I hate divorce, says the Lord" (Malachi 2:16). If a couple, however, have not truly made God a part of their marriage, they are not likely to seek his will concerning the termination of it. That is why a continuous relationship with God in prayer, Scripture study, worship, and fellowship within a Christian community of faith is an essential part of the marriage covenant from the very beginning. ❦

*T*ODAY'S THOUGHT: *What do you, as a couple, need to do to make God a more vital part of your covenant?*

*L*OVE

I will give to the Lord the thanks due to his righteousness.
Psalm 7:17

Some Christian organizations provide their supporters with a thank-offering box, where they can put coins of gratitude for things that happen in their lives. It is a way to recognize the providence of God, and to show our thankfulness to him. When the box becomes full, or at a designated time each year, the contents of the box are emptied, and the money (or a check representing it) is sent to the sponsoring organization.

How about making a love box to express gratitude to God for marriage? When your spouse washes the dishes, makes up the bed, irons clothes, or runs an errand, it's time to be grateful and to place a coin in the love box. When you feel gratitude to God for some major aspect of your marriage (the birth of a child, for instance), make a big contribution to the love box.

Once a year, preferably on your wedding anniversary, take out the contents of the love box and decide what to do with the money. Maybe you can help pay for a family vacation or purchase something special for your home. Or you could contribute to a Christian organization that stands for marriage and family values. ❧

*T*ODAY'S THOUGHT: *Is it time to make a love box for your home? Why or why not?*

*L*OVE

My mouth will tell of thy righteous acts. Psalm 71:15

Feelings are very important, especially within the marriage relationship. But, as we've discussed earlier, balance is essential. There is a tendency in contemporary society to make feelings the primary test in ethics and morality: If it feels good and no one is going to get hurt, do it!

God values feelings greatly. If it were not for his abundant love for us, he would not have sent his Son to die on a cross for our sins. But God is also one who acts. There is a time to quit relying so much on our feelings and to get busy doing what God would have us do.

Perhaps we don't feel very loving toward our spouse or our children. At such times we need to act ourselves into a new way of feeling instead of feeling ourselves into a new way of acting. If we wait for the feeling, it may never come. Yet, by taking the action God would have us choose, the feeling will follow. ❧

*T*ODAY'S THOUGHT: *What feeling do you need to act yourself into?*

*L*OVE

Therefore a man leaves his father and his mother and cleaves to his wife, and they become one flesh. Genesis 2:24

Each spouse in the marriage is a precious child of God, with his or her own personality, friends, vocation, life. There should be nothing in marriage that diminishes the giftedness God has granted to each spouse.

Marriage, however, brings into existence a new entity: the couple. Although each spouse maintains everything that God created him or her to be, there now also exists something greater than the two individuals who comprise it. The great wonder of marriage is that one plus one equals more than two.

As two people "become one flesh," this unique, God-given relationship happens. Wholeness becomes possible in a way that would not be so by the two individuals living separately. Marriage is an institution ordained by God, filled with potential for good, including the birth of children and the forming of family. It is an arrangement worth working on to make it all that it can be. 🍎

*T*ODAY'S THOUGHT: *What do other people see when they look at your marriage?*

MARCH 5 · *L*OVE

For where you have envy and selfish ambition, there you find disorder and every evil practice. James 3:16 NIV

Marriages typically begin with the couple being so "in love" that they idealize the relationship and are not wary of the internal and external dangers that work against it. The biggest internal problem is selfishness.

Once the fresh glow of the relationship has begun to wear off, selfishness raises its ugly head. The spouses begin to fight for their rights. The husband wants to keep on doing those things he always did before the marriage, such as "going out with the guys," and the wife has her own set of demands.

Some of these fights for rights are proper, even healthy. But for a marriage to be all that it should be, much more than the proverbial fifty-fifty proposition is involved. God is a partner in the marriage, and husband and wife are each answerable to him as well as to each other. Understanding basic selfishness as the number-one enemy and learning ways to deal with it is at the cornerstone of every successful marriage. ❦

*T*ODAY'S THOUGHT: *Are there any ways in which you are being selfish in your relationship? If so, what can you do about it?*

*L*OVE

The acts of the sinful nature are obvious: sexual immorality, impurity. Galatians 5:19 NIV

In addition to those internal things, such as selfishness, that work against marriage, there are also many external factors. Perhaps the most serious external enemy today is the media. Marriage and family values are ridiculed, and divorce is accepted as normal in movies, on TV, and in magazines and books. Fornication ("living together") and adultery ("having an affair") are seen simply as legitimate (sometimes even preferable) choices.

We fool ourselves if we fail to see that these ways of the world are really at war with Christian marriage. Our casual acceptance can lead to apathy toward these destructive forces. If we try to ignore them, we may find we are actually supporting them by our silence, inaction, and perhaps even assent.

The Bible teaches something very different from the current cultural standards, and we must learn to use what it says as our measuring rod against what is socially acceptable in our day. Scripture not only gives us guidelines for marriage and family life, but motivates us to stand against the world's value system. ❦

*T*ODAY'S THOUGHT: *What is God asking you to do?*

*L*OVE

For which of you, desiring to build a tower, does not first sit down and count the cost, whether he has enough to complete it?
Luke 14:28

In this passage, Jesus is dealing with unrealistic expectations, another internal enemy of marriage.

As we get to know one another better in order to make the choice to marry, we tend to see each other's best side. Also, perhaps because of youth, naïveté, or physical attraction, we overlook a lot of things.

Realizing that the one we have married is not everything we thought he or she would be is not reason for despair. It simply means that the marriage has reached a new stage, one of give-and-take and adjustment. Of course our spouse has faults; we did marry a human being, didn't we? Now is the time to learn to overlook a few things—and to look for the good qualities that we didn't realize were there when we married! ❦

*T*ODAY'S THOUGHT: *What endearing quality does your spouse have that you didn't know about at the time of your marriage?*

LOVE

He said to them, "An enemy has done this." Matthew 13:28

In Matthew 13, an enemy had sown weeds among the wheat. And over the last three days, we have looked at weeds sown among the wheat of our marriage. We have seen that basic selfishness is probably the greatest internal enemy and that the media may be the worst external foe of our day. We also saw that unrealistic expectations can be the seeds of our undoing. We have examined these weeds not to be negative about marriage, but to keep us from being blindsided.

Some marriages are complacent and seemingly untroubled for years, existing only at a surface level, with each spouse going his or her own way. Then trouble occurs and the couple doesn't even know how to communicate concern, confusion, and pain. It is much better to understand the dynamics of marriage from the first, including those things that work against marriage. Not only does this make for healthier marriages, but we are better able to spot trouble areas and much more equipped to deal with them. ❧

*T*ODAY'S THOUGHT: *What are some enemies of marriage that haven't yet been mentioned?*

LOVE

Jesus spoke . . . , saying, "What do you think?" Matthew 17:25

Living in Florida provides us with glorious weather through the winter months, but summer, which can be from April to October, is hot and humid. For people who can afford to do so, the answer always seems to be a summer home in the mountains. Many rush into finding such a place and become responsible for another piece of property they can enjoy only for a few days at a time because of their responsibilities back home.

In one of his books, Keith Miller tells the story of a friend who was having marriage difficulties. The wife insisted they needed a bigger house, so, after much resistance, the husband finally gave in and bought one. Soon after the couple moved in, the husband told Keith, "It isn't the house." It's a shame that they couldn't see their communication problem until they had tried everything else! Sometimes we also don't take the time to stop and think.

When faced with problems in our marriage and life in general, often we simply need to give time for probing thought and searching prayer to get to the bottom of the difficulty rather than going out and doing something. ❦

*T*ODAY'S THOUGHT: *What in your marriage relationship needs fresh thought and prayer?*

*L*OVE

Rejoice always . . . give thanks in all circumstances.
1 Thessalonians 5:16, 18

Do we really believe that God is in charge of our lives, our marriage, our family? Do we really know that, because God has us in his hands, he is working all things together for our good (Romans 8:28)? Why, then, do we often worry rather than rejoice?

The entire New Testament testifies that God loves each of us personally, deeply, and intimately. So great is the intensity of his care for us that no circumstance is too small for his attention. Everything that God demonstrates in Jesus Christ proves his love for us.

God's plan for our life together is to guide us through every circumstance, good and evil, so that we may remain united as husband and wife—and ultimately united with him in the glories of heaven. In the meantime, we will face irritation, pain, and even tragedy; but none of those can separate us from the love of God. Even when we don't feel like rejoicing, we can still express our gratitude to God for his love. Because we know that he loves us, we can be thankful. ❦

*T*ODAY'S THOUGHT: *What do you especially need to thank God for today?*

MARCH 11 LOVE

By this all men will know that you are my disciples, if you have love for one another. John 13:35

When a friend of ours was in an airport, he saw a little girl who persisted in trying to give candy away, although no one would take it. Finally, our friend began to feel sorry for her and was about to say something when her mother came and whisked her off. *It's just like God and his grace,* our friend thought. *God stands ready to give his grace freely to all, and we ignore him.*

God is always there, giving away his love. All he expects of us is that we return that love to him and to one another. In the marriage relationship we have a special opportunity to give away our love, with the Lord as our example.

Love is something for us to give away freely, no strings attached, just like the little girl in the airport. It is an act of faith, and the more faith we have in God, the more love we will be able to give. ❧

*T*ODAY'S THOUGHT: *What has faith in God taught you about love?*

LOVE

He who finds his life will lose it, and he who loses his life for my sake will find it. Matthew 10:39

There is much in life that is risky. Stepping on a plane is a risk; succeeding in a particular vocation is a risk. Therefore, it isn't surprising that Jesus calls us to the ultimate risk in seeking to follow him.

In marriage we face the risk of surrender as we give our life into the hands of each other and God. The more we trust in that relationship, the more we are willing to risk. As we become increasingly dependent on one another, we love more, and our love bears more fruit. It has been said that there are no guarantees in the risky business of loving one another, but that love is never wasted.

In his great hymn to the glory of love, Paul says that love "does not insist on its own way; it is not irritable or resentful; it does not rejoice at wrong, . . . bears all things, believes all things, hopes all things, endures all things" (1 Corinthians 13:5-7). Such love comes from the risk we take when we commit ourselves to one another in the covenant of marriage. ❦

TODAY'S THOUGHT: *What risks are you taking because of your love for your spouse?*

May the God of peace himself sanctify you wholly.
1 Thessalonians 5:23

Life itself is often a hassle. Our jobs and relationships with associates are fraught with problems. And then there are marriage and family complications and responsibilities! No wonder we sometimes identify with Paul when he lamented, "I do not do the good I want, but the evil I do not want is what I do" (Romans 7:19). God's call to be perfect can easily lead to despair.

Every Christian, faced with the fact that his or her life and marriage are far from what God calls them to be, can have these sentiments. So what are we to do? Paul answers that question for us: God himself will sanctify us wholly. If we cannot, in ourselves, produce the fruit of righteousness, God will do it.

In his letter to the Philippians, Paul says, "I am sure that he [God] who began a good work in you will bring it to completion at the day of Jesus Christ" (1:6). Those of us who have accepted Jesus Christ as the Lord and Savior of our life and have entered into a covenant with God and spouse in holy matrimony have made commitments. As a result of those commitments, God has taken upon himself the responsibility of bringing us to himself and, in the process, sanctifying our lives and our marriages. ❦

*T*ODAY'S THOUGHT: *What life struggle do you need to release to God?*

*L*OVE

Do not quench the Spirit. 1 Thessalonians 5:19

One of the symbols of the Holy Spirit is fire. It is the fire that cleanses, purifies, ignites with passion and zeal, and motivates into action. It warms the soul, enlightens the mind, and speaks to the emotions with enthusiasm and joy. It causes natural people to perform the supernatural as they are empowered by God to do his work in the world.

Here Paul is warning the Thessalonians not to put out this fire from the Holy Spirit. Unfortunately, it isn't difficult to quench the Spirit. When we reject a nudge from the Holy Spirit to show love to our spouse or children in some particular way, we quench that Spirit. And the more we quench the Spirit, the less often we perceive those nudges. Likewise, the more we yield to the Spirit, the more perceptive we become in receiving the guidance the Lord would give us through his Spirit.

For our marriage to be all that God wants it to be, we should be increasingly perceptive of the Holy Spirit, responding to the Spirit, not quenching him. Furthermore, it is extremely important that we not quench the Spirit in our spouse by failing to take seriously the guidance our spouse receives from God. 🍃

*T*ODAY'S THOUGHT: *What can you do to encourage, rather than quench, the Holy Spirit in your marriage?*

MARCH 15 LOVE

Owe no one anything, except to love one another. Romans 13:8

This admonition from Paul seems contrary to our present day, in which we are encouraged to be credit consumers. The average debt of Americans has risen dramatically over the last fifty years. Is there anyone left who always pays cash?

Borrowing was customary in Paul's time as well. Perhaps that is why he asks Christians to reflect on what they owe to others. Owing money creates an obligation to the person or institution. As married couples who struggle to stay within a budget and to provide for the future, we realize Paul is talking about something common to us all.

We are also bound in nonmonetary ways. We owe employers honest labor, our spouse fidelity, people we have offended apologies. In these relationships we are either bound by constraints or we are able to respond freely. Paul is saying that if we fulfill the law of love, we can be out of bondage and able to respond freely. This is especially important in the most intimate relationship in which we live, the one with our spouse and children. ❧

TODAY'S THOUGHT: *How do you fulfill the law of love and avoid bondage?*

*L*OVE

In the world you have tribulation; but be of good cheer, I have overcome the world. John 16:33

People who have worked in industry know what *downtime* is. Downtime happens when equipment fails and the manufacturing process comes to a screeching halt. People stand around wringing their hands, and valuable production time is lost.

Depression is our body's "downtime." According to studies, twice as many women as men suffer from depression. Regardless of the cause, moods of sadness are a part of life today. Very few of us totally escape "downtime." It can be serious, and it is not to be taken lightly within marriage. We should be sensitive and understanding when depression afflicts our family and be as helpful as we can in helping the depressed person overcome the condition.

Periods of depression are seldom broken quickly. Patience is needed, and tender loving care is essential. Fortunately, each day is a new opportunity to break free of "downtime," to remember Jesus' promise in times of tribulation: "Be of good cheer, I have overcome the world." Jesus is working to bring about healing. ❧

*T*ODAY'S THOUGHT: *Is depression a problem for you and/or your spouse? If so, what can you do about it—together?*

*L*OVE

That you may be made worthy of the kingdom of God, for which you are suffering. 2 Thessalonians 1:5

People sometimes say, "Suffering is an opportunity for personal growth." Such people may mean well, but saying those words to us in the midst of our suffering rings quite hollow. Suffering, by its nature, is a lonely and harrowing experience.

In 2 Thessalonians 1, Paul says there are two things that make a difference in times of pain. The first is support from loved ones who stand by us (not preaching to us, like Job's "comforters") so that we know we are not alone. The second is a consciousness of God's presence and love.

In times of illness or other physical suffering, we may find it hard to pray and to read Scripture. Sometimes we begin to question the presence, perhaps even the goodness, of God. That's why it's especially important for us to be there for a suffering loved one. We can be God's presence to him or her. ❦

*T*ODAY'S THOUGHT: *When have you suffered? How did your spouse bring you comfort at that time?*

*L*OVE

He who believes in the Son has eternal life. John 3:36

Those words, basic to the Christian faith, so easily roll off our tongue. But how seriously do we take this relationship with God?

Since our metropolitan area isn't large enough to support a National Football League team or a major league baseball team, local residents have gone absolutely wild over our newly acquired National Basketball Association team. Thousands hold in awe these dozen tall men as though they were gods. No lack of money, energy, or time is spent on the games. Activities have to be scheduled around the games so there will be no conflict. Nothing is taken as seriously as the games.

What would our world be like if everyone took Christ that seriously? Moreover, what would our marriage be like if we took it that seriously? When Christ is taken seriously, miracles happen. And when we take our marriage seriously, we'll be amazed at the relational changes. ❦

*T*ODAY'S THOUGHT: *What will you do today to demonstrate how seriously you take your marriage?*

MARCH 19 LOVE

May the God of hope fill you with all joy and peace in believing,
so that by the power of the Holy Spirit you may abound in hope.
Romans 15:13

Those who have had the opportunity to see Monticello, the home of Thomas Jefferson in Charlottesville, Virginia, may have noticed the ring given to Jefferson's daughter by the British ambassador to France. Engraved on it are the words "I love and I hope." That would be a good motto for Christian marriages.

The words on the ring were not only a beautiful expression of love between two people, but are, in a broader sense, expressive of Paul's prayer quoted above. The idea is that by the power of the Holy Spirit, the love of God may so fill us that we abound in hope.

We live in a "post-Christian" era, when values are constantly questioned. The Christian faith is ridiculed, and immorality is rampant. At times like this, we especially need hope in our marriage and in the Christian community. We can't solve these problems overnight; we can only deal with each challenge as it comes. Paul calls us to do that in hope, filled with the love of God. ❧

TODAY'S THOUGHT: *How can you manifest*
hope in times of trial?

MARCH 20 *LOVE*

We always pray for you, that our God may make you worthy of his call, and may fulfil every good resolve and work of faith by his power. 2 Thessalonians 1:11

In a society where we are constantly bombarded by news from around the world, most of us have developed the fine art of selective listening. We skim most of the publications that come our way and read only what is immediately relevant. We crave entertainment because it relieves the stress. We feel guilty because we don't think we adequately keep up with what is going on around us.

The pace of our lives and the demands of our schedules keep us constantly on the move. As someone put it, "I seem to just go from one event to another all day long." Yet, all this busyness doesn't produce satisfaction.

In answer to "the tyranny of the urgent," Paul gives us some comforting words. We can be made worthy of our call and fulfill every good resolve and work by the power of God. All we need to do is reassess our priorities, making sure our actions are in accordance with God's will for us. Our primary calling is to our spouse. Are we willing to take a break from our hectic schedules and decide what, from God's point of view, is really important? ❦

*T*ODAY'S THOUGHT: *How can you prioritize your time for the benefit of your spouse?*

I waited patiently for the Lord. Psalm 40:1

Patience is a prerequisite for the Christian who prays, and especially for the one who is married. Most of us have patience in varying measure. There are times when the urgency is real, and we act, perhaps shooting an arrow prayer to God such as, *Lord, please guide me quickly!*

Yet the wind blows where it will, which is a picturesque way of saying that God moves in his own time. It is for that moment that we wait. God's timing doesn't always suit our schedule, but only his timing is perfect.

We all have some measure of impatience. Use your impatience to persist rather than to give up. The psalmist says, "I waited patiently for the Lord; he inclined to me and heard my cry." Then the psalm goes on to say that God sets our feet on a rock, makes our step secure, and puts a new song in our mouth. Now that is promised assurance—if we will be patient and listen. ❧

*T*ODAY'S THOUGHT: *What challenge do you and your spouse face today that calls for patient, listening prayer?*

LOVE

Love one another with brotherly affection; outdo one another in showing honor. Romans 12:10

In his book *Fire in Coventry*, Stephen Verney wrote, "We must not only approach other people with the love of God in our hearts, but we must know how to express it." To illustrate his point, he told about a schoolmaster who was teaching his children about religion. "What did Jesus come into the world for?" he asked. When there was no answer, he roared the answer to them: "Love!" Then he walked around the room hitting each child over the head as he continued to roar, "Love! Love! Love!"

We live in a time when there is a lot of love talk, but very little loving action. Love is not love if it isn't manifested in a loving way. In Romans 12:9-18 Paul gives a practical, nuts-and-bolts view of love in action.

Marriage and family life provide us with the ideal setting for putting Paul's guidelines for love into action. ❦

*T*ODAY'S THOUGHT: *Read Romans 12:9-18.*
In what way will you show love in action to your spouse today?

*L*OVE

This is the day which the Lord has made; let us rejoice and be glad in it. Psalm 118:24

How about beginning a day with Psalm 118:24, just to get things off to the right start by acknowledging your utter dependence on God and being joyful and grateful?

Then thank him for all he does: for your spouse and all that he or she means to you; for any children you might have and the blessing they are to you; for everything else you can think of.

As the day progresses, look for God's hand in everything that happens. Even when little disasters occur, seek to learn what God might be trying to teach you. Look for special significance in the common events of the day and for God's love in the faces of everyone you meet. Then return God's love to them. Try to act as Jesus would toward all people. Then, before you go to sleep, assess the day. Ask God's forgiveness for the ways in which you didn't live up to expectations. Rejoice and be glad in everything else. ❧

*T*ODAY'S THOUGHT: *Give the above exercise a try!*

*L*OVE

Put away the foreign gods which are among you, and incline your heart to the Lord. Joshua 24:23

The foreign gods discussed in Joshua were very obvious items. Cast in bronze or gold, they had a prominent place in the temple or home. Today's foreign gods are more subtle, but just as destructive. Our god may be the television set, sports activities, alcohol, or other indulgences.

Joshua implored the people to get rid of their foreign gods and incline their hearts toward their Maker. A closer look at the meaning of *incline* reveals that its first definition is "to bow." What a powerful image that creates as it relates to worshiping the one true living God! Inclining is not a casual nod of recognition of our relationship with God, but a physical act of submission.

As married people who are in a covenant relationship with God and our spouse, we especially need to weigh our habits, lifestyle, and desires against our complete devotion and obedience to God. If our hearts are bowed toward something other than our heavenly Father, we need to make a change. ❦

*T*ODAY'S THOUGHT: *Are any foreign gods creeping into your life? If so, identify them and weigh them against your obedience to God.*

Should we pay them, or should we not? Mark 12:15

When a friend's daughter graduated from college, she secured a well-paying job in their hometown.

After failing to find a place to live, she asked her parents if she could live at home. The parents, to teach her responsibility, agreed to the arrangement, but only if she would pay appropriate room and board. After much objection, the girl finally agreed to do so. When, two years later, she found a place of her own, her parents presented her with a check totalling the amounts she had paid them, plus interest. "Why did I ever object to the deal you made with me?" the surprised girl asked. "The more you made me put into it, the more I got out of it."

The more we put into our marriage, the more we will get out of it. Investing ourselves fully in our marriage means involvement. Just like the wealthy person who flicks a dollar into the collection plate on Sundays, we can "tip" God and our marriage. Or we can give sacrificially by totally offering ourselves. Tips and small deposits usually bring in small achievements. Sacrificial giving results in blessings. ❦

*T*ODAY'S THOUGHT: *How much are you really putting into your marriage?*

LOVE

Finally, brethren, pray for us. 2 Thessalonians 3:1

As Paul brings his second letter to the Thessalonians to a close, he asks for prayer, saying, in essence, "I see the marvelous work God is doing with you and among you. As you continue to stand strong in the midst of persecution, pray for us that we, also, may stand strong in the persecution we endure."

Paul is paying these Christians a high compliment. Even the strongest leaders cannot stand alone and succeed. We need each other, and we especially need to pray for each other. It is not inappropriate to admit we're mutually dependent on one another. Indeed, God has designed it that way (see 1 Corinthians 12).

There are levels of prayer support that should always be in the mind of married Christians. First we pray for our spouse, then for our children and the rest of the family. An important part of our mutual support is being confident that our spouse is also praying for us. But we also need to pray for Christian leaders who face the sort of persecution that beset Paul. As we pray for others in our home and in the Christian community, we take a stand for marriage and family values. ❦

TODAY'S THOUGHT: *How can you pray more effectively for marriage and family values?*

LOVE

Then Satan answered the Lord, "Does Job fear God for nought?" Job 1:9

Job had been blessed in a great many ways and was, at the same time, a model of righteousness.

Satan took the position with God that Job was righteous because he had everything going for him—of course he loved God! But what would happen when everything was taken from him?

In this instance, Satan asked the right question. For the test of faith, like the test of a marriage, is not how faith handles prosperity, health, and all the good things life has to offer, but how it handles adversity, sickness, and the bad things that happen to good people. In our marriage vows, we took each other for better and for worse. We can handle the better; how about the worse?

We will probably never face all the disasters that befell Job. However, we fool ourselves if we do not realize that our life together as husband and wife will encounter the worst of times along with the best of times. If our marriage and faith are built on the foundation that Jesus Christ provides, we can cope with the bad along with the good. 🍎

*T*ODAY'S THOUGHT: *How does your faith support you in the worst of times?*

*L*OVE

Hast thou not put a hedge about him and his house and all that he has, on every side? Job 1:10

In the beginning of the story, Satan points out that God has protected Job and his family by putting a fence of security around them.

No wonder he's righteous, Satan says. But let's look at the righteousness of Job.

It's obvious that Job not only prayed for his children (he had seven sons and three daughters), but carried his prayers for protection into action. When his children had been eating and drinking on feast days, Job would offer burnt offerings "according to the number of them all" (verse 5) in case they had sinned in the course of the festivities.

In this sense, Job is certainly a model for Christian parents. We should pray daily and fervently for our children. We should be sensitive to their particular needs, asking God to meet those needs. We should also pray for a fence of protection around them each day. And, like Job, we should be willing to fast and make other spiritual sacrifices on their behalf. ❦

*T*ODAY'S THOUGHT: *If you have children, how can you pray more effectively for them?*

*L*OVE

Martha, Martha, you are anxious and troubled about many things. Luke 10:41

Good marriages take work. Over the next few days we'll be looking at some of the things that interfere with good marriages so that we may be wary of them and take whatever actions are needed to overcome them.

The first trap involves the activities that can capture our time and attention. In the quoted verse, Jesus cautions Martha about being so involved in household activities (although she had a good purpose — taking care of Jesus) that she has no time to really hear what he has to say.

Married couples can easily become overly involved in activities for the benefit of the church and community but to the detriment of their marriage. People who see such couples think they have the ideal marriage: They're fine, giving people, doing good things. But, often, these marriages are the most troubled. The couple may have become obligated to so many good things that they don't have time to work on their relationship. Some involvement in activities is healthy. But we must be careful to maintain a balance. 🍂

*T*ODAY'S THOUGHT: *Do you need to review your commitments in order to have a balanced life and time for your spouse?*

*L*OVE

Perseverance must finish its work so that you may be mature.
James 1:4 NIV

The second obstacle to a healthy marriage is children. There are many Christian couples who, wanting to be good parents, carry it to an extreme. They focus on the children to the exclusion of the marriage relationship and everything else.

Some parents focus so totally on their children's lives and accomplishments that one writer has labeled it "Christian Shintoism" (family worship). These parents arrest their own growth to maturity in marriage and their faith because they live vicariously through the children. This can be particularly dangerous to the marriage when the children leave home and move away. People who have been married for as many as twenty-five years get divorced when the "empty-nest syndrome" occurs.

It is entirely appropriate to devote time and attention to our children, particularly because we have them at home for such a short time. But we shouldn't let our relationship with the children become a substitute for our relationship with one another. ❦

*T*ODAY'S THOUGHT: *Is this a problem for you or your spouse?*

Do you love me more than these? John 21:15

Another obstacle to successful marriage is, ironically, being wholly focused on one another.

This is the problem of "us two, just me and you." But as Christians, we are to love Jesus more than we love our spouse.

Couples can become so enamored with one another, especially if they happen to have similar interests, that there is no room for Jesus. Their activities together become more important than participating in church programs; worship attendance is occasional; praying and studying Scripture interferes with more interesting activities; faith dies.

No matter how excited a couple may be with one another, particularly in the early days of marriage or even in the newfound freedom that occurs when children leave home, a marriage relationship not centered in Jesus is almost certainly doomed to failure. "Except for Jesus, our marriage never would have made it" is the statement of many successfully married Christian couples. No matter how much we seem to love one another, if the primary love of Jesus is not there, there will be arrested growth, an unstable foundation, and, when problems occur, an inadequate means of handling them. So we must seek to put Jesus first—in all relationships. ❦

*T*ODAY'S THOUGHT: *How vital a part does Jesus play in your marriage?*

April

LOVE

You became an example. 1 Thessalonians 1:7

Just as we are examples to our children, our parents have been examples to us—some good, some not. Most of us are a mixture of good and bad examples.

As we continue to look at obstacles to successful marriage, a major one can be our parents. If either spouse is the child of parents who divorced, we particularly need to break any influence that might have on our marriage. Otherwise, in times of trial, it will be too easy to say, "Divorce is certainly an option; our parents did it." But there are also many other ways in which our parents can be a negative influence on our marriage.

We tend to be bound by the way our parents did things. If our parents bickered with one another, we will tend to do the same. If our parents handled disagreements and anger with the "silent treatment," we will be tempted to follow that model. But the Lord wants us to break through the negative influences on our marriage and build only on the good examples our parents have given us. The first step in making the break is realizing that these influences exist and naming them for what they are. ❧

*T*ODAY'S THOUGHT: *What negative models,
if any, have you brought into your marriage from
your parents? How are you going to keep from
following those models in your own marriage?*

LOVE

Male and female he created them. Genesis 1:27

Another obstacle to successful marriage is the basic design differences between men and women. Some men have to be reminded that their wives aren't just guys who happen to smell good! Perhaps our greatest communication difficulties between husband and wife result from these inherent differences between men and women.

Women tend to be relational, men objective. Men tend to be thinkers, women feelers. Women tend to get absorbed in details while men look for the bottom line.

Here, again, the important thing is realizing these differences and learning how to live with them. That's the first step. But there's also an extremely positive side to our differences: We can complement one another. When the husband is too focused on thinking, he may well miss something his feelings should be telling him. His wife, on the other hand, will more easily perceive those feelings. Better decisions can be made when both thinking and feeling are given due weight. This can only happen if each spouse is willing to listen to the other with heart and head, realizing basic differences. 🍎

*T*ODAY'S THOUGHT: *How can you improve communication with your spouse?*

LOVE

Do nothing out of selfish ambition. Philippians 2:3 NIV

If either husband or wife (or worst of all, both) is primarily driven by the desire to fulfill personal needs, they face another major obstacle to successful marriage. In our day and age, it's easy to get on the fast track, running over the bodies of our spouse and children to get where we are going.

Writer Keith Miller tells a story about a father who always brought work home with him and therefore had no time to play ball with his son. When the child asked his mother what the problem was, the mother said, defensively, "Son, your father has so much to do that he simply can't get it done at work and has to get caught up on it here at home." The child responded, "Well, why don't they put him in a slower group?"

Many of us need to slow down and reassess what our real priorities should be. Selfish ambition and happy marriage simply don't mix. It is entirely proper for the wage earner(s) in the family to want to do their job and do it well. It is right to want to provide security for our family by the work we do. But it's another thing altogether to want success for its own sake at the expense of those to whom we have a primary obligation in marriage. ❦

*T*ODAY'S THOUGHT: *Are you unnecessarily allowing your work to interfere with your marriage? If so, what will you do about it?*

LOVE

The Lord bless you and keep you. Numbers 6:24

The ancient blessing set forth in Numbers 6:24-26 became very popular in Christian churches following the Reformation. Lately, through the writings of Gary Smalley and others, it has become a way in which fathers bless their children daily. Likewise, it is a way in which married couples can ask the Lord's blessing on each other.

Such a blessing is an intentional act of speaking God's favor and power into someone's life, often accompanied by the laying on of hands. It is the kind of blessing spoken by Isaac to his son Jacob, and in turn by Jacob to his sons (Genesis 49). It is the type of blessing Jesus gave to his disciples (Luke 24:50) and to the children (Mark 10:16).

As Christians, it is our responsibility to engender a deep love of God within our home. It is especially important to convey to children that our love of God is primary in life. One of the simplest and most effective ways to help our children know and love God is to pray a blessing on them daily, with the laying on of hands. This gives them a regular and concrete encounter with God's power and protection. We can do the same with our spouse. ❧

*T*ODAY'S THOUGHT: *Do you pray a blessing on your family? If not, how can you be more intentional about it?*

Bless me, even me also, O my father! Genesis 27:34

Following the ancient tradition, many Christian fathers today are blessing their children in the manner we considered yesterday.

Each night before bedtime, they lay their hands on the child's head and say the blessing in Numbers 6:24-26. This also can be personalized by adding the child's name and by closing with a specific blessing desired on the child's behalf that day.

It has been the common experience of parents who have used this method of blessing their children that children begin to seek the blessing. For instance, if a child is going to bed early, he or she will come to the parent and ask for the blessing. Or if the father is going on a business trip, the child might ask for a blessing to last until his return, or request that he call each night and give his blessing.

With all the distractions that exist in our world, it is extremely important to keep ourselves and our families focused on God and his providence. The common failing of Jews throughout the Old Testament was that they simply forgot about God and their obligations to him, and contemporary Christians seem to fall into the same trap. But blessings regularly given within the family help to offset this problem. ❦

*T*ODAY'S THOUGHT: *How will you begin to bless your family each day?*

LOVE

When we are cursed, we bless. 1 Corinthians 4:12 NIV

God is a God of blessings. He wants the best for us, and he blesses us in a great many ways each day, even when we fail to recognize them. As his people in the world today, we are to pass his blessings on to others, especially to our family.

When we ridicule, we are cursing rather than blessing. "Reckless words pierce like a sword, but the tongue of the wise brings healing" (Proverbs 12:18 NIV). We have the daily choice of speaking words of life or death to our spouse and children. We speak death when we destroy their self-esteem. And, since sins of omission can be as great or greater than sins of commission, we also "speak" death when we fail to encourage them when they need it.

What a privilege it is to speak words of life, to bless those we love. There are so many ways we can show our gratitude for them and for God, who made them a part of our lives. One of those ways is to speak gracious words at appropriate times. 🍒

*T*ODAY'S THOUGHT: *What words of blessing would God have you say to your spouse and/or children?*

LOVE

Son, go and work in the vineyard today. Matthew 21:28

Some of us have a tendency to live in the past; others always focus on the future. But, as a friend of ours says, "Yesterday is a cancelled check, and tomorrow is only a promissory note." Today is the only day we have; yesterday is gone, and it isn't yet tomorrow.

Life is not a waiting room. It is an opportunity to serve God and our spouse and children. The only time we have to live is now, and God wants us to go and work in our marriage vineyard. Until we are willing to be intentional about the things at hand, we will go on wandering in the abyss of an indeterminable future.

There is something that God wants to happen in our lives today for the benefit of our family. There is something he wants happening in our relationship with him. And these "somethings" are first priority—they are things worth living for. ❦

*T*ODAY'S THOUGHT: *What do you have to live for?*

LOVE

Now may the Lord of peace himself give you peace at all times in all ways. 2 Thessalonians 3:16

Paul's volatile second letter to the Thessalonians ends with a benediction of peace. Certain sections of the letter remind us of Jesus' words, "I have not come to bring peace, but a sword" (Matthew 10:34). However, Paul wants to end his letter with words that remind us of Jesus when he said, "Peace I leave with you" (John 14:27).

Paul calls Jesus the "Lord of peace," emphasizing that controversies within the church should always be viewed as necessary tensions on the way to deeper unity. The same can be said for marriages. Married life will always be filled with disagreements and the need for compromise. It, as well as the church, is a testing ground on which we give and take as we seek unity. Christ's goal for the church and for Christian marriages is that we "may be one" (John 17:11).

Christian homes should be centers of peace, but not at the cost of honesty. Honesty is what disturbs the tranquility of marriage as we express our true feelings to one another, in love, and try to work through them to unity. But the peace that is then achieved is peace indeed. ❦

TODAY'S THOUGHT: *Do you "keep peace" or "make peace" in your home?*

LOVE

But there are also many other things which Jesus did.
John 21:25

Those who value Christian marriage cannot help but be disappointed that Jesus didn't say more about it. Of course he dealt with life issues, and those necessarily involve marriage. (The biblical bases for the teachings in this book confirm that.) But we don't seem to have many helpful biblical role models.

Peter was married, but he almost seems to have gone off and left his wife. The patriarchs of the Old Testament aren't much help; they practiced polygamy and (to say the least!) devalued women. The prophets were, for the most part, loners, including John the Baptist. And, of course, Jesus and Paul never married.

The Acts of the Apostles ends rather abruptly with the twenty-eighth chapter. But we can imagine that it continues with a chapter 29, through the lives of Christians from that time forward. We who are married Christians today, living by biblical principles, become the role models for those to come. What a responsibility! What an opportunity! ❧

*T*ODAY'S THOUGHT: *What couples have been role models of Christian marriage for you?*

LOVE

This man began to build, and was not able to finish. Luke 14:30

When an assistant clergyman was hired, the senior pastor encouraged him to get involved with the people. Several afternoons later he arrived at the church looking forlorn and bedraggled. "What happened to you?" asked the senior pastor. "Well, sir," the assistant replied, "I have just taken it upon myself to tackle the problem you have with the older people in the congregation." "I have no problems with the older people in this church" was the response. "Oh," said the assistant, "I think you do now."

Unless we sit down and count the cost before we rush off to undertake some objective, we will be unable to finish what we start.

God has given us a plan for Christian marriage. We entered into that plan by way of a covenant with our loved one and with God. The conditions of that covenant were spelled out in the words we exchanged at our wedding, supplemented by what we learn through Scripture and the teachings of the church. If we impetuously rush off in another direction, we'll bring chaos. But as long as we proceed within those guidelines, we find fulfillment in marriage. ❦

*T*ODAY'S THOUGHT: *What do you need to "think through" in your relationship with your spouse?*

The simple go on, and suffer for it. Proverbs 22:3

The saying "Into every life some rain must fall" certainly is true of married life. There is no way to avoid the pain and suffering that are a part of living.

But pain can be the doorway to healing. We ignore it at our peril: "The simple go on, and suffer for it." The wise, however, realize that there is a message in the pain. Christian counselor Dr. Paul Tournier said he hoped his patients wouldn't get rid of their pain until they knew the meaning of it.

Our inner pain acts as an alarm system to warn us of impending danger. Rather than reacting to the alarm by grabbing our valuables and running for our lives, we need to analyze calmly what the problem is and begin to work toward a solution. One of the seductions of modern life is that the conveniences and distractions we have tend to mask the pain. If we try to ignore the pain or stuff it down within us, it will simply pop up in some more serious way. If we, instead, allow the pain to happen, we have a much better chance of dealing with it successfully. ❧

*T*ODAY'S THOUGHT: *With what pain do you need to deal?*

APRIL 12 LOVE

Those controlled by the sinful nature cannot please God.
Romans 8:8 NIV

Many marriages disintegrate because of addictions or compulsions of either husband or wife. A huge percentage of people are addicted to alcohol, drugs, work, eating, gambling, or something equally threatening to marriage and family life. Perhaps a great many more are controlled by compulsions that become the primary driving force in their lives.

When an addiction or compulsion becomes our god, we may say, and actually believe, that we are a faithful Christian and a faithful spouse; but, in actuality, we are engaged in pagan worship of some substance, habit, or sin. We are likewise untrue to our spouse because we love something else more than him or her. We must all do a reality check to see if such a problem exists in our life or marriage.

Denial is a process by which we take thoughts and feelings that are unacceptable to the image of who we think we are and stuff them down in our subconscious. If we are in denial concerning an addiction or compulsion, we need to be honest. There are many programs available to help us root out and deal with these addictions or compulsions so they will no longer control us. ❧

*T*ODAY'S THOUGHT: *Do you have a god other than God? If so, what will you do about it?*

And gave us the ministry of reconciliation. 2 Corinthians 5:18

We live in a time when, increasingly, lay people are becoming aware that they also are called to ministry. As 2 Corinthians 5 points out, we are specifically called to a ministry of reconciliation. We are here in this world to love others for Christ, and to bring them into relationship with him.

Our marriage is our primary ministry, and looking at it as such opens all sorts of possibilities. Because it is not really our ministry, but Christ's, we realize we are serving our spouse as Christ would serve him or her. That not only raises our love and care for our spouse to a whole new level, it assures us that, as we minister, we are not doing it in our own strength but by the power of God!

One note of caution: Let's not get too functional about ministering to our spouse (i.e., doing things as opposed to loving and listening). As one spouse said, "Will you please stop ministering to me and just love me?" 🍎

*T*ODAY'S THOUGHT: *How can you treat your marriage more as a ministry?*

LOVE

The boundary lines have fallen for me in pleasant places.
Psalm 16:6 NIV

The more whole we are as persons, the better our marriage will be. One important aspect of wholeness is having healthy boundaries—understanding personal limits and the right to personal space. Boundaries prevent us from obligating ourselves to do things we shouldn't be doing in the first place and from being taken advantage of by others.

Some Christians shy away from the idea of having boundaries because they believe we always need to be available to God and to our fellow human beings; they see the exercising of boundaries as sheer selfishness. Remember, however, that we impose boundaries on our children for their own health and protection. We don't allow them to do certain things we feel they are incapable of—or to make certain decisions on their own. Similarly, the boundaries we're discussing are for our own health and protection.

We are little good to our spouse and family if we allow ourselves to be drained physically, emotionally, or spiritually. ❦

*T*ODAY'S THOUGHT: *Do you exercise reasonable boundaries?*

So God created man in his own image. Genesis 1:27

Let's talk more about boundaries. Because wholeness of the individuals in a marriage relationship enhances the marriage itself, the more realistic our individual self-images are, the healthier the marriage will be. We need to remind ourselves that God created us in his own image and that we devalue God when we devalue ourselves.

People who do not have good self-images often do not have sound boundaries. They either try to earn acceptance from others (thus, theoretically becoming more acceptable to themselves) by overdoing, or their negative self-image causes them to be hostile to others and to erect unreasonable boundaries (walls) to prevent others from becoming a constructive part of their lives. Such behavior is not only unhealthy to the individual, it's destructive to the marriage.

People with realistic self-images, on the other hand, normally have good boundaries. By the grace of God, they are able to discern what reasonable restrictions to impose on their time and energy for their own protection and health. They know when to say no. So, for the benefit of our marriage, and our life in general, we need to realize the importance of boundaries and to work on any self-image problems we may have. ❦

*T*ODAY'S THOUGHT: *What image do you have of yourself?*

LOVE

Thou hast granted me life and steadfast love. Job 10:12

Just as boundaries exist to protect us individually that we might become whole persons, there are also boundaries we should exercise as married couples and Christian families.

Some boundaries of this nature are obvious. There are certain things we will not do (i.e., commit adultery) and places we will not go (i.e., pornographic movie houses) as Christians. But there are other important boundaries that aren't so obvious. These have to do with realistically assessing what we can do and can't do, what we need and don't need, who we are and who we aren't.

God has granted us life and a household of love in the midst of a chaotic world. In order for God to use us as a healthy example of how he wants his people to live, we need to be realistic about what we should and should not be doing. Just as we can be taken advantage of individually, to our (and our marriage's) detriment, we, as a Christian couple and family, can be abused by society's—and even the church's—demands. As others seek to get us involved, we need to be prayerful and realistic. ❦

*T*ODAY'S THOUGHT: *Are you being unfairly imposed on in any areas? How can you prevent this from happening in the future?*

The fire will test the quality of each man's work.
1 Corinthians 3:13 NIV

Think of people you know who have lost their spouse by death. Some of them have extremely happy memories of that loved one and their life together. Others are filled with remorse about things that should have been done, words that should have been said. Still others fall somewhere in between those two emotions. These feelings speak of the quality of married life.

In this age of "divorcitis" we honor people who have been married long years. Perhaps we should celebrate even more every year of a marriage that exhibits the qualities God wants of Christian marriage, even if it is only the first or third or tenth anniversary.

What makes a quality marriage? First, having Jesus Christ at the center of it. Second, seeing marriage as your ministry. Other essential qualities are honesty, open communication, being willing to work, understanding love is a decision rather than a feeling, and taking the time to worship, pray, and study Scripture together. These attributes and attitudes produce quality worthy of being tested by fire. 🐦

*T*ODAY'S THOUGHT: *Appraise the quality of your marriage.*

LOVE

The whole body, supported and held together by its ligaments and sinews, grows as God causes it to grow. Colossians 2:19 NIV

In a day when divorce seems an easy option, we need support from the body of Christ to help hold our marriages together. Too many Christian couples have treated their marriage as a private affair, unwilling to share problems with others who might have helped, until the situation has gone too far to save the marriage.

Obviously, we must use discretion in sharing with others marital problems we may be having. However, we need to remember that when we took our wedding vows, the people who witnessed those vows (mainly our church family) committed themselves to support us.

We should avail ourselves of all the church has to offer in support of our marriage. Private counseling by clergy or trained lay people is one option. Another option is small groups that pray and study the Bible together, becoming "families within the family of Christ" where all know they are loved and can be vulnerable in sharing. In addition, many churches offer courses on healthy marriage and parenting. These are ways our marriage can be "supported and held together . . . as God causes it to grow." ❧

*T*ODAY'S THOUGHT: *In what ways are you seeking support from the church for your marriage?*

Happy are those whose greatest desire is to do what God requires.
Matthew 5:6 TEV

It has been said that to be psychologically healthy we need creative, meaningful work, a purpose in life, and our needs met (to the extent that these things are possible for us). Our greatest desire should be to do what God requires, because that is at the heart of purpose in life. But it is helpful, from time to time, to back off and prayerfully reflect upon our life, its purpose, and the extent to which we are doing what God wants us to do. That doesn't mean we should always be seeking change; most often, God reveals how he wants to use us more creatively and effectively just where we are.

As married people, we need to support each other in reaching psychological wholeness. We should constantly be thinking, *How can I help my spouse achieve creative, meaningful work, a purpose in life, and have his/her needs met?* ❧

*T*ODAY'S THOUGHT: *What is your purpose in life? Is it being fulfilled? Why or why not?*

Each man has his own gift from God. 1 Corinthians 7:7 NIV

Paul makes this statement in connection with marriage. Our spouse is a gift from God, and there is nothing we should cherish as greatly! We need only look around—at all those who have never married, or whose marriages have ended in divorce because they believed they had the wrong spouse—to know how precious a gift we have in our spouse.

How do we properly deal with a gift? First, we express our appreciation to the giver. (Have we let God know lately how much we appreciate the gift of our spouse?) Next, we unwrap it. (To what extent have we unwrapped or set free our precious loved one?) Then, we examine the gift. (Examining means getting to know, understanding how something works, etc. Have we examined our spouse?)

Finally, we put the gift to use. We use it in the manner that the giver intended it to be used. In the case of our marriage partner, Jesus is our example of how to "use" the one to whom we owe the greatest debt of love. The model Jesus gave us is a model of serving. ❧

*T*ODAY'S THOUGHT: *What can you do to show how much you appreciate your spouse as a God-given gift?*

Therefore a man leaves his father and his mother and cleaves to his wife. Genesis 2:24

In recent years there has been a trend to blame parents, to a great extent, for all our problems. But, if we are honest, *we* have probably brought into our marriage feelings about our parents that adversely affect our relationship with our spouse.

A mistake some people make is deciding, as a primary goal in life, not to be like one or both of their parents. Perhaps their parents were particularly dominating, and, as a result, that person decides he or she will never be dominating. But if we allow that goal to become the primary focus of our life, we will indeed become dominating (even if it's in a passive-aggressive way).

The answer is not to focus on being unlike all the negative things we saw in our parents, but to forgive them. Forgiveness is at the core of the Christian faith; it is why Jesus died for us. If we can truly forgive our parents, we can come to love and appreciate them (whether or not they are still living). Instead of seeing only the bad, we begin to see their good qualities. Then we can use these good qualities, and not the bad, as patterns for our own marriage. 🍒

*T*ODAY'S THOUGHT: *Do you need to forgive your parents for any negative influence they may have had in your life? If so, ask God to help you forgive them.*

LOVE

Cleaves to his wife, and they become one flesh. Genesis 2:24

The NIV substitutes the word *united* for *cleaves.* A footnote reference is then made to Malachi 2:15 which says, "Has not [the Lord] made them one? In flesh and spirit they are his." Clearly, uniting or cleaving is to be permanent in nature. Once we have left our father and our mother, we become the number-one priority to one another for life.

"Becoming one flesh" deals with the matter of exclusivity. In the marriage relationship we belong wholly to one another. We will each have friends, both male and female, but there is no room for romance between us and anyone else but our spouse. A married person shouldn't even flirt with someone of the opposite sex.

These standards are very different from worldly standards. The so-called sexual revolution of the sixties brought into question our understanding of love and marriage, and changes in social mores, often much more subtle than the excesses of the sixties, have continued to erode the way the majority of people, even Christians, think about marriage. Yet the standards set by God are worth standing up for at any cost. ❦

*T*ODAY'S THOUGHT: *What are you doing to stand up for the Christian concept of marriage?*

Even my close friend, whom I trusted. Psalm 41:9 NIV

Trust is at the heart of any relationship. It has to be built over time because it has to do with reputation. We are either known to be trustworthy, or we are suspect, based on past performance. We have to earn trust by showing, over and over again, that we are worthy of trust.

So it is in marriage. The fact that we wed shows an amazing degree of trust. Yet, into every marriage come those things about ourself that we aren't sure we can share fully with our spouse, that we don't want anyone to know. We wonder if our spouse will still love us if we tell him or her.

If we have grown, through our marriage, to the point where we trust each other completely, and we know our spouse loves us regardless of our failings, we'll be much more willing to share. As a friend of ours said of his wife, "She has the key to my heart; she can walk in and out of it anytime she likes." ❦

*T*ODAY'S THOUGHT: *What is the trust level between you and your spouse?*

I was afraid, because I was naked; and I hid myself.
Genesis 3:10

These words from Genesis are in marked contrast to Genesis 2:25: "And the man and his wife were both naked, and were not ashamed." What happened in the intervening nine verses of Scripture? Adam and Eve violated the command of God and ate the forbidden apple.

Sin brings shame. That is the reason Adam and Eve knew they were naked. There are, in a sense, at least two kinds of shame. The first kind of shame is that experienced by Adam and Eve and all of us who have lived subsequently. It is a result of sins we have committed and things we have done wrong or failed to do that we should have done. Our shame calls the matter to our attention so we can ask forgiveness and deal with the shame constructively.

However, many people bring into marriage another kind of shame: the "shame voices" of their past that are not the result of unforgiven sin. Whether we regard them as the work of Satan or as the voices of people (or ourselves, when we haven't lived up to our own expectations) who have judged us in the past, they are not healthy and need to be rejected. False shame is harmful to ourself and our marriage, but real shame can bring healing. 🍒

*T*ODAY'S THOUGHT: *Are there any shame factors you need to deal with?*

The woman whom thou gavest to be with me. . . . The serpent beguiled me. Genesis 3:12-13

Excuses, excuses! If Adam and Eve had just confessed, God would have forgiven them. But what did they do instead? Adam blamed God for giving him the woman who gave him the apple. Eve blamed the snake for enticing her. They rationalized, justified, and blamed someone else.

Are there similar patterns in our relationship with God and our spouse? If we sin against God, do we sometimes find a way to blame it on our spouse? "God, the reason we didn't get to church on Sunday was because Mary forgot to set the alarm clock." "Lord, I wouldn't have gone to that filthy movie if John hadn't convinced me that it was family entertainment despite its industry rating."

Unfortunately, most of us have been gifted with great imagination in concocting reasons for failing God and our spouse. But God doesn't want our rationalizations, and neither does our loved one. God is in the business of forgiving, and we should give our spouse that opportunity as well. If we will just admit our part in anything that shouldn't have been done, not only will we feel better, but we'll more likely reach a satisfactory conclusion. Adam and Eve are our examples—bad ones! 🍎

*T*ODAY'S THOUGHT: *Is there anything you need to confess?*

I will betroth you to me in faithfulness; and you shall know the Lord. Hosea 2:20

Have we been faithful in our relationships? That is what the Lord wants to know—not how much money we've earned, how many awards we've won, what status in life we've attained. In that sense, God is no respecter of persons.

What does it mean to be faithful to our spouse? Obviously it means not engaging in any sort of love affair with anyone else. But it goes much further than that. Our faithfulness to God means praising him, thanking him, being completely open and honest with him, and seeking to live in accordance with his will for us. Shouldn't our faithfulness to our loved one be like that?

If our relationship in marriage is all that it should be, we will be conscious of honoring our spouse by appropriate praise and thanksgiving (including many hugs and kisses). We will be open and honest in our communication. And, consistent with God's own will for us, we will seek to know and follow our spouse's deep needs and desires. That's faithfulness! ❦

TODAY'S THOUGHT: *How would you rate yourself on the faithfulness scale?*

Mary has chosen the good portion, which shall not be taken away from her. Luke 10:42

A well-known author had just been taken to his room in a hotel, only to realize he had no tip for the bellman. "I hate to tell you this," said the man, "but I only have twenty-seven cents in my pocket. However, I'll be glad to give you an autographed copy of my new book." The bellman thought on that choice only for a moment: "If you don't mind, I'll take the twenty-seven cents."

Life is one long series of choices, and married life is no exception. And, as the saying goes, failure to make a choice is a choice. Choices are simply something we can't avoid.

In Luke 10:42, Mary had chosen the way of love. Rather than running around doing the things her sister Martha wanted her to do, she devoted herself fully to Jesus. She simply wanted to be with him, to hear him, to show her love for him. Likewise, we can choose the way of love. Often that means negotiation and compromise. It means loving our spouse enough to work through the choices we have to make that will affect our marriage and family. The best choices are those we arrive at together after full and thoughtful communication. ❦

TODAY'S THOUGHT: *How do you and your spouse make important decisions?*

Each person is tempted when he is lured and enticed by his own desire. James 1:14

Dr. William Barclay has said that every person is a walking civil war, and the problem is the temptations we face. Paul, in Romans 7:22-23, talks about the war between good and evil always going on within himself. It is a common experience of us all, and the tendency is to want to blame the predicament on God, on circumstances, or on someone else (especially our spouse).

There are temptations that lead us away from our spouse (such as lusting after someone else or putting too much time into activities that separate us from our loved one). There are other temptations that have no direct bearing on our marriage, but violate our relationship with God (such as cheating on our income taxes or expense account).

We can either learn and grow by the way we handle temptations, or we can sin and suffer the consequences. The more we give in to or allow ourselves to entertain temptation, the weaker in resistance we become. Conversely, the more we resist temptation, the stronger we are to resist it next time. ❦

*T*ODAY'S THOUGHT: *Are you currently dealing with any temptations? If so, identify them—and work at resisting them.*

Beloved, let us love one another. 1 John 4:7

A friend tells the story of a man who was sailing with his two children when their boat sank. The daughter could not swim, but the son could float on his back. The father told him to do so, while he swam the daughter safely to shore. When the father returned with the boat owner in another boat to pick up the son, the son was still confidently floating on his back. When the boat owner helped the boy out of the water, he asked him if he had been afraid. "No. My dad loves me, and he promised he would come back" was the reply.

That is the sort of confidence our loved ones can have in us if we regularly, consistently show how much we love them. What we cannot supply in talents, material possessions, or good looks, we can supply in steady, loving care toward our spouse and children.

All of us need to know that we are loved, that we are not taken for granted. Are we doing our share to let our family know how much we love them, in specific ways? Not by "buying them off" with presents and money, but by giving them the most precious thing we have to give: ourself? That takes time and attention, and it means being willing to listen, with our ears and our heart. It also allows them to "float along," knowing they are loved. ❦

*J*ODAY'S THOUGHT: *How confident do you think your family is of your love?*

LOVE

His steadfast love endures for ever. Psalm 136:1

Civic leaders were planning a marriage and family confer-
ence and wanted to invite the person they believed to be the
outstanding speaker on the subject. The problem, however,
was that because the man was in such demand, it would be
difficult to get him. "Why do we have to get him?" asked
someone. "Does he have a monopoly on marriage?"

"No," answered another, "marriage has a monopoly on
him."

As we look at the marriages of our friends, of our parents
and their friends, how much devotion to marriage can we
see? Some show such dedication, such complete commitment, that marriage has a monopoly on them. Does our
marriage have a monopoly on us?

True health and wholeness in our relationship with our
spouse lies in allowing ourself to be taken over by the
covenant that binds us together. When this happens, nothing can compete with our marriage. This doesn't mean that
our lives become so focused on one another that we lose our
individual identity, but that our priorities will be right, and
everything will fall into its proper place. ❦

*T*ODAY'S THOUGHT: *What couple has
modeled for you a "marriage that has a monopoly
on them"?*

May

MAY 1 Love

He who walks blamelessly, and does what is right, and speaks truth from his heart. Psalm 15:2

There is a story about a man whose wife suspected they had mice in their house. The husband didn't take the problem very seriously, but said he would get the mousetrap. When he got ready to set it, however, he found he had no cheese, so he set the trap with a picture of cheese he clipped out of a magazine. The next morning he found he had caught a picture of a mouse!

We cannot walk blamelessly, do what is right, and speak the truth unless we first get to the heart of the problem. When difficulty occurs in marriage, we tend to start finding solutions rather than taking the time and effort to find the real difficulty.

Often the problem has to do with the communication between husband and wife (or lack thereof). But, instead of then communicating about the problem, we compound it by jumping to conclusions. We need to take the time to define the problem and take stock of the situation. After all, our marriage is worth it. ❦

*T*ODAY'S THOUGHT: *How can you, as a couple, avoid jumping to conclusions instead of analyzing the problem?*

Love

Now the whole earth had one language. Genesis 11:1

It is hard to conceive of the world having one language because even when husband and wife speak English it often seems like two different languages. Norm Evans, who teaches on "love language," says there are five different aspects of loving communication:

1. Words, by which we build one another up
2. Gifts, as a way of expressing love tangibly
3. Acts of service, whereby we express love in deed
4. Meaningful time, caring enough to really listen
5. Physical touch, such as hugs

All these aspects of loving communication are important, and all should be shown to one another from time to time. But, according to Evans, problems arise because only one of these means of communication is top priority for each person. Some especially need love to be shown by words; others by physical touch. We must learn to express ourselves to our spouse, particularly when he or she is in need of our love, in the way that's most meaningful to him or her. Thus, it's important for each of us to know which form of love language our spouse prefers. ❦

*T*ODAY'S THOUGHT: *What is your form of love language? How about your spouse's?*

Love

He called a little child and had him stand among them.
Matthew 18:2 NIV

By bringing a child and putting him among the disciples, Jesus was demonstrating something very important about the kingdom of God. According to Norm Evans, Jesus was getting down on our level: "Whoever welcomes a little child like this in my name welcomes me" (Matthew 18:5).

As we communicate with our spouse and children, it's important to be on the same level with them emotionally, spiritually, and sometimes physically (a child needs eye contact from a parent when a crucial issue is being dealt with). As we learned yesterday, it's helpful to speak in their particular love language. But it's also important to recognize that a quantity of time is necessary if we're going to have quality time.

Norm Evans says we each have a "love tank" that needs to be kept as full as possible. We fill each other's love tank by our willingness to be "on the same level" with our spouse and children. ❦

*T*ODAY'S THOUGHT: *How full is your spouse's love tank?*

Love

But for the man there was not found a helper fit for him.
Genesis 2:20

Next we'll spend a few days looking at specific things the Bible says about marriage. Genesis 2:20-24 tells of the creation of woman to become a partner for Adam. In Genesis, the issue of sexuality is complicated. It sometimes is seen as fundamental and wholesome, at other times with doubt and distress. But that is the nature of the sex urge: The deepest and most enduring human relationships are rooted in it, yet many of the fiercest human passions and darkest crimes also come out of it.

This situation should not surprise us, for this double side of sexuality runs throughout history. Sex can be used for manipulation and intrigue. It can become an obsession that needs satisfaction regardless of the consequences. Or, when properly understood and exercised, it can be expressed in marriage or sublimated into courageous action and quiet adoration.

Sexuality is divinely ordained. As the slowly maturing experience of the people of the Old Testament revealed, and as all of Scripture expresses, the way in which genuine sexuality is best served is through monogamous marriage. ❦

*T*ODAY'S THOUGHT: *What does sexuality being divinely ordained mean to you?*

Love

He made . . . a woman and brought her to the man. Genesis 2:22

How may the marriage of one man and one woman be such that all God has in mind for them may flourish? It requires utter devotion to each other and a willingness to live and love in accordance with the will of God "as long as they both shall live."

From a biblical point of view, the one word that expresses what marriage is all about is *companionship.* Two different personalities each develop to the fullest by giving and receiving the utmost that both can share. A marriage that doesn't have this kind of mutuality won't reach its highest possibility.

True marriage, the marriage of two Christian people seeking to serve God, is between a man and a woman who bring their different gifts in equal honor and equal exercise. The greater opportunities that women have today can lift marriage nearer to the divine intention. A great marriage is a partnership of true mutuality, not only of body, but of mind and spirit, seeking to understand God's purposes and then live them out to his glory. ❦

*T*ODAY'S THOUGHT: *To what extent is your marriage a true partnership?*

MAY 6 *Love*

Therefore a man leaves his father and his mother and cleaves to his wife. Genesis 2:24

Poet and writer G. A. Studdert-Kennedy once wrote: "Love is the joyous conflict of two or more free, self-conscious persons who rejoice in one another's individualities and . . . through the clash of mind on mind and will on will work out an ever-increasing but never finally completed unity. . . . And the primary school of this vital and vitalizing love is the home."

Home itself, however, will not produce and maintain such unity. It has to be a home that is held together by something more than itself. The presence of God must be of such consciousness and force that individuals are held harmoniously together.

Too many homes began as havens of love, but, once the romance ended, became battlefields in which differing personalities fought for their own territory regardless of the consequences. This can too easily happen if there is not an obedience to God. When we look to God for his grace in dealing with our differences, we will become seekers and searchers through prayer, Bible study, and worship, of God's highest calling to us. Then we can truly be a home. ❧

*T*ODAY'S THOUGHT: *Is your house a home?*

Love

So they are no longer two but one. Matthew 19:6

Having looked specifically at some things the Old Testament says about marriage, let's now turn to some things Jesus said and did.

Jesus' position is based on God's ideal for marriage as set forth in Genesis 2:24. This Jewish ideal provides the basis for the Christian ideal.

The Jewish term for marriage was *kiddushin,* meaning "sanctification" or "consecration." It was used to describe something that had been dedicated for God's own possession and use. Anything that was absolutely surrendered to God was kiddushin.

This means that, in marriage, the husband is dedicated and consecrated to the wife and the wife to the husband. Each becomes the exclusive possession of the other, just as an offering or sacrifice to God became God's exclusive possession. Kiddushin is what Jesus meant when he said that a man shall leave his father and mother and be joined to his wife in one flesh. He was speaking of the total giving of self to each other in marriage. ❦

*T*ODAY'S THOUGHT: *To what extent are you the exclusive possession of your spouse?*

Love

Whoever divorces his wife, except for unchastity, and marries another, commits adultery. Matthew 19:9

Sexual relations are important to marriage, but the total unity Jesus calls us to means that marriage is not given just for the purpose of one act but for all acts in life. Sex is not the whole of the relationship. Any union entered into just to satisfy sexual desires is doomed to failure. Marriage is not so that people can do just one thing together, but all things together.

Ideally, marriage is the total union of two personalities. There are, unfortunately, many marriages in which one person is dominant and the other subservient. This is not union; it is slavery! There are other marriages where the spouses exist in a sort of armed neutrality, where there is constant tension and collision between needs and desires. This also is not union; it is the Third World War. In other marriages two people live together in a sort of resigned acceptance of their differences and, for the most part, go their own individual way and do their own individual thing; this is married singleness.

The ideal is the state in which two people find the completion of their personalities. Each spouse brings to the marriage certain gifts to be shared in a life patterned by thoughtful and prayerful compromise, creative dealing with challenge, and spiritual and mental growth. ❦

*T*ODAY'S THOUGHT: *Evaluate your marriage. Is it the ideal complement of personalities, or one of the other possibilities mentioned?*

Love

For your hardness of heart Moses allowed you to divorce your wives, but from the beginning it was not so. Matthew 19:8

As Jesus continues to teach about marriage, he refers to why the Jews with whom he was debating were allowed, under the Mosaic law, to divorce. It was not to have been that way, from the beginning. Jesus speaks to us strongly against divorce.

Marriage is to be a sharing of all life circumstances. We covenant to love and care for one another "for better, for worse." When people are first married, they often have an idealized picture of each other; they have seen each other at their best. However, after they have been married for a while, they begin to see each other at their worst: when they are tired and irritable, when there doesn't seem to be enough money to pay the bills, when there are problems with the children. It is so easy to say yes to the better and so hard not to say no to the worse.

Yet, divorce is not an option for the Christian. Neither is "living together" (fornication) before marriage. (Statistics show, incidentally, that couples who cohabit before marriage are more likely to divorce than those who do not.) The answer is not to forsake our Christian standards but to decide that we are going to accept the bad with the good because we have promised God we would. By his grace and guidance we can work through our differences and find the ultimate unity that God wants in our marriage. ❧

*T*ODAY'S THOUGHT: *How do you deal with the "for worse" in marriage?*

Love

Therefore what God has joined together, let man not separate.
Matthew 19:6 NIV

Jesus is teaching that the basis of marriage is togetherness, and the foundation of togetherness is consideration. If a marriage is to succeed, it must be grounded in a genuine desire on the part of each person to be considerate of the other. The spouses need to think more of each other than of themselves.

Selfishness is the death of any real relationship, and this is especially true for those of us who are bound together in holy matrimony. Every time we selfishly insist on our own way we drive a wedge into our marriage. Every decision we make without consulting our spouse because it may involve compromise endangers the relationship. Selfishness is the deadly enemy of marriage.

The true basis of marriage is not complicated: It is simply a love that is willing to serve, listen, and to try to understand. It is a love that is always able to forgive. Jesus shows us, not only through his teachings on marriage but in all principles of Christian living, that it is in giving that we receive and in dying to self that we are raised to a new level of living. ❦

*T*ODAY'S THOUGHT: *Does selfishness injure*
your marriage in any areas?

Love

Jesus and his disciples had also been invited to the wedding.
John 2:2 NIV

We have looked at what Jesus taught about marriage; now we see him at one—the wedding at Cana—and it was here that he performed his first miracle, turning water into wine.

In Palestine, a wedding was a truly notable occasion. The wedding festivities lasted far more than a day. The ceremony itself took place in the evening, after a feast. Following the ceremony, the couple were led to their home. By that time it would be dark, and they were conducted, a canopy over their heads, through the streets by the light of flaming torches. They would be taken by the longest possible route so that many people would be able to wish them well. Rather than going away on a honeymoon, they stayed at home and had an open house for a week for their family and friends to visit them. During this time they were treated like a king and queen, despite their physical poverty.

The fact that Jesus' first miracle occurred at a wedding puts his seal of approval on marriage in a special way. His graciousness in dealing with what was a problem and could have been an embarrassment lets us know how important the occasion was to him. As Christians, we didn't have to go through the ritual told about in this story, but we have the joy of knowing that Jesus was at our wedding as well! ❦

*T*ODAY'S THOUGHT: *To what extent were you conscious of Jesus' presence at your wedding?*

Love

For this reason a man will leave his father and mother and be united to his wife, and the two will become one flesh.
Ephesians 5:31 NIV

Paul's teachings on marriage have been a problem for many because, at least in his early letters, he seems to be against it. In actuality, at that time Paul was of the opinion that Christ's return was imminent; therefore, he felt the entire focus of the Christian should be on telling the Good News of Jesus Christ, rather than marrying and settling down.

According to Dr. William Barclay, it is in Ephesians 5:22-33 that Paul's real thoughts on marriage come to the surface. This is also one of the most contested passages in the Bible because it has been used by some Christian husbands to dominate their wives. But, again according to Dr. Barclay, that happens when the emphasis of the passage is entirely misplaced.

The problem comes at verses 22 and 23, where wives are told to be subject to their husbands, and the husband is said to be the head of the wife. These verses are not to be quoted in isolation, but considered in light of the entire passage. The basis of the passage is not control but love. Paul is talking about the kind of love husbands and wives should have toward one another. We will look at that kind of love over the next two days. 🦅

*T*ODAY'S THOUGHT: *How do you interpret the Ephesians passage?*

Love

For the husband is the head of the wife as Christ is the head of the church. Ephesians 5:23 NIV

The love of the husband for the wife is to be a sacrificial love. He is to love her as Christ loved the church and gave himself for her. This is the epitome of unselfish love.

Paul teaches that the husband has responsibilities. Being the spiritual head of the wife and the household does not mean being a tyrant. In fact, it's just the opposite: It means the husband is duty bound to provide certain things, including physical and spiritual protection for his wife and family. The mature husband looks at Ephesians 5:23 and says, "Lord, you have given me responsibility for my family; help me to see the many things I need to do to provide for them, and give me the grace and strength to do so."

Most of all, the husband has the responsibility to love. He is to love his wife as Christ loved the church. Christ gave his life for the church, and a husband is to give his life for his wife. That does not mean being nailed to a cross as Christ was, but giving ourself day and night for the rest of our life for the good of our wife and family. ❦

*T*ODAY'S THOUGHT: *What are some specific responsibilities of a Christian husband?*

Love

Husbands, love your wives, as Christ loved the church.
Ephesians 5:25

The command that husbands love their wives as Christ loves the church not only implies sacrifice, but other things as well.

The husband's love for his wife is to be a purifying love. Paul talks about how Jesus makes the church "holy, cleansing her by the washing with water through the word" (verse 26 NIV). By the washing of baptism and the confession of faith, Jesus sought to make for himself a cleansed and consecrated church. The husband brings this element to marriage when he holds himself as an example of moral purity.

The husband's love is also to be a caring love. "Husbands should love their wives as their own bodies" (verse 28). Just as we are attentive to, and considerate of, our own body, so should the husband care for his wife.

The husband's love should be an undying love. "Each one of you also must love his wife as he loves himself" (verse 33 NIV). Because of this love, a man will leave his father and mother and be joined to his wife—permanently. Just as we will always love ourselves, so the husband is always to love his wife. 🥀

*T*ODAY'S THOUGHT: *What is your*
understanding now of what Paul thought about
Christian marriage?

Love

I will stand at my watch and station myself. Habakkuk 2:1 NIV

Let's consider some practical applications to what Paul teaches about the responsibilities of husbands.

Too often, husbands simply become family spectators. When a psychiatrist asked a little boy what his father did, wanting to learn the man's occupation, the boy replied, "He watches." "You mean he is a nightwatchman?" the psychiatrist asked. "No," the little boy responded, "he just watches." "Well, what does he watch?" "He watches football games on television; he watches me do chores around the house and my sister do the dishes; he watches my mother cook the meals and tell me and my sister what to do; mainly, he just watches."

Most Christian women want their husband to be the spiritual head of the household. But that cannot happen unless husbands resist the temptation to use a hard day at work as an excuse for becoming watchers instead of leaders. When the wife does not work outside of the home, she often feels that the husband is entitled to his rest and is unwilling to challenge the "spectatoritis" he is exhibiting. Husbands have a responsibility to break the habit themselves. 🐝

*T*ODAY'S THOUGHT: *Is spectatoritis a problem in your household?*

MAY 16

Love

Touch no unclean thing; go out from the midst of her, purify yourselves. Isaiah 52:11

A couple of days ago, reference was made to the need for husbands to exhibit a purifying love. The spiritual protection that a husband should be providing to the household certainly includes his maintaining personal holiness.

In one sense, the husband's spiritual protection of the household is like an umbrella held over it to prevent Satan from intruding in Christ's territory. As long as the husband keeps his own life pure and protects the household by his prayers, Satan is thwarted. When the reverse happens, and the husband becomes guilty of impurity of thought and/or action, the umbrella springs leaks and no longer provides the needed protection.

No situation such as this is permanently fatal, however. We are all guilty of sin and fall into temptations that are detrimental to the spiritual well-being of our family. Thank God, we can go to him in prayer, repent, be forgiven, and reestablish the protective environment the family needs. The point is that our personal holiness (husbands and wives!) is important to God. If we expect God's spiritual protection of our household, there is a responsibility on the part of husbands to take their spiritual leadership seriously. ❦

*T*ODAY'S THOUGHT: *What is the status of the umbrella in your household?*

Love

As a father has compassion on his children. Psalm 103:13 NIV

While dealing with the responsibilities of husbands, it would be well to look at some related obligations of fathers to their children, specifically to their daughters and their sons.

If a father shows an unhealthy interest in the anatomy of women, it can have a very adverse effect on his daughter. If the man reads magazines with pictures of nude women or comments admiringly about scantily clad women at the beach, for instance, it gives the daughter a message: "Dad likes sexy looking women." Often, despite the father's own voyeurism, the last thing he wants is for his own daughter to "grow up too fast." So, the result is a disastrously mixed message. The daughter wants to look sexy to please her father, and he reacts, often violently, against her attempts.

Likewise, a father needs to realize that he is the number one male role model for his son during the son's formative years. If there are things a person doesn't like about himself as a husband and father, he had better correct them as soon as possible, or he may well see them repeated in the life of his son. A father who has compassion for his children will be willing to take the simple steps necessary to create a wholesome environment for them. 🌿

*T*ODAY'S THOUGHT: *Is there anything that needs to be done to "clean up the act" in your home?*

Love

My house shall be called a house of prayer. Mark 11:17

Although Jesus spoke these words concerning the temple in Jerusalem, it is certainly true that if our house is to be his, we need to make it a house of prayer. Over the last several days we have directed our attention to husbands and fathers; now we turn primarily to the woman's responsibility.

When the husband accepts his duty to be spiritual head of the household, that doesn't mean all spiritual responsibility falls on him. As the primary keeper of the home, it is the duty of the wife to pray for the benefit of the home. Normally, she will spend more time there than her husband; thus, she should keep it saturated in prayer.

Furthermore, it is usually the wife who has primary responsibility for the decor of the home. She is the one who will probably choose the pictures, slogans, quotes, and symbols that appear around the house. These items can be faith builders for the family and for friends and strangers who visit (again, balance is important; overkill can have a negative effect). God is a vital part of our marriage covenant, and our devotion to him should be obvious to all who come into our home. ❧

*T*ODAY'S THOUGHT: *What impression would a stranger get concerning your faith if visiting your home?*

I will pull down my barns, and build larger ones. Luke 12:18

The main cause of divorce is not physical abuse and addictions; it is intimacy killers.

The word *intimate* means "belonging to or characteristic of one's deepest nature; marked by a very close association, contact or familiarity; of a very personal and private nature." Holy matrimony is intended to be the ultimate intimate relationship. Our goal in looking at intimacy killers over the next few days is so we can identify and combat them.

Busyness is a major intimacy killer, and this is particularly true now that many husbands and wives both work outside of the home. We are always finding more barns to pull down so we can build larger ones. If we allow the busyness of our jobs and/or our civic and social activities to exhaust us, we have no energy left for our spouse and children. Busyness means stressful lives, and stress kills intimacy. We can even get so involved in good Christian work that we forget the great work God has for us: our marriage. God does not want us to be lazy; he wants us active. We need, however, to weigh the things we have to do against the way God wants us to be. And, most of all, God wants us to be intimately related with our spouse. ❦

*T*ODAY'S THOUGHT: *What busyness do you need to curtail?*

Love

These you ought to have done, without neglecting the others.
Luke 11:42

Neglect is another major intimacy killer. Here we are not talking about abandonment of our loved one or even making a wife a golf widow. That sort of neglect is too obvious; it is the more subtle forms of neglect that destroy intimacy.

We need to care creatively for one another. A busy executive once forgot his wife's birthday, their anniversary, and Mother's Day—all in one year. Chagrined at his neglect, he instructed his secretary never to let that happen again. Now that isn't creative caring; that's just passing the buck! Instead, we need to make the deliberate choice to find time to play, talk, and have sexual relations. We can't simply wait for the mood to strike us; we have to care enough for one another to take the time to plan, and plan creatively.

It is true that little things mean a lot. Because we love our spouse, we should be willing to use our mind and heart to discover those little things that make a big difference to our loved one. Even marriages that seem to have died can be resurrected by replacing complacent neglect with creative caring. Neglect can be defeated if we are willing to make the effort. ❦

TODAY'S THOUGHT: *In what ways might you be neglecting your spouse?*

Love

Complete my joy by being of the same mind, having the same love, being in full accord and of one mind. Philippians 2:2

Other intimacy killers include lack of effective communication. Husbands, particularly, seem to be ignorant of good relational skills, resulting in angry and desperate wives. Yet women, despite their tendency to focus more on relationships and intimacy, can also be poor communicators. Because men are such reasoning creatures, they expect their wives to at least attempt order and logic in what they are trying to communicate.

For a husband and wife to be of the same mind, they need to work at effective communication. Often it is helpful simply to repeat, in a gentle and nonjudgmental way, what your spouse has said to you, to see if what you heard was really what he or she said.

Ungodly attitudes are also intimacy killers. One definition of sin is maintaining attitudes or behaviors that tend to destroy relationships. We may actually be unconscious of some behaviors of this type that we routinely exhibit. Ungodly attitudes about sex can, if not checked, lead to fantasizing about intercourse with someone other than our spouse; and that, in turn, can easily lead to the betrayal of adultery. From time to time, we need a reality check about any ungodly attitudes we may be exhibiting. ❦

TODAY'S THOUGHT: Is it time for a reality check about ungodly attitudes? How much do you trust your spouse to help you see these?

Love

Be kind to one another, tenderhearted. Ephesians 4:32

Taking one another for granted, even becoming hard-hearted, can be a major intimacy killer. There are few things worse than regarding your spouse, or being regarded by your spouse, as an old shoe—something comfortable to be around but not very exciting and certainly not worthy of any special attention.

When Paul outlines rules for Christian living in Ephesians 4 and 5, he gives some good advice that applies well to marriage: "Let no evil talk come out of your mouths, but only such as is good for edifying, as fits the occasion, that it may impart grace to those who hear" (Ephesians 4:29). We need to show basic kindness and consideration—affirmation that builds up—to our loved one, not criticism that tears down.

"Let all bitterness and wrath and anger and clamor and slander be put away from you, with all malice, and be kind to one another, tenderhearted, forgiving one another, as God in Christ forgave you" (verses 31-32). Tenderheartedness is the opposite of the "old shoe" feeling. Rather than taking our loved one for granted, we care enough to avoid unkind words and treatment. When we fail, we ask forgiveness. That builds intimacy rather than killing it. ❦

*T*ODAY'S THOUGHT: *Have you been taking anything for granted that is worthy of time and attention?*

Love

O Lord, you have searched me and you know me.
Psalm 139:1 NIV

The final major intimacy killer we'll examine is past wounds and hurts we've brought into our marriage. We all come into marriage with baggage. Some of it is helpful, much of it is not. God, who knows our "going in and coming out," can help us discover and then find healing for this negative baggage.

According to psychiatrists, low self-esteem is the most prevalent emotional problem of our day. It alone can be a major intimacy killer in a marriage. Jesus told us to love others as we love ourselves; but, if we do not love ourselves, how can we be intimate with another? Those who have low self-esteem are convinced they are not worthy and that there are really bad things about themselves they don't want their spouse to discover.

A bad self-image can manifest itself in three ways: building protective walls a loved one cannot penetrate; becoming a sponge who almost seeks to absorb condemnation (always ready to accept fault for anything that happens in the relationship); adopting a passive-aggressive attitude (when we're too unsure to make a decision, but ever ready to complain about the decisions thereby forced by our spouse). A bad self-image can only be cured by learning to love and care for ourselves because God made us in his image. ❧

*T*ODAY'S THOUGHT: *Psalm 139 is an excellent remedy for a bad self-image. Read it whenever you feel bad about yourself.*

Love

Give to every one who begs from you. Luke 6:30

If we are honest about our relationship in marriage, there are times when we need to get and other times when we need to give. Two of our most basic urges are to give and to get. Few of us are all givers or all getters; we are driven in one direction one time, the other another time. Sometimes our need for security, privacy, or intimacy is primary; other times our need to help, affirm, support, or share moves into first place.

There are several things we can learn from this to strengthen our marriage. The first is that although "it is more blessed to give than receive," we are not being honest if we don't admit that we do have needs "to get," and that it is appropriate to let our spouse know those needs when they are there. Often, our loved one is thereby able to fulfill a need to give (to us).

Having said that, however, it is also important to analyze any tendency we might have to want always to be a "getter" rather than a "giver," or at least to be solely a "getter" in some aspect of our lives. If we only seek from life what will benefit ourselves, we miss a basic Christian principle that's essential not only for our happiness but for the happiness of those we love: It *is* more blessed to give than to receive, because giving is contrary to our sin nature (which would have us hold on to everything we have, always seeking more). It is only as we work against our sin nature that we grow in the wholeness God wants for us. ❦

*T*ODAY'S THOUGHT: *To what extent are you a giver? a getter?*

MAY 25 *Love*

For everything there is a season and a time for every matter under heaven. Ecclesiastes 3:1

One of our friends is very conscious of living one day at a time — and living it fully. One of his questions to others often is: "What are the two least important days of the week?" The answer: "Yesterday and tomorrow."

If we maintained time in a bank account, today's time is all we have to spend. The saying "Today is the first day of the rest of your life" is literally true.

Many people, after the time has passed, regret what they did not do for or with their spouse and children. As we reflect on the account of time God provides us, there is no room for regrets about the past. That time has been spent, for good or for ill. This day is the time we have now, and now is the time to be thinking of how we can show our love to our spouse, our children, and our other loved ones. ❦

*T*ODAY'S THOUGHT: *How can you best spend love this day?*

Love

The Lord is my shepherd. Psalm 23:1

If, when we are out walking, we meet a friendly dog and rub its ears or pat its back, it will invariably want to follow us. Our own pets will, from time to time, come to us to be caressed and loved. Apparently sheep do the same thing; sometime during the day they come to the shepherd for him to show them some undivided attention so they will know they are valued and loved by him.

Although we human beings don't like being compared to dogs and sheep, we also want to know that the Great Shepherd loves us and is present with us individually, and as a married couple. We need daily affirmation and reassurance from God. This can come through prayer, Bible study, worship, and in other ways; but, regardless of how we get it, we need it on a continuing basis. When we grow desperate, it's not because of a particular problem we face but because we have lost consciousness of God's presence in our life. Our number-one goal becomes reestablishing that relationship with God.

The same principle is true in our relationship with our spouse. If we are feeling uneasy and can't quite put our finger on what the problem is, it may well be that we are out of relationship with our spouse. We need a hug or kiss, that affirmation and reassurance only our loved one can give us. ❧

*T*ODAY'S THOUGHT: *What loving touch do you especially need to get or give this day?*

MAY 27 *Love*

Men of Galilee, why do you stand looking into heaven? Acts 1:11

This passage from the Acts of the Apostles is about Jesus' ascension into heaven.

The angels are telling the apostles, in a sense, to get about their business instead of just standing around looking.

Relationships are like gardens: They need a lot of attention. The marriage relationship especially needs tender, loving care. Marriages fall apart because of neglect. If we are just standing around looking up at the sky rather than tending the garden of love the Lord has provided us, we'll suffer the consequences. Weeds may get in among the good fruit of our marriage, or locusts may come to rob us of our love for one another.

Like a garden, marriage is work. We can't get by with tending only "in season"; it needs nurture year round. Yet, also like a garden, loving care produces abundant fruit. The beauty of the love relationship is like flowers of infinite variety and beauty. Growth within marriage is like fruit trees that need pruning and that become scarred by time and weather, but produce increasingly better fruit. Wholeness in marriage comes from a bumper crop that only love can produce. 🍎

*T*ODAY'S THOUGHT: *How is your garden doing?*

You will know the truth, and the truth will make you free.
John 8:32

Mark Twain, the great American novelist, once defined faith as believing in something you know really isn't true. Author Jim Peterson has noted, however, that a valid faith is just the opposite: It must be based on truth.

Nothing is more important to our relationship in marriage than honesty and the whole truth. Denial, evasion, and half-truths just muddy the water of communication and, more than that, destroy trust. God put us together so we can become whole people by our interaction, building a level of trust that can become a model for a growing trust in God. Real interaction is thwarted, and trust is impaired, when there is any form of deception. We endanger our relationship with our spouse and with God.

Sometimes we're tempted to withhold truth in order to not hurt our spouse. However, if we are growing together as we should, we are becoming so transparent to one another that we're found out easily enough. Our spouse senses something (even subconsciously) that lets him or her know that things are not right. When we then try to untangle the web of deceit, we often make matters worse. Truth is best. 🐝

*T*ODAY'S THOUGHT: *Have you ever lied to your spouse? What was the result?*

And he sent them out to preach the kingdom of God and to heal.
Luke 9:2

Some years ago, a friend of ours began to grasp more fully the love and power of the Lord in the world around her. She was confronted with stories of Jesus' healing miracles and wanted to believe he would heal in our day. She knew that he could heal, but she had never had a firsthand experience of his healing power.

About that time, her husband experienced such severe pain that they were sure there was something terribly wrong with him. He was scheduled to see a specialist. Prayer was sought, and their pastor laid hands on him and prayed that God would heal and strengthen him. When the tests were performed, they revealed nothing serious, and a troubling rash on the husband's hand had disappeared as well.

The healing her husband experienced gave our friend more trust in God. But it also taught her that, although we should always seek medical help when we need it, our first thought should be to pray for our spouse or our children. If we are to be Jesus to one another, we should pray for our loved ones' healing just as Jesus himself would have done. ❦

*T*ODAY'S THOUGHT: *Is it customary for you to pray for healing for your spouse? Why or why not?*

MAY *30* *Love*

Whoever serves me must follow me. John 12:26 NIV

The same friend mentioned yesterday had another experience that illustrates the parallels between our relationship with the Lord and that with our spouse.

"On several occasions," she wrote, "our family has moved across the country, necessitating driving in separate cars. Because my husband has greater experience in cross-country driving than I, I was content to follow him on these trips. For me, following required many elements. Among them was a willingness to submit to my husband's plan, attentiveness to his timing, and openness to changes in direction. In short, I had to trust in him as leader in the belief that he wanted the best for me, that his decisions were wise and offered safety, and that, at the point of arrival, there would be a happy reunion."

As Christians who are married, we will not only see similarities between this story and things that have happened in our lives, we will also note how the elements of following a spouse's lead can show us how, more effectively, to follow the Lord's lead. In our willingness to trust him and follow where he leads, there are also requirements to be met. But we can be sure we will be with him at the end of the journey, and that it will be a supremely happy reunion. ❦

*T*ODAY'S THOUGHT: *In what specific ways do you follow Jesus?*

MAY *31*

Love

O Lord, I am oppressed; be thou my security! Isaiah 38:14

People are very security conscious today.

The root of the difficulty is probably the drug problem in our country. When people get hooked on drugs, they have to find some way to pay for their habit. The result is often breaking and entering houses to steal whatever of value they can find. Thus, home security systems have become a big business. We can keep our homes safe and secure relatively easily.

Marriage, however, is anything but easy, safe, and secure. It is difficult, hazardous, and frightening. Marriage does not offer security; it offers wholeness. Safety and security are a prison for the timid; marriage is a blessing that brings freedom, wrapped in risk. Divorce offers temporary escape and lifelong pain and regret; growing in the marriage relationship offers temporary pain and turmoil, but lifelong happiness.

We are pilgrims on a journey, vulnerable and exposed. If we remain alive to the dangers around us and willing to face risk after risk, it can be an exciting journey of growth and discovery. We face fear, not behind the walls of "home security systems," but by looking it in the face together, by the grace of God. The ways of the world will invariably oppress us, but we must remember that our security is in the Lord. 🍎

*T*ODAY'S THOUGHT: *Are you facing any fear as a couple right now? If so, take time to pray — together.*

June

LOVE

Seek the Lord and his strength. 1 Chronicles 16:11

We have been going through strange times. In the sixties, people became antiestablishment in order to free themselves from the "bondages of authority" and "find themselves." "Baby boomers," it is said, are mainly interested in having their needs met. Neither route is the one God wants for us. Wholly selfish self-seeking will always result in despair, because selfishness is a dead-end street.

But there is a positive side of self-seeking that many are finding today in coping with alcoholism and other addictions. This isn't wholly selfish; it happens most effectively when the person has simply reached the end of his or her rope and is desperate for help. Healing comes when the person realizes that only God can really help. These people may not have known what they were getting into when they started the journey; but, if they're going to finish it, they will have learned to "seek the Lord and his strength."

There can also be healthy self-seeking within marriage. A healthy marriage is built on the spouses coming to know more about themselves, each other, and their relationship as a couple. But, again, that seeking is best centered in the realization that the kingdom of God must take priority, and then the rest follows from his grace (Luke 12:31). 🍂

*T*ODAY'S THOUGHT: *What does it mean to seek the kingdom of God?*

We like sheep have gone astray. Isaiah 53:6

Jesus often used sheep, one of the most stupid of animals, to illustrate his point. Sheep truly have to be "kept," or they will get into trouble every time.

Perhaps it is an embarrassment to us that Jesus, in referring to sheep, was exposing the foibles of human nature. Sheep, for instance, pay no attention to where they are going. They nibble their way into trouble before they realize what they've done.

Unfortunately, we also can nibble our way into trouble in our marriages. We overlook this, fail to confront that, in our spouse or our children. We decide it's not necessary to go to church every Sunday or to say our prayers and read our Bible every day. We buy a bigger house than we can afford or otherwise get into substantial debt because everyone else seems to be doing it. We rationalize, surely it won't hurt to take the children to see that movie despite the rating it has been given; after all, they've heard all those words, and the violence and sex aren't real but just make-believe. A little flirting with the next-door neighbor is nothing more than that and certainly will come to nothing. Nibble, nibble. If we are aware that every nibble takes us closer to trouble, we will go out of our way to be "kept" by Jesus. 🐑

*T*ODAY'S THOUGHT: *Is there any nibbling going on in your life?*

My heart is in turmoil, and is never still; days of affliction come to meet me. Job 30:27

Allow us to illustrate this teaching with a corny joke. A golf ball landed on an anthill. The golfer had such a poor swing that he had chopped up the anthill and killed all the ants but two, but still hadn't hit the ball. One ant said to the other, "If we want to survive, we'd better get on the ball."

Days of affliction do come upon us in marriage. In the normal course of events of two people trying to live together in intimacy, there will be turmoil. But, rather than cursing it, it is helpful to realize its purpose and to tackle it with courage and determination. Turmoil in marriage is there to help us grow.

When we aren't experiencing difficulties, we become complacent. We are likely to be less attentive to one another. We'll be less intentional about our marriage and the job of keeping it "on course." Without struggle and strain, we can fall easy prey to dumb errors. We won't be as alert as we should be. Rough times, on the other hand, produce the toughness and endurance that are needed to shape our relationship into everything that God intends it to be. In reality, tough times help us to "get on the ball." 🐛

*T*ODAY'S THOUGHT: *Have you faced tough times in your marriage? Are you experiencing them now?*

LOVE

For as we share abundantly in Christ's sufferings, so through Christ we share abundantly in comfort too. 2 Corinthians 1:5

There is, of course, a limit to the difficulties we face in marriage. If marriage were only a continuous series of disasters, it would lead to depression and hopelessness. Fortunately, that is seldom the case. The sufferings are more than counterbalanced with joy.

When we are weighted down by the burdens of life, it is good to remember that the lowest ebb is the turning of the tide. When we feel that everything is working against us and we can hold on no longer, things will probably start to get better. "This too will pass."

In times of intense and lasting trouble, there are two important factors working in our favor. The first is that, as a married couple, we are sharing the experience together. We have each other to lean on rather than having to battle it out in loneliness and separation. The second is that God is with us. With his help, we can steer through any storm. Every storm ultimately blows itself out; all tempests cease. And, in the midst, is the love of God. He is there to comfort and to guide us. We are not alone. ❧

*T*ODAY'S THOUGHT: *When has the love of your spouse and God helped you through a particularly rough time?*

He who does not love does not know God; for God is love.
1 John 4:8

Augustine said, "God loves each one of us as though there were only one of us." If I were the only person left in the world, Jesus would still have died for me. That's how much God loves us. His love is beyond our ability to comprehend.

If we understand that the source of our life and being is love, and that love gives us hope and joy, there is no way we can praise God enough for his love. And he is the one who stirs our own love of and devotion to him! If we truly give ourselves to God, he becomes our dwelling place, our focus, our center.

Just as Christ has shown us what the love of God is all about, we are to show that love to each other in holy matrimony. Each of us can be a model of God's love to the other, to our children, and to those with whom we come into contact day by day. "He who does not love does not know God" could be reversed to say, "He who does love shows his love of God." The only way we can clearly demonstrate that we know God and his love is to reflect it to others—and most of all, to our spouse. 🐚

*T*ODAY'S THOUGHT: *What love have you shown recently?*

Blessed are you poor. Luke 6:20

In the marriage relationship, money is important. It costs a lot to live. The old saying that "two can live as cheaply as one" may have some truth to it, but even a frugal couple will have a hard time living cheaply today. We can, however, become too focused on money and forget what is most important.

A friend put it this way: "By the time I was thirty years old, I had accomplished all my life's goals. I had a wonderful wife and three healthy children. We lived in a dream home that we had built, and it had all the trimmings. We belonged to the right clubs. We enjoyed luxurious vacations in Europe. We attended church every Sunday and enjoyed the Christian fellowship.

"I was in the securities business, managing my newly gained wealth and helping others attain financial independence. I had everything I wanted, and yet I was miserable. I experienced a great sense of dis-ease. I was rich, but I was poor in spirit. I had concentrated on the wrong security business. I lacked the one thing I needed: a personal relationship with Jesus Christ. Fortunately, in the poverty on my spirit, I found what I needed." No amount of wealth can compensate for a marriage centered in a personal relationship with the Lord. ❦

*T*ODAY'S THOUGHT: *Are you focusing too much on something other than your relationship with God and your spouse?*

LOVE

Those servants went out into the streets and gathered all whom they found, both bad and good; so the wedding hall was filled with guests. Matthew 22:10

A friend of ours who is a great Christian leader once had, as a weekend house guest, the president of the United States. Many people envied him, whether they had voted for that particular president or not. What an honor—it was something that could happen only to a very few fortunate individuals. There was much conversation about what it must have been like to have such an important guest.

But if he were asked if the president were the most important person he had ever had in his home, my friend would have replied in the negative. The president had been his guest, but the Lord was there as a permanent resident!

Knowing that Jesus Christ wants to be part of our home helps us realize how important we are to God. He should be the head of our household and the heart of our home. There is no one, no matter how famous, who can ever match him. No matter who might grace the homes of people we know or read about, they can never have such an important personage among them—unless they also have Jesus there as a permanent resident. ❦

*T*ODAY'S THOUGHT: *In what ways is Jesus a resident in your home?*

Remember then what you received and heard. Revelation 3:3

A great deal of life depends on our memory. Married couples have the benefit of helping each other remember; or, on the other hand, we can remind our spouse of things he or she would rather forget!

We tend to remember what is important to us. For the most part, we have a choice of focus: We can choose to store in our memory banks what we want to retain. Yet, there are also things that force themselves upon us in life in such a dramatic or tragic way that we seem unable to forget them regardless of how hard we try.

If we focus our attention on godly things (doing the will of God, making the most of our marriage, concentrating on our spouse and children and their needs rather than our own selfish desires) we can begin to heal our memories constructively. Much of the trash, and some of the pain of unfortunate past events, will simply be lost from lack of recall. The good and positive things that God wants ever before us will be there for ready reference. From this day forward, the choice is ours to develop a wholesome and helpful memory. ❦

*J*ODAY'S THOUGHT: *What positive memories do you need to begin building today?*

In the image of God he created him; male and female he created them. Genesis 1:27

It can be argued that neither an individual man nor an individual woman fully reflects the image of God; the fullness of God's image is only in husband and wife together. Without a spouse we are alone, incomplete.

In the Genesis story, the rib of man was extracted for the purpose of creating woman. As a result, man is incomplete without woman, and vice versa. The symbol of Adam's rib represents the intimacy and companionship that can be found only in a man and woman who are married to one another.

The need for companionship and intimacy is at the core of our being, and can be found only in the complement of husband and wife. Our inherent differentness (i.e., between male and female) is what makes the completeness. This not only is physically true by virtue of the way God made us, but emotionally, psychologically, and spiritually true. By nature men and women tend to feel things differently, to think differently, to see things differently, often creating obstacles to communication. But as we strive to overcome these obstacles, we bring wholeness to what we both feel, think, and see. ❧

*T*ODAY'S THOUGHT: *In what ways does your spouse bring wholeness to your marriage?*

They heard the sound of the Lord God walking in the garden.
Genesis 3:8

Just as companionship and intimacy between husband and wife are necessary in order to represent fully the image of God, so companionship and intimacy between the married couple and God are necessary for there to be holy matrimony. Christian marriage cannot be sustained independent of intimacy with God.

The concept of God walking in the Garden of Eden is a picture of the relationship that was intended between God and human beings. Humans are the crown of God's creation. All that God provided before he made mankind was for the benefit of mankind. He has given people dominion over the earth, and we are its stewards.

As God's people on this earth, we have a major responsibility. While the world is redefining family as any group that cares about me, we who live in companionship and intimacy with each other and with God are models for the way God wants the earth inhabited, nurtured, and guided. We cannot attain the status that God wants for us by demanding our rights or extolling our virtues. We can do it only by obedience to God, as he directs us. And that relationship is totally dependent on our intimacy and companionship with him. ❧

*T*ODAY'S THOUGHT: *Why do you think holy matrimony isn't regarded as highly as it should be in our day?*

Each of us should please his neighbor for his good, to build him up. Romans 15:2 NIV

The Bible talks a lot about responsibility to our neighbor, and there is no one who is more a neighbor to us than our spouse. We are told that self-image is the biggest emotional problem today. Thus, each of us should do all we reasonably can to build up the self-image of our neighbor, our spouse.

Perhaps the greatest image builder is steady and persistent love. Words of love are of little value unless they are supported by actions that show love. Occasional spurts of attention have little effect, particularly when they are done to offset an offense committed or an important matter overlooked. Just as trust can only be built by proving trustworthiness over a period of time, our spouse's self-image can only be improved by our love if we show that love regularly and continuously.

Affirming our loved one is one specific way of building a good self-image; refraining from criticism is another. However, honesty has to be at the base of these actions. There is little good in phony affirmations or in the squelching of issues that need to be discussed. Sensitivity is the key. If we love our spouse as we should, we will miss few opportunities to affirm, and we will criticize only when failure to do so would be the greater crime. ❦

*T*ODAY'S THOUGHT: *How steady and persistent are you in showing love to your spouse?*

LOVE

Encourage one another with these words.
1 Thessalonians 4:18 NIV

A teacher once tried an experiment on her class. She congratulated them on the excellent work they were doing. "Of course," she said, "I expected this of you because you are all exceptional students." Actually, the only thing exceptional about them was that they were fortunate enough to be in her class. Nonetheless, they believed the teacher and began to perform as exceptional students. A little encouragement goes a long way.

The same principle can work in our marriages. Believing in another person, giving encouragement and support, truly works wonders. Men and women often feel inadequate in their sexual performance; let your spouse know he or she is a great lover. Men sometimes sense that they are not providing for their wife, at least in the manner that the wife had anticipated, so women, let your husband know he is an excellent provider. Women often feel they are a failure as a parent; men, tell your wife what a good mother she is.

One of the special blessings of the marriage relationship is that it provides people with a built-in opportunity to encourage one another, to build each other up to face a world that is often, to say the least, inhospitable. ❦

*T*ODAY'S THOUGHT: *What encouragement do you need to give to your spouse right now?*

For our struggle is not against flesh and blood, but against the rulers, against the authorities, against the powers of this dark world and against the spiritual forces of evil in the heavenly realms. Ephesians 6:12 NIV

Perhaps the most famous quote that came out of the last major conflict our nation was involved in was, "If you know the enemy and know yourself, you need not fear one hundred battles." At a time when marriage and family life seem to be under attack in our nation, it is important for us to know ourselves and to know the enemy.

What does it mean to know ourselves? First, it means we're honest about who we are and aren't—as individuals and as marriage partners. Second, just as soldiers need to understand warfare and how to conduct it properly, we must understand marriage according to God's purposes for it.

What does it mean to know the enemy? We must realize the enemy is not a person or people; it is the evil one whose whole purpose is to try to defeat that which God has ordained. C. S. Lewis once said that there are two equal errors people make concerning Satan: one is to take him too seriously, and the other is not to take him seriously enough! We are at war. In every squabble, problem, or crisis that surfaces in our marriage, we need to ask ourselves, *What's going on here?* Often we will be able to discern that it's simply a trap Satan has set for us; and if we resist the devil, he will flee (James 4:7). ❧

*T*ODAY'S THOUGHT: *To what extent are you conscious of Satan's hand in problems that occur in your marriage?*

A man who had died was being carried out, the only son of his mother, and she was a widow. Luke 7:12

A woman in the congregation had dealt with the loss of her husband in a very grace-filled way. The pastor came to her one day and asked her to minister to other widows in the congregation. "You've been through it," he told the widow. "You know what it's all about."

We all will experience grief through the loss of loved ones. When we married, we basically doubled the number of people who would fall into that category. Ultimately, one of us will lose the other to death. As Christians, we know that death is simply entry into the larger and more glorious life, but those of us who are left behind will be lonely—and we will grieve.

Friends who have been through grief therapy following the loss of a loved one say they are encouraged not to focus too much on either the bad times or the good times they and their loved one had together. It is difficult enough to deal with the grief that accompanies the loss without compounding it with negative thoughts. On the other hand, giving attention only to the good times causes a person to idealize the relationship and never be able to overcome the grief. In grief, as in all things in life, there must be balance. ❦

TODAY'S THOUGHT: *Have you lost a loved one? If so, how have you handled grief?*

JUNE *15* LOVE

Weep with those who weep. Romans 12:15

Married Christian couples face many kinds of grief other than the death of a loved one. We are more sensitive to the pain of others. And, if we are also parents, we are aware of the grief we carry concerning the difficulties any of our children have.

Many of us have a tendency to minimize the pain our children face. Because we've been through similar pain when we were young, we know everything will work out in the long run. That can be a big mistake. The pain is real to the child; if it isn't real to us, the child won't feel loved.

The sharing of another's pain is a profound part of the Christian life. This is especially true in our relationship with our spouse and children. We know we are loved when our pain is shared by another at a deep, personal level. To try to avoid pain is to deny the importance of life and of the person who is in pain. But tears of shared grief water the roots of love. ❦

*T*ODAY'S THOUGHT: *When was the last time you cried?*

LOVE

Look at what is before your eyes. 2 Corinthians 10:7

At some marriage-improvement programs, couples spend five minutes giving undivided attention to each other. During that time, they can't take their eyes off each other. For some, it's the first time they've clearly communicated.

Our facial expressions, body language, and eye contact convey more to the other person about what we are really thinking and feeling than our words do. This is why some people have an aversion to talking on the phone when dealing with a delicate matter. The more we genuinely attempt to give our full attention to another person, the more effectively we will communicate with him or her.

The most effective way to communicate with children is to get down on their eye level. It shows that we are accommodating ourselves to them, and that we are serious about what they are saying or what we want to say to them. This, of course, is what Jesus was all about: God getting down on eye level with humankind. ❦

*T*ODAY'S THOUGHT: *When was the last time you gave your spouse undivided attention?*

And Samuel grew, and the Lord was with him. 1 Samuel 3:19

From time to time we should reflect on our life and whether we are living it in accordance with God's purposes for us. As Christian married people, this is particularly important because we not only answer to God for ourselves but also for the way we have treated the loved ones he has given to us.

One way to carry out a self-examination is to think about our various roles in life, and evaluate them as honestly and objectively as possible. Do you have true friends or just longtime acquaintances? Do you have relationships or only contacts? Have you acquired reasonably needed items or amassed possessions? Do you have a home or only a house? Do you have a ministry or just a job? Do you have a family or just dependents?

We must also ask ourselves, *Am I all that my spouse and children deserve?* A key part of the answer lies in whether the Lord has been with you. If you have been going your own way and doing your own thing, you have not been the person God wants you to be. If, on the other hand, you have sought the Lord and tried to follow him in all that you do, your loved ones could not ask more of you. ❧

*T*ODAY'S THOUGHT: *Is it time for a self-examination?*

LOVE

I mention you always in my prayers. Romans 1:9

Asking the blessing at meals has always been a part of our life together. When the children were small, we sometimes ran into some static when they were hungry and the prayers were long. Once, when we looked up at the end of the prayers, all three had their fingers stuck in their ears!

Acknowledging our dependence on God by way of asking the blessing at meals is a habit all Christian families should follow. Even when eating in a restaurant, it is the proper thing to do. Some would regard that as ostentatious, but not if done in humility and reverence. We affirm the faith of our Christian brothers and sisters when they see us openly and devotedly at prayer, and we witness to others of our sincerity of faith.

Within the Christian family itself, we model to one another our dependence on God by our communal prayers. Married couples who ask the blessing at every meal constantly keep before themselves the priority of God in their lives. And Christian parents who do the same are building a healthy habit into their children. ❦

*T*ODAY'S THOUGHT: *How committed are you to asking the Lord's blessing at every meal, no matter where it's eaten?*

A sower went out to sow his seed. Luke 8:5

Farmers are the biggest gamblers in the world. Their lives are at constant risk because they have so little control over the crop that will be produced from the seed they sow.

The biggest factor in successful farming is undoubtedly the weather, over which farmers have no control. The condition of the soil and the quality of the seed are somewhat, but far from wholly, in the farmers' power. They can take measures against pests of various kinds, but they cannot completely thwart them. And when they do have a bumper crop, so does everyone else, and the price drops!

Now, this is not to say that the work of farmers is inconsequential; the opposite is true. If it were not for farmers doing their best to contribute to the end product, nothing would be produced. But the illustration puts things in perspective. Our lives and marriages are dependent on God. We are gamblers, at risk in our relationships. But if we truly depend on God while doing the best we can with what he gives us, we can produce a bountiful harvest. ❧

*T*ODAY'S THOUGHT: *In marriage, what is your part? God's part?*

For attaining wisdom and discipline; for understanding words of insight. Proverbs 1:2 NIV

A healthy marriage means good communication between husband and wife. Let's look at three aspects of good communication.

Sensitivity to the pain our spouse is in will guide us in how effectively we can communicate with him or her. There are times when our loved one could say, "My hurt is so loud I cannot hear what you are saying." In these situations, words will always fail. Such times call for empathy, listening, and patience.

Good communicators are aware of their feelings and able to express them. How we feel is at least as important as what we think. Knowing our own feelings and being able to tell our loved one about them can be extremely helpful.

We tend to interpret our spouse's emotions by the way we feel them. This may not be accurate. Although there are times when our loved one's feelings call for empathy, there are other times when we need to be sufficiently detached from his or her feelings to be able to discern them properly. A right interpretation of the feelings of the other is essential to being able to respond appropriately. If we are sensitive listeners, aware of our own feelings and able to express them, and we work on learning how to interpret our spouse's emotions, we're on our way to effective communication in marriage. ❦

*T*ODAY'S THOUGHT: *How can these guidelines for effective communication help you?*

Speak tenderly to her. Hosea 2:14

Words and actions of a negative, punitive, or even malicious nature, often resulting from anger, can grievously injure our relationship with our family. Although we need to be honest in our words and actions, we must be sensitive to what we should say and do. Our action or response should be appropriate to the situation.

Our innate possessiveness adds to the problem. Often we will do and say things to our loved ones we would never think of saying or doing to anyone else.

First we need to ask ourselves whether, because of the familiarity we have with those of our own household, we are habitually unpleasant in our words and actions toward them. It is the sort of thing we can fall into because we are having a rough time at work or other things aren't going our way. If we're OK in that regard, we should ask next whether we overreact when we become angry. Do we treat our spouse and children with at least the respect and dignity we would a friend or fellow employee? In all situations, we need to remember that family members are our loved ones, God's gifts to us. ❧

*T*ODAY'S THOUGHT: *Are your words and actions toward your loved ones appropriate to the occasion?*

Be angry but do not sin; do not let the sun go down on your anger. Ephesians 4:26

There is no excuse for selfish anger. A bad temper and general unpleasantness are wrong. However, what we sometimes refer to as *righteous indignation* is a form of anger that is honest and can be constructive. We should always hate sin, and we should be angry about the injustices that are suffered by others. However, we should not let even righteous indignation drive us to inappropriate words and actions.

When we become cross with our loved ones, how should we deal with the situation effectively? It is best to deal with the anger immediately. As long as feelings of hostility exist within the home, there will be tension, lack of communication, and trouble will persist. The longer the anger continues, the more bitter it becomes (and thus Paul's sound advice never to let the sun set on our anger).

One of the best pieces of advice we received before our marriage was always to sleep in a double bed. (We were married, incidentally, before it was common for couples to have king- and queen-size beds.) There is something about sleeping in a double bed that makes it almost impossible to remain angry—that is, to remain angry and get any sleep! ❦

TODAY'S THOUGHT: *How do you deal with anger in your home?*

What causes fights and quarrels among you? Don't they come from your desires that battle within you? James 4:1 NIV

How do we deal with fights and quarrels when they occur between us? A friend told us he has a simple solution for handling things he has done that offend his wife.

"First," he said, "I concede. Then I apologize. Finally, I grovel." More serious steps to resolving conflicts between husbands and wives are: confrontation, communication, and negotiation.

If we are going to resolve anything, the first step is getting it out in the open. Few people really like confrontation, especially with our partner for life. Yet, honesty must be at the heart of the relationship, and honesty requires the courage to face the issue.

To deal with any issue, we must communicate. Silence won't make it go away. We have to talk it through. It needs time and attention.

In the end, negotiations can also be essential. If the matter has been one of serious disagreement, compromise may be the only solution. That can only happen with give and take. If we are willing to handle conflict with confrontation, communication, and negotiation, our differences can be resolved. ❧

TODAY'S THOUGHT: *How do you currently handle conflict?*

Offer to God a sacrifice of thanksgiving. Psalm 50:14

Most of us started our marriages by writing a great many thank-you notes for presents. Then, if we had babies, we found ourselves again sending notes of thanksgiving to the many people who gave us baby gifts or sent letters of congratulations. If we are honest, we probably regard thank-you notes as something of a nuisance.

Stories abound, however, of the wonderful results that thank-you notes produce. Perhaps we take time to write someone who has been special to us in shaping our lives for good: a teacher, someone who helped on our journey of faith, a former neighbor or friend. If you have received such notes in the past, you know what they mean. Sometimes they seem to be received just at the right moment, when you can say, "Thanks, I needed that!"

Consider sending thank-you notes to people who have helped your marriage become what it is: maybe the person who introduced you to your spouse, clergy who instructed you in marriage and/or conducted the wedding service, those who have given you advice and encouragement along the way. Taking time to send such thank-you notes can truly be a sacrifice well pleasing to God. And, most of all, we must remember to thank him! ❦

*T*ODAY'S THOUGHT: *To whom are you especially thankful for your marriage?*

For this people's heart has grown dull. Acts 28:27

One of the traps marriage can fall into is dull routine, what we often refer to as "being in a rut." With as many demands as life puts upon us, we may see home as simply a safe haven where we can watch television or otherwise try to escape. If so, there is little effort to be creative in showing our love and attention to one another.

A man once shot at a grizzly bear and missed. The bear started after him. "What did you do?" asked his friend. "I ran as fast as I could, but the bear was catching up with me. Then I saw this tree limb, but it was ten feet up in the air. I had no choice, so I jumped for it." "Were you able to reach the limb?" the friend asked. "Actually, I missed it on the way up," was the reply, "but I caught it on the way back down."

Unfortunately, we, like the hunter, sometimes need an impending disaster to cause us to leap for our best, to break the dull routine, and to reach the goals that God has for us and our marriage. 🍎

*T*ODAY'S THOUGHT: *Are you in a rut in your marriage? If so, how might you escape?*

Thy word is a lamp to my feet and a light to my path.
Psalm 119:105

A friend of ours was a financial consultant to the clergy pension organization of our denomination. He was a man who lived by the Word of God in all areas of life. One day he and a fellow business commuter were on the train to New York City, rejoicing in a stock market rally that had greatly benefitted the pension fund and the businessman's personal financial situation. Suddenly the man turned to our friend and said, "The problem I have with you is that you're happy about the stock market because of the aged, widows, and orphans; my interest is pure greed."

Our friend lived by a different value system because he received his guidance about what's really important in life from Scripture. The Bible truly is the Christian's lamp to our feet and light to our path. It contains guidelines for our life together as married couples, as parents, and as God's people. We need only seek in order to find the answers God will provide. To receive that guidance, however, we have to be familiar with the book, not just running there in times of desperation. The Bible needs to be an integral part of our life together. ❦

*T*ODAY'S THOUGHT: *In what ways is the Bible a guidebook for you and your spouse?*

LOVE

Jesus had compassion on them and touched their eyes.
Matthew 20:34 NIV

A flood became so severe that the owner of a house had to climb onto the roof. When friends came by in a rowboat and offered him rescue, he refused, saying, "No, the Good Lord will take care of me." He said the same thing to the people who came in a motorboat, and later to the people who came in a helicopter to try to save him. When he drowned and went to heaven, he asked the Lord why he hadn't saved him. The reply: "I sent a rowboat, a motorboat, and a helicopter!"

God uses us to reach one another for him. How often we need to be reached with a loving touch. And when that human touch is motivated by the love of God, it is as if he is touching us also.

Within the framework of marriage and family life, there is both the need and opportunity for many loving touches. Kisses and hugs can bring joy, warmth, intimacy, healing, comfort, encouragement, strength, confidence, sympathy, peace, assurance, affirmation, self-worth, hope, trust, and so much more. No investment of ourselves in the lives of the ones we love produces so great a result. ❦

*T*ODAY'S THOUGHT: *How is your loving touch?*

My dove, my perfect one, is [the] only one. Song of Solomon 6:9

The average person probably tends to idealize the size of his or her spouse. If we don't have our loved one's clothes sizes written on a piece of paper, we are likely to be unrealistic in choosing something for our spouse. Although our choice might be flattering, it would be better to have it right (so our spouse doesn't have to exchange it later!).

Because we love our spouse, we perhaps see him or her as perfect. We might, like the writer of the Song of Solomon, say of our spouse, "Who is this that looks forth like the dawn, fair as the moon, bright as the sun?" (Song of Solomon 6:10). Do we, however, carry this profound admiration into the practical aspects of life?

Do we, for instance, carry with us the measurements of our spouse so that we know what size of clothes to buy for him or her? Do we know what our loved one likes and doesn't like to eat? Do we know what our spouse considers fun? These are some of the ways in which we can show that, to us, our loved one really is perfect. ❧

*T*ODAY'S THOUGHT: *How do you honor your spouse as perfect?*

No one who puts his hand to the plow and looks back is fit for the kingdom of God. Luke 9:62

Baseball's Yogi Berra once remarked, "If you don't know where you're going, you're liable to end up someplace else." Can you imagine driving a rototiller while looking back over your shoulder the whole time? Or driving your car while looking at the passenger in the backseat? At one level, Jesus is telling us to keep our eyes on the road to make sure we know where we're headed, that our eyes are on the goal.

At a deeper level, Jesus is warning us that a broken promise is worse than no promise at all. If we promise to follow Jesus and then turn our back on him, we've betrayed our word and broken our relationship with God. Likewise, we made a commitment to our spouse and to God at the time of our wedding. If we, in any way, turn our back on that promise, we betray our word and break our relationship.

Marriage is, in many respects, like putting our hands to the plow. There is a field to be tilled and cared for, a crop to be grown, a harvest to be gathered. Just like the farmer tending his field and his crop, we are to be about the work of marriage on a constant basis. There is never time to let up or look back. It is true that "he who sows sparingly will also reap sparingly, and he who sows bountifully will also reap bountifully" (2 Corinthians 9:6). Let us sow, tend, and reap bountifully. ❦

*T*ODAY'S THOUGHT: *In what ways are you working on your marriage?*

LOVE

Heal the sick ... and say to them, "The kingdom of God has come near to you." Luke 10:9

Jesus told his disciples to go into the villages of Galilee to heal the sick and bring wholeness to the mentally ill. Then he instructed them to announce where the healing power came from. The wonderful cures were neither of human origin nor the product of human skill, but the signs of a new era in history. Like the first rays of sunshine at dawn, they were evidence of the kingdom of God.

By "the kingdom of God," Jesus meant the reign of God on earth, the active power of God at work in the human situation. When God appeared in human form, when Jesus walked the dusty roads of Palestine, God's healing rule began to affect human history in a decisive new way.

The availability of God's healing power has special significance for us as married Christians. It not only means relationships can be healed within the family structure, but that the physical, emotional, and spiritual healing of individuals is also possible. Through prayer, we can seek all sorts of healing between and among our loved ones, and know that God will answer. His answer may not always be what we pray for ("For my thoughts are not your thoughts, neither are your ways my ways," says the Lord in Isaiah 55:8), but however God chooses to work will be the most healing thing for that person. ❦

*T*ODAY'S THOUGHT: *What healing do you need to pray for in your family today?*

July

LOVE

Only one thing is needed. Luke 10:42 NIV

According to sociologists, Americans are now working 138 hours more per year than in the mid-sixties. Yet, others criticize us for laziness. The answer is not working harder. Doctors often refer to the type A lifestyle of many Americans as "hurry sickness." We are a busy, busy culture that doesn't seem to know when to slow down.

The culture Jesus lived in placed relationships over productivity. Yet, even then, some people were caught up in the "hurry sickness." In Luke 10:38-42, we find the story of Martha, who lets herself get rattled by unexpected company. Because she is a perfectionist, she responds compulsively. Jesus loves Martha, but he praises her sister Mary for sitting quietly at his feet and listening.

As Jesus tells Martha, "Only one thing is needed." We need to set aside our worries and distractions and be present with our loved one. It's too easy to justify our own compulsions by saying we are doing them for the benefit of our spouse and children. If our busyness in fulfilling that compulsion takes us away from the presence of our loved ones or makes us cross in their presence because of all we've done, we've caught "hurry sickness." We need, instead, to slow down and sit quietly at their feet. ❦

*T*ODAY'S THOUGHT: *Have you caught "hurry sickness"? Do you need to slow down?*

JULY 2 LOVE

Fathers, do not provoke your children, lest they become discouraged. Colossians 3:21

Fatherhood is in trouble. Workaholic fathers ignore their families. Alcoholic fathers abuse their families. Psychologists say that 90 percent of American families are dysfunctional. Actually, the figure is 100 percent; it's called original sin!

Fathers tend to get the blame. Patriarchy, as reflected especially in the Old Testament, is associated with fatherhood and is condemned by many as an oppressive system. People have trouble praying to God as Father because of the bad experiences they have had with their earthly father.

Fathers were rotten in biblical times too. That's why God needs to educate men in good fathering. From beginning to end, the Bible is a history of God's patient and relentless retraining of fathers.

God's loving care is the model for human fatherhood. Above all, God doesn't want his children to lose heart. Those of us who are Christian fathers need to look to him as our guide in trying to be the fathers God calls us to be. Those of us who are mothers need to support our husbands in any way we can to help them be godly fathers. We also need to let God be our guide to godly motherhood. ❦

*T*ODAY'S THOUGHT: *How can you encourage your children, rather than discouraging them?*

JULY 3

For where two or three are gathered in my name, there am I in the midst of them. Matthew 18:20

What a simple, beautiful promise—and challenge! Here Jesus isn't talking in parables as he often did; he speaks clearly and straight to the point. If we do this, Jesus will be in our midst. Although he's always present when we worship in church services, he promises to be with us in a special way when only two or three are gathered in his name.

For eleven years we traveled all over the United States and abroad, leading "Prayer in Practice" workshops. The idea was not only to teach about prayer, but to get people doing it! One of the primary objectives was to form prayer groups so two or three would continue in prayer long after we had left.

The most important prayer group is the husband and wife. The next most important prayer group is the whole family praying together. We strongly recommend that married couples find some way to have effective prayer time together each day. Establishing a period of prayer, other than the blessing at meals and at bedtime, may be difficult, yet it's extremely worthwhile. ❦

TODAY'S THOUGHT: *What can you do to have more prayer time together?*

*L*OVE

He who is not with me is against me. Luke 11:23

We cannot be lukewarm. Are we with Jesus or against him? Just being "for" him apparently is not enough. Jesus is saying, "If you are not doing the things I have told you to do, then you are not simply neutral, you are literally against me."

What has Jesus told us to do? Feed the hungry, visit the sick and those in prison, take care of widows and orphans, clothe the naked. But his great command is to love God and to love one another. If we truly love in that way, the rest will follow. Nothing will be impossible for us. Our ministry will unfold, and it will become clear who needs our love and how we are to give it. We will be demonstrating that we are truly "with" Jesus.

Loving is not easy, particularly when it means showing love to those around us, all day every day. Yet, this is our greatest calling. Of course we are "for" our spouse and children, but are we "with" them? Are we loving them by doing and saying all the things that Jesus would have us do and say? Being "with" Jesus means being "with" our spouse and children. ❦

*T*ODAY'S THOUGHT: *Are you lukewarm in your relationship with your spouse or children? If so, what will you do?*

Seek his kingdom, and these things will be given to you as well.
Luke 12:31 NIV

A friend writes, "Having recently retired, I sometimes find myself wondering if there will be enough income in case I live as long as many of my ancestors have. Did I build my barn big enough and did I fill it with the right 'things'?

"Or, on the other hand, have I set aside too much treasure for myself? In the parable (Luke 12:13-31), Jesus calls the man a fool for taking such good care of himself. Am I merely rationalizing to say that I'm far from being a wealthy person and that I'm just making things reasonably comfortable for myself? I do want to serve the Lord."

These questions are ones all of us have to ask, not only at retirement, but as we decide how to be good stewards of what we have. As we think about a new house or a new car or begin to prepare for future education, as we decide how much to pledge to the Lord's work for the coming year, as we deal with the mountain of requests we get from worthwhile organizations, what do we do? We seek God's kingdom; we seek to be in relationship with him, growing in the knowledge and love of him day by day. Through prayer, Bible study, worship, and fellowship with other Christians, it becomes more clear how to answer questions about money, possessions, and the future. ❦

TODAY'S THOUGHT: *How do you handle questions about your needs and the needs of others?*

JULY 6 $\mathcal{L}$OVE

But no human being can tame the tongue—a restless evil, full of deadly poison. With it we bless the Lord and Father, and with it we curse men, who are made in the likeness of God.
James 3:8-9

We all wrestle with the "taming of the tongue." We can use our tongues in blessed ways: to speak the truth in love, to encourage one another, to pray and confess, to build up, teach, inspire, and exhort. But we also can use our tongues to distort truth and to bring pain and humiliation to others. We can all recall times in our lives when our casual gossip, convenient exaggeration, shading of the truth, and even withholding of speech when we should have said something in someone's defense have been the source of pain and broken relationships.

Only God can reform our thoughts and speech to more properly reflect his image—if we are willing to confess our misuse of this great and dangerous gift and to ask his forgiveness. We also need to ask forgiveness of those we have hurt through the misuse of our tongue, beginning with our own loved ones. 🍎

$\mathcal{T}$ODAY'S THOUGHT: *Have you misused your tongue lately? If so, confess that sin to God—and ask your spouse or child for forgiveness.*

JULY 7 ℒOVE

Always be prepared to make a defense to any one who calls you to account for the hope that is in you, yet do it with gentleness and reverence. 1 Peter 3:15

We Christians are to be prepared to share with others what Christ means to us. We don't have to do that defensively or offensively; instead, we are to share with gentleness and reverence. The title of Joyce Neville's book says it all: *How to Share Your Faith without Being Offensive.*

What we have to share is the hope that is in us. There is reason for Christians to be hopeful. The world can be filled with chaos and disaster; our friends can be facing illness and a myriad of other problems; we can be in similar difficulties in our own lives. Yet, because God is with us, we know that present problems are not the end of the story. We need to share with others that with the bad there is always the good; and that good is indeed very good.

What we have said about our faith could also be said about our marriage. We need always to be prepared to share the hope that is in us as a married couple. No matter how bad things are around us, we have each other and God as an integral part of our togetherness; we are all three partners in the covenant of holy matrimony. People need to know that too. ❦

TODAY'S THOUGHT: *When have you had a chance to share the hope you have in Christ?*

LOVE

Bear one another's burdens, and so fulfill the law of Christ.
Galatians 6:2

Old Testament law did not come to an end with Christ; instead, he came to fulfill the law. But, in Christ, we see "law" in a new way. Rather than being able to see only the letter of the law (the trap the Pharisees had fallen into), Jesus made it clear we have to obey the spirit of the law as well. At the heart of the spirit of the law is loving God and loving neighbor as self. That certainly includes bearing one another's burdens. Jesus never said that the Christian life would be easy.

Often we may feel that it's enough to carry our own burdens, much less take on someone else's. Yet, bearing one another's burdens is at the heart of marriage and family. The principle of burden bearing has some very positive aspects. First, it is a privilege to share the burden of another person, particularly one we love. Second, we know the load won't be too heavy because Jesus carries it with us (Matthew 11:29-30). Finally, we also know that, when the burden is ours, our loved ones and our Christian brothers and sisters will be helping us with the load, for that is the law of Christ. ❦

*T*ODAY'S THOUGHT: *What burden(s) are you helping your loved ones carry today?*

JULY 9 LOVE

Do you not know that you are God's temple and that God's Spirit dwells in you? 1 Corinthians 3:16

How differently we Christians would live if we were always fully conscious that we are temples of the Holy Spirit because the Spirit of God dwells within us.

Christian married people need to be especially sensitive to this teaching of Paul's. Today there is much arrogance, even among Christians, concerning sexual behavior. The attitude is that whatever is done between consenting adults is nobody else's business. Would we feel that way if we were truly conscious that we are temples of the Holy Spirit? Whenever we disobey the law of Christ, we defile the temple, we injure the soul, and there is no health in us. Only as the Christian family upholds a godly lifestyle will further moral degeneration in our country be avoided.

The good news is that the indwelling Christ can guide us away from sinful behavior, sustain us in times of weakness and temptation, pick us up when we fall, and forgive us when we sin. ❦

*T*ODAY'S THOUGHT: *What would you do differently if you were always conscious of the Holy Spirit within?*

*L*OVE

In him we have redemption through his blood, the forgiveness of our trespasses, according to the riches of his grace. Ephesians 1:7

Although, as we noted yesterday, we are temples of the Holy Spirit, we are also Christians under construction. A little button, popular some years ago, said, "Please be patient. God isn't finished with me yet." A friend stated this in another way: "God loves me just as I am, but he likes me too much to let me stay this way."

Thank God he forgives us. God loves us so much that he was willing to come among us in Jesus Christ and let us do our very worst to him. Then he redeemed us with his precious blood, shed on our behalf. "According to the riches of his grace," we have been redeemed from the pawnshop of a wasted life, and we are forgiven when we repent of the fact that we have gone astray. Then we and God, in a joint effort, can get about the job of constructing us into the person he calls us to be.

God also is constructing our marriages into what he wants them to be. Because of the closeness of our relationship within the bond of marriage, there are often things for which we need forgiveness from one another and from God. Fortunately for us, God is in the business of forgiveness. He is also there to help us build constructively on the foundation of our repentance. ❦

*T*ODAY'S THOUGHT: *What, for you, are "the riches of his grace"?*

*L*OVE

But be doers of the word, and not hearers only. James 1:22

Studying Scripture regularly is certainly one of the primary things we should do in order to grow in our relationship with God and with each other. We can be especially thankful that, in our day, there are many translations that speak to our particular needs. It is through Scripture that we know about God and how he wants us to live.

But James is calling us to a step beyond Bible study. It is not enough simply to hear God through Scripture. Our Bible study is really of no value unless it changes our lives.

There are habits God wants us to form or break. There are particular actions God wants us to take or avoid. Most of all, there is a lifestyle he wants us to adopt as a Christian married couple, something very different from the lifestyle depicted for us by the world. God wants us to do what the Bible instructs us to do. And he wants us to do it together so we may reflect to the world what wholeness is. ❦

*T*ODAY'S THOUGHT: *What have you learned from Scripture that God wants you to do this very day?*

LOVE

Have this mind among yourselves, which you have in Christ Jesus. Philippians 2:5

The goal of Christian living should be to attain the mind of Christ. Although we cannot reach this goal in our lifetime, it is certainly worthy of pursuit.

Many of us are spoiled. For the most part, we have it rather easy in life; we are accustomed to instant everything. Sometimes we'd like to have our Christianity easy and convenient too. Those who aren't willing to spend time studying Scripture in order to learn what the mind of Christ is with regard to various matters will say, "What Christ is all about is love, so all we have to do is show love to everyone."

That statement is true; but Jesus, Paul, and others give us, in Scripture, a picture of love that is much more demanding than simply saying yes to everyone. Christ's love is tough love—the kind of love we need in order to be shaped and molded into the people God created us to be. This truth is especially important within the framework of marriage and family, for it is there that tough love must be most expertly practiced. As we attain the mind of Christ, we'll become increasingly able to show and receive tough love in our home. ❦

*T*ODAY'S THOUGHT: *Have you exercised—or received—tough love? If so, give an example.*

LOVE

Why do we endanger ourselves every hour?
1 Corinthians 15:30 NIV

There are four characteristics that, when manifested in marriage, spell danger (and often lead to divorce).

If they appear in our relationship, they need to be counteracted. They tend to take place in sequence: criticism, contempt, defensiveness, and withdrawal.

Criticism, if it goes unchecked, can ultimately lead to contempt between individuals. The one who is doing the criticizing can conclude that the one being criticized really is contemptible; the weight of error laid upon the other adds up to contempt of the other. The person being criticized can also be led to contempt of the one doing the criticizing, as a defense against the pain created by the criticism. In most cases, however, criticism by one leads to retaliatory criticism by the other, building contempt one against the other.

Likewise, bearing the abuse of criticism can lead a person to defensiveness and, ultimately, withdrawal. When withdrawal takes place, the opportunity for communication is destroyed.

The solution? Don't criticize in the first place. Criticism involves judging the other person and has no place in marriage. When our spouse falls short of our expectations in some regard, we must let him or her know how that makes us feel. In order to reconcile differences and heal wounds, we need to communicate with one another. ❧

*T*ODAY'S THOUGHT: *Have you ever felt that your spouse has failed you? If so, how did you handle it?*

JULY *14* *LOVE*

The Pharisees and the lawyers rejected the purpose of God for themselves. Luke 7:30

What arrogance on the part of anyone who rejects the purposes of God for their life! That, of course, is why Jesus so often denounced the Pharisees and the lawyers who were constantly putting him to the test. They had made up their minds what God wanted from them, and they were not open to any new revelation of God's will.

While it is easy to dismiss the actions of the lawyers and Pharisees of Jesus' time, are we not guilty of the same arrogance when we fail to seek God's counsel? Perhaps we believe that the matter before us is too trivial for God. Or we feel we are too busy to pray. Whatever the reason, God beckons us to come to him with all of ourselves and all of our lives.

Because our marriage union represents to the world the relationship between Christ and the church, it's particularly important that we seek God's will for our lives.

God is always reaching out, seeking us, never too busy for us. Nothing is too small or of too little importance to God. He is ready, willing, and able to share his bountiful grace and mercies with us. We are heirs of his kingdom, on a special mission. We should never hesitate to tell our Father of our fears or our needs. ❦

*T*ODAY'S THOUGHT: *What is God's purpose for you, as a married couple?*

*L*OVE

Therefore encourage one another and build one another up.
1 Thessalonians 5:11

In the passage that leads to today's verse, Paul makes it clear that, as Christians, we are members of the body of Christ. As such, we are both interdependent and interrelated.

Paul exhorts us to "encourage one another." How do we do that? By being Christ to one another. We get glimpses of what Paul means in a Christian marriage, where a man and woman become one in Christ and are called to build each other up and to be available for each other.

With marriage as the example, we can see what we are called to be in all relationships. God knows we will not be able to meet such a high standard, even in marriage. We can, however, hold up our spouse, our children, our parents, and our brothers and sisters in Christ, asking God to protect and guide them. And, moreover, we can build them up by our words and actions as we affirm them for who they are and show our love to them in a multitude of ways. ❦

*T*ODAY'S THOUGHT: *Whom do you need to build up?*

*L*OVE

*Your iniquities have made a separation between you and your
God.* Isaiah 59:2

As Christian married couples, we need to be mindful not only
of barriers between us and God, but between one another as
well. When our communication with one another faces a
barrier, whether as a result of our own iniquities or because of
factors over which we seem to have no control, our relationship with God often begins to break down as well.

We have been dealing, and will continue to deal, with
communication barriers because they can be serious imped-
iments to a good marriage. Perhaps it would be helpful, over
the next few days, to consider a number of them so you can
assess which ones you might especially need to look out for
in your marriage.

We will look at four categories of communication barriers:

1. Natural barriers (differences we have brought into the
   marriage over which we had no control: for instance,
   gender and culture)
2. Lifestyle barriers (problems created by the way we
   choose to live)
3. Emotional barriers (difficulties between us that get in
   the way)
4. Poor communication skills

At the outset, let's resolve to do all we can to break down
any of these barriers that may exist. To fail to try is indeed
"iniquity." ❦

*T*ODAY'S THOUGHT: *How committed are you
to good communication with your spouse?*

*L*OVE

In the image of God he created him; male and female he created them. Genesis 1:27

The very fact we stay married to one another should be sufficient proof of the grace of God. Perhaps the most basic natural barrier to communication in marriage is the difference between males and females. A great deal of the time, we simply tend to approach things from opposite points of view. The key is to recognize these differences, given to us by God in creation, and realize they exist for a purpose (sanctification, as we are constantly challenged by these differences, and wholeness, so that, together, we can reflect the image of God).

Another natural communication barrier we bring into the marriage is the role models that others (normally, our parents) have been for us. If they have been negative role models, we need to consciously reject what lingering influences still control us.

Cultural (even regional) differences can also be a communication barrier. Even if you've been "next-door sweethearts" since third grade, you've each grown up in a different environment. We are shaped by the traditions, priorities, and beliefs of our forebears. These aren't things to resolve; rather they are things to understand, appreciate, and reach compromises on. ❦

*T*ODAY'S THOUGHT: *How do you deal with the natural barriers to communication in your marriage?*

*L*OVE

For every matter has its time and way. Ecclesiastes 8:6

Our lifestyle can also have a major impact on the time and way we communicate with one another. Obviously our vocation, particularly if there are two vocations outside the home, influences how much time we have together, and the nature of that time (whether we're attentive or tired). Likewise, other forms of busyness, such as involvement in civic and church activities, although commendable in and of themselves, can deprive us of time and attention to one another and be a barrier to effective communication.

Our children can also be a barrier. Although they are certainly deserving of our love and consideration, our spouse must come first.

Finally, our own personal preferences and priorities will affect the time and manner in which we communicate with our spouse. Couch potatoes who are addicted to television and sports enthusiasts who leave football widows are among those who have little time left for good communication.

These are barriers we can do something about. It is a matter of getting our priorities straight. Regardless of our good works, the time we need with our children and for rest and relaxation, time and attention to our spouse should always come first. 🍂

*T*ODAY'S THOUGHT: *How do you deal with lifestyle barriers to effective communication?*

For all his days are full of pain. Ecclesiastes 2:23

Emotional barriers to good communication also need due consideration. When our "days are full of pain," it is hard to communicate effectively because our emotions get in the way.

It is impossible to converse in a loving and useful way when we are filled with anger, pain, and frustration. These types of emotional interference simply block communication. We are more likely to explode than to talk. Although true feelings should not be hidden from our spouse, we sometimes need a cooling-off period. We can probably express our true feelings more rationally and more effectively when our temper and feelings are under control. We need to remember how precious our spouse is to God (and to us, when we're not angry!) in order to prevent us from lashing out in a way we will later regret.

Another emotional barrier happens when we try to avoid talking about areas that always lead to conflict and pain. An example could be our loved one's work situation, bad dietary habits, or difficulty with parents. These are matters that, from time to time, need to be discussed. Here, sensitivity to one another is the key; we should pray about how to deal with the subject responsibly, yet as gently as possible, and then have the fortitude to do it. ❦

*T*ODAY'S THOUGHT: *How do you deal with emotional barriers?*

LOVE

On the day of judgment men will render account for every careless word they utter. Matthew 12:36

The final barrier we will examine is poor communication skills. The primary skill in communicating is the ability to listen—with our heart and mind as well as our ears! Reaching conclusions too quickly and cutting our spouse off in midsentence are examples of communication barriers that occur because of ineffective listening. If, on the other hand, our spouse knows we really care what he or she has to say by the attentiveness of our listening, most of the barriers will come crashing down.

Careless thinking and the careless words that result are another example of poor communication skills. We need to think before we speak. We owe that to our spouse, knowing how deeply we can hurt our loved one by a careless remark. (If you doubt this, think of the emotional scar tissue you carry from something someone carelessly let slip about you.)

Finally, we need to be conscious of our body language. We can follow all the rules of effective communication and still fail to be in touch with one another if we don't communicate interest by our body language. If our spouse can read into our stance, look, and other mannerisms a message that belies our words, we're still in trouble. The key to communication is listening, thinking, and body language that shows we care about what the other person thinks and feels. ❦

*T*ODAY'S THOUGHT: *What are you doing to improve your communication skills?*

LOVE

If I . . . have not love, I am a noisy gong or a clanging cymbal.
1 Corinthians 13:1

Paul's description of love in 1 Corinthians 13 is one of the most beautiful passages in the Bible. And, as married Christians, it speaks volumes to us of how we are to show love to one another. Like so many poetic pieces in the Bible and elsewhere, however, we can become so familiar with the words and/or spellbound by their beauty that we miss the message.

A helpful exercise is to look at this passage of Scripture in light of the specific things it says love is or is not. What are the elements of love as defined by Paul? Underline them in your Bible, or make a copy of the passage on a sheet of paper and underline the words there. For instance, underline "Love is patient and kind" (verse 4). Then ask yourself, What does it mean to be patient and kind toward my spouse? How do I show these traits?

Now, once the elements of love are underlined and can be looked at individually, pray that God will show you what each one means in relationship to your spouse. Find out what God would have you do or be in order to be love to your loved one and not just another noisy gong or clanging cymbal. ❧

TODAY'S THOUGHT: *Take time to do the exercise.*

JULY 22 *LOVE*

Watch at all times. Luke 21:36

The passage from which this verse comes has to do with standing before the Son of Man at the time of judgment. The thought of standing before a judge is terrifying for most of us. Knowing that the judge is going to pass final judgment is too much for even the strongest person. Thus, Jesus calls us to watch. We don't know when judgment may come upon us. We are exhorted to live as though it could come at any time.

As Christian married people, we not only have to be able to answer to God for ourselves but also for our marriage and family. God has given us something very precious and special, and "every one to whom much is given, of him will much be required" (Luke 12:48).

Jesus' call is to self-examination. We are to be alert against falling into complacency. It's too easy to get caught up in the demands of everyday life. Often we get too busy to have time for God. We fail to stay alert. Our intentions are never realized.

Jesus reminds us that now is the time to examine the fruit of his life in us. Each day is an opportunity to start afresh. God calls us to grow in relationship with him, to grow in relationship with our spouse, and to be a good steward of our family and everything else he has entrusted to our care. ❦

*T*ODAY'S THOUGHT: *Are you prepared?*

LOVE

For not all have faith. But the Lord is faithful.
2 Thessalonians 3:2-3

Faith, if it is real, is seen in its fruit. Many of us seem to leave our faith at the door of the church when we leave on Sundays. There is not as much correlation as there should be between our faith and our family life. Many simply don't know how to use their Christian faith as a guide to decision making at home.

In his Second Letter to the Thessalonians, Paul tells us that we must "never tire of doing what is right" (3:13 NIV). This exhortation is aimed at the problem of our losing heart when dealing with idle brothers and sisters. It is easy to wonder why we must act like a Christian family while we see others ignoring all the moral standards, or simply being idle, and yet seemingly being rewarded.

What Paul is really addressing is the complete integration of our faith into our lives, our work, and our family. It will seem, at times, that the idle prosper and the immoral get what they want without paying the price. But those evaluations are based on a worldly point of view that is not consistent with our faith. As we become better able to see things from God's point of view, we see that our faith is the foundation for all decision making, and that the rewards are on a higher plane than what the world can see, taste, or smell. ❦

TODAY'S THOUGHT: *What, for you, is truly a reward?*

*L*OVE

A prudent wife is from the Lord. Proverbs 19:14

Today's verse could just as well say that a prudent husband is also from the Lord. God wants us to think well of our spouse. How we refer to our loved one in the company of others says quite a bit about how we really feel about him or her. If our loved one is on our mind as he or she should always be, and if we speak of him or her in a favorable way, our consciousness of our loved one and what he or she means to us will grow. Unfortunately, the reverse can be true.

Some people simply never say anything about their spouse. You wouldn't know they were married unless you had seen them together or saw a wedding ring on their finger. What does that say about what marriage means to that person?

Other people only make reference to "my wife" or "my husband," as though the spouse were some sort of possession. They never mention their spouse's name. What does that say about what marriage means to that person?

Fortunately, others often refer to their spouse, and always by name and in a favorable (or at least not unfavorable) way. They see the loved one as a part of themselves, not as a possession, but in a covenant relationship. They know that they are incomplete without their spouse. What does that say about what marriage means to that person? ❦

*T*ODAY'S THOUGHT: *Which description fits you?*

JULY 25 LOVE

This is the disciple who is bearing witness to these things, and who has written these things; and we know that his testimony is true. John 21:24

We have a friend who gets up at 5:30 in the morning to watch, on cable television, a thirty-minute journey to some distant part of the world. He has traveled quite a bit in the past, so some of the "television trips" are to places he is familiar with, and they bring back memories. Other "trips" are to places he has not been, but they become real to him through the miracle of modern communication. Seeing is believing.

The Gospel of John is based on the testimony of the beloved disciple and close companion of Jesus. In the verse above, we are told that the Gospel is not mere speculation or some vague picture of what really happened. We are assured it was based on the witness of someone who was there and saw and heard the things reported. Seeing is believing.

We also are called to witness to Christ. And, as Christian married people, we are called to witness to Christ within the family and as a family. We can be living examples of the kind of people God calls us to be. To others, we can be ones who, because of Jesus and by his grace, show forth growth toward wholeness to a broken and sinful world. Seeing is believing. ❦

*T*ODAY'S THOUGHT: *In what ways can you witness to others?*

Love

An angel of the Lord appeared to Joseph in a dream.
Matthew 2:13

Dreams were a common means of communication between God and his people in the Bible. Dreamlike visions also occurred, such as Peter's experience in Acts 10:9-23. Prophecies, acted-out parables, and many other means of communication are shown to us through Scripture whereby God let his people know what he wanted them to do.

As married couples and families study the Bible together, pray, and share spiritual insights with one another, it becomes obvious how rich and varied are the ways in which God tries to reach us. The experiences of God in the lives of our loved ones can expand our spiritual horizons and make us increasingly conscious of God's presence within the family circle day by day. God truly speaks to us through one another.

Each of us is as spiritually different from one another as we are physically different. And God has a special way to communicate with each of us. Within the marriage, and within the family, it is extremely important for us to recognize and respect each others' spirituality. One way is not better than another, and the variety of ways God speaks to us within the family framework is another sign of the wholeness that marriage and family life provides us. ❦

*T*ODAY'S THOUGHT: *Reflect on the spiritual gifts your spouse brings to the marriage relationship.*

*L*OVE

If any one thirst, let him come to me and drink.   John 7:37

Because television news can take us anywhere a disaster is striking or has struck, we are familiar with the devastation wrought by hurricanes. Despite the amount of water that is contained in a hurricane, those who are left homeless following the tragedy often experience a critical need for water. It is the one thing we must have in order to live, and natural disasters tend to destroy or contaminate water supplies.

There is no substitute for the basic need that the human body has for water. Wars have been fought over water and sources of water. In the settling of the American West, water was often a major consideration, and the need for it sometimes led to violence.

Jesus speaks of a different kind of water: water that is more important to us than the physical water we drink. Jesus brings spiritual water that can nourish the soul. It is water we don't have to fight over; it is free to all.

As we reflect on how vital both physical and spiritual water are to us, let us remember how vital we are to each other. Couples who have been married for many years may become so close to one another that when one dies, often the other dies shortly thereafter. We are that precious to one another. ❦

*T*ODAY'S THOUGHT: *What would your life be like without your spouse?*

If any case arises . . . which is too difficult for you.
Deuteronomy 17:8

In married life there are constant decisions to be made and problems to be solved. Some cause stress; others are almost welcomed as a challenge; still others fall somewhere in between. It is helpful to be aware of which problems are really traumatic for us as a couple to deal with, and which ones are not. That is the purpose of the following exercise.

On a piece of paper, list all the problem-solving issues you face from time to time as a married couple. Examples could be relationships with in-laws, how to discipline the children, where to go on vacation, when to have sex, how to pray together, how to invest money, how much money to set aside as savings, how to develop a family budget, how to spend our leisure time, who should do what chores, how to allot contributions to various causes, what civic activities to be involved in, whom to vote for in elections, whether or not to have a pet, and how to decorate the house.

After you and your spouse have completed such a list, make duplicate copies of it. Then individually mark on your own copy whether the issue, for you, is (1) easy; (2) moderate; or (3) difficult. Discuss the results with your spouse. 🍂

*T*ODAY'S THOUGHT: *Why not try the exercise now?*

*L*OVE

Judge righteously between a man and his brother.
Deuteronomy 1:16

It has been said that we unconsciously project onto others our natural and learned behaviors. These are the things that affect the way we think, what our inclinations and prejudices are, how we judge others, and how we react to what happens to us. They are such an inherent part of us that we assume that others think and feel the same way (which, of course, they do not!).

When others, especially those we love the most, do not respond the way we would respond, our first impulse is to take it as intentional action on their part. Too often we fail to see they are merely acting out of their own natural and learned behaviors.

To keep this situation from becoming too big a problem between husbands and wives, there are things we can do about it. The most obvious solution is getting to know one another as fully as we can. We should share regularly on a personal level those things that have shaped the way we think and feel, even if we have to use gimmicks to do so (such as what our highest and lowest moments have been during the last week, or yesterday). And, when we have the opportunity, we should have ourselves scored by way of personality type indicators and similar exercises that will help each of us understand why we and our loved one think and feel the way we do. ❦

*T*ODAY'S THOUGHT: *How much do you know about your spouse's natural and learned behaviors?*

*L*OVE

If any one of you is without sin, let him be the first to throw a stone. John 8:7 NIV

The passage from which this verse comes is one of the most intriguing in the Bible. A woman caught in adultery has been brought before Jesus for him to judge her. Instead, Jesus bends down and writes something (we're not told what) on the ground with his finger. Perhaps he was just letting some time pass, to allow those who were testing him by trying to force him to judge the woman deal with themselves and what they were planning to do. A good time for a little self-examination.

Stones are abundant in Israel, and it's no wonder they were used as weapons in the stories we read in the Bible.

Our modern life affords many "stones" for our use. Our words as well as our actions are like stones when they are thrown at others. Within the marriage and family relationship it is especially tempting to throw stones of insult or retaliation at our loved ones when things aren't going our way. What a wonderful example this story can be to us when we are inclined to throw one of these stones. It tells us, first, to stop and think about what we are doing; and, second, to question whether we are so sinless as to be entitled to stone another, particularly someone we love. ❦

*T*ODAY'S THOUGHT: *"People who live in glass houses should never throw stones." What does this quote say to you?*

JULY 31 LOVE

Jesus said to them, "I am the bread of life." John 6:35

In Jesus' time, bread meant much more than it does to us in our contemporary Western world. If someone mentions bread to us, we recognize it as a staple of our diet, but not a necessity. Our imagination runs wild with all the varieties of composition, ingredients, shape, size, taste, etc., of bread that are available to us. To those to whom Jesus spoke, bread meant life.

Jesus is always trying to bring his followers, including us, back to the basics. He is also trying to communicate on a level that his hearers can understand.

As the Lord's Prayer reminds us, there is something daily about bread. We recall that the manna in the wilderness could not be stored; it came a day at a time. God wants us to know that we have to rely on him day by day for our spiritual and physical needs.

There is also something very daily about marriage. It is an integral part of our life, and there's nothing more important to our life than our marriage. It is the bread of our existence. We want it to remain fresh, to never grow stale. Just as the Israelites in the wilderness, and the people of Jesus' day, could not take bread for granted, neither should we take our marriage for granted. ❦

*T*ODAY'S THOUGHT: *Are you taking any aspect of your marriage for granted?*

August

LOVE

In thy presence there is fulness of joy. Psalm 16:11

Over the next five days we'll be looking at bridges to effective communication. The first bridge is presence. If we want to communicate effectively with our loved ones, we must make ourselves present to them in mind, body, *and* spirit. It's not very helpful, for instance, to be physically present but have our mind on other things.

Being available and approachable is essential. Not only do we need to provide the time our loved ones need to be with us, but they need to know that the door to our mind and heart is always open. If they feel they'll be intruding on our time or that we are in no mood to hear them, they'll be reluctant to communicate with us. We need to be fully approachable.

We should also be patient. Patience is the first characteristic of love listed by Paul in 1 Corinthians 13. If we want to build and maintain an atmosphere of respect in the home, we must be gentle and forbearing, not rationing our availability, but giving it freely and unselfishly to those we love. ❦

*T*ODAY'S THOUGHT: *How present are you to your spouse and children?*

Pay attention to him and listen to what he says.
Exodus 23:21 NIV

The second bridge to effective communication is listening. A good listener is one who places maximum value on what is going to be said. He or she listens as though the success or failure of the family is at stake.

The good listener listens with more than the ear. He or she comes to know each member of the family so well that what is said can be processed accurately. We come to understand how the loved one experiences life, and therefore exactly what that person means by what is said. For instance, some people are excitable and tend to overstate the situation; others are subdued and tend to understate it. Thus, what is said needs to be considered in light of who is saying it.

Yet, the good listener accepts with an open mind what others have to say. Preliminarily judging the person or the topic can impede effective listening. Until we have heard the whole story, we cannot properly process the information. In order to hear the whole story, we must have an open mind — and a listening ear. ❦

*T*ODAY'S THOUGHT: *How good a listener are you?*

LOVE

The Lord God has opened my ear. Isaiah 50:5

The third bridge to effective communication is openness, which we began to touch on yesterday. Openmindedness, as we saw, is necessary in order not to prejudge what is being conveyed to us. But there is much more to openness than openmindedness.

First, we need to allow our loved ones their own private thoughts and feelings. We tend to think that they should think like we think and what we think! That is an unjust and unrealistic restriction to lay upon them, and it impedes our communication with them.

Second, we need to respect their rights and opinions. If the members of our family have had an opportunity to take a personality or temperament exercise, and we have seen the results, we know how differently we can feel and think about matters within our own household. For there to be good communication, differences must be respected.

Third, we need to realize we all will change over a period of time. Almost anyone with grown children will attest to the fact that they had an attitude toward discipline that reversed itself when they began to have children of their own! ❦

*T*ODAY'S THOUGHT: *How open are you in communicating with loved ones?*

Turn from your fierce anger; relent and do not bring disaster on your people. Exodus 32:12 NIV

A fourth bridge is the mental and emotional adjustments we need to make once communication has begun. A first step is to treat each of our loved ones and each situation they are telling us about as uniquely as possible. In other words, we shouldn't load our hearing with a lot of outdated baggage.

Next, we need to see the matter from our loved one's point of view. It's so easy to see things through the eyes of our own preconceived notions. But as long as we're doing that, we aren't truly hearing what the other person is saying. Our loved one's words come out of their own emotional background and experience, not ours.

As the conversation progresses, it's essential to clear up misunderstandings as quickly and effectively as possible. Rather than arguing about matters that simply aren't clear, it is much more effective to say, "Let me repeat what I think you're saying." Often, misunderstandings result from thinking we have heard one word when our loved one has said another, or from misinterpreting the emphasis or feeling our loved one has put into the words. By stopping for clarification as the discussion progresses, we keep from compounding any misunderstanding that may exist. ❦

*T*ODAY'S THOUGHT: *How effective are you at keeping discussions on track?*

Many waters cannot quench love. Song of Solomon 8:7

The final bridge to effective communication is conveying warmth to our loved ones. There is no substitute for letting them know we love them, even in the midst of the most heated disagreements. It's not a bad idea to pray as a discussion begins to reach fever pitch, because that can allow us to control our tempers and continue to show love even when we must disagree.

By using a warm and friendly tone of voice and refusing to become riled, we communicate much more effectively. Politeness is basic to all human relations, and it's essential in communicating with our loved ones. There is no excuse for foul language or other improprieties (such as sarcasm) that will simply compound the problem.

Trust, of course, is at the foundation of good communication. If our loved ones know we trust them, we can expect good communication. How we communicate with them reflects the trust that's there. If we always question their motives or doubt what they tell us, they know we don't trust them. If we accept and believe what they say, even if we disagree, they know we trust them. ❧

*T*ODAY'S THOUGHT: *Do your loved ones know you love them, even in the midst of disagreements?*

LOVE

Let everything that breathes praise the Lord! Psalm 150:6

Praise is defined as "an expression of warm approval and admiration." In worldly terms, praise is a limited commodity, often reserved only for the best performances or finest productions. We are often told that if we don't ration our praise, it will become shallow and meaningless.

The psalmist's interpretation of praise is on an entirely different level because he's talking about praise directed to God, rather than human beings. Our praise of God need not be limited to times of worship or when we feel particularly blessed. He is always and forever deserving of our praise.

The praise of our spouse also doesn't need to be limited to the "best performances and finest productions." Although praise, even of the one we love, should not be so automatic that it has no meaning, we should never miss an opportunity to recognize and appreciate our spouse for all he or she does and is. Taking the time to praise our loved one costs us very little and means so much to the one receiving the praise. We live in a time when there is a lot of negativism, even cynicism, and there is no balm more comforting to the feelings of our loved one than to receive our appreciation and praise. ❦

*T*ODAY'S THOUGHT: *Do you give your spouse (and children) adequate praise?*

LOVE

I am He who blots out your transgressions for my own sake, and I will not remember your sins. Isaiah 43:25

Candidates in political campaigns inevitably have unpleasant details of their past revealed. Youthful indiscretions, skeletons in the closet, and common mistakes become the stuff of headlines and tabloid articles. A candidate's past is exposed like an open book for all the world to see.

All of us have past mistakes we wish had never happened. The memories often cause guilt, remorse, and even anger. We plague ourselves with, "If only . . . " For many of us, these dusty skeletons rattle in the back of our mind for a lifetime.

When we bring these painful memories into the marriage relationship, we lay an unfair burden upon that relationship. There is enough to contend with in the intimacy of day-to-day living with one another without carrying the unnecessary weight of the past.

God has already forgiven us of our confessed sins; that is the reason Jesus died on the cross. God blots out our sins and remembers them no more. He gives us a new life, free of the burdens of past mistakes. This is the kind of life he wants us to share with our spouse. ❧

*T*ODAY'S THOUGHT: *What past sin(s) do you need to confess and forget?*

LOVE

I remember . . . your love as a bride, how you followed me in the wilderness. Jeremiah 2:2

In this verse, God is reminding his people that they are his first love and have been as a bride to him. Marriage is the model of the relationship that is to exist between God and his people.

Every Christian couple is a "church in miniature." Every Christian home is a "home church." What do we think of when we think of "church"? Worship, certainly. Christian education, prayer, and Bible study. Fellowship. Service. Nurturing others in the love of God; providing help spiritually, physically, and emotionally. Those, and perhaps many other things, are "church" to us as Christians.

What, then, should our "home church" look like? Well, first of all, it would be a place where the things mentioned above take place. For instance, regardless of how good a Sunday school program our congregation provides, the most and best Christian education still takes place in the home as children see us model what life in Christ is all about. Above and beyond those specifics, the Christian home should be a holy place. That doesn't mean we can't have fun or that it has to look like "house beautiful" all the time; it just means that it's a place where God dwells, and that anyone present knows it's God's house. 🍎

*T*ODAY'S THOUGHT: *How can you make your home more truly a place where God dwells?*

LOVE

It is not good that the man should be alone. Genesis 2:18

A downward spiral can happen when a marriage moves from intimacy to aloneness. It works this way. One of us has expectations that we want our spouse to share. What we experience, however, is disappointment; our spouse not only doesn't have the same expectations, but perhaps almost opposite ones. This can be true whether we are talking about what restaurant we prefer to go to on a special occasion, or where the children should go to school.

Faced with the disappointment, we then try to change our spouse. We wish our loved one didn't think and feel the way he or she does, and we try to manipulate our spouse's thinking to match our own. We argue, we cajole. We meet with resistance that gets more and more firmly embedded against us. As a result, we feel defeated and alone. When this happens over and over, married life is in danger.

The solution is to share expectations openly from the start without trying to coax the other to our point of view. We simply explore where each other is on the matter. If we have no preconceived desire to make our loved one agree with us, and truly want to come to a mutual understanding and solution, there is no reason for disappointment. It always makes sense to talk things through. ❦

*T*ODAY'S THOUGHT: *How can you more effectively share your expectations without getting into conflict?*

But we pray God that you may not do wrong. 2 Corinthians 13:7

Despite the best advice, times come when there seems no way to resolve a difference between us in marriage. What's more, sometimes it seems impossible to avoid the issue reaching a point at which we say hurtful things we'll later regret. At those times, it's always appropriate to suggest stopping to pray about the matter.

Saying "let's pray about this" is a vulnerable act of love. It is a willingness to allow God to speak to us rather than forcing the issue and scoring our points in the debate. If it's a sincere request, it's also a way of admitting that we might be wrong and that God will speak that corrective to our spouse, if not to us. (Of course, we have to be willing to allow the truth to come, through prayer, to our spouse.)

Submitting to prayer in times of conflict has many benefits. First, it acknowledges God's partnership in the marriage. Second, it allows him to speak to the matter. Third, it puts us in a quieter and more receptive mood to hear him and each other. Ultimately, it allows us to respond rather than react. ❦

*T*ODAY'S THOUGHT: *How do you feel about stopping to pray when you and your spouse are on the verge of a disagreement?*

I say, "My bed will comfort me, my couch will ease my complaint." Job 7:13

Mark Twain, the great American novelist, had such an acid tongue and used such foul language that his wife continually reprimanded him about it. One day, when she got particularly angry with him, she assaulted him with the worst curse words she could come up with. When she had finished, Twain just laughed and said, "Honey, you know the words, but you don't know the tune."

We've looked at ways to deal with disagreements and even rules for fair fighting. One thing that also needs to be considered is where not to argue.

There are two places in any Christian household that should be especially sacred, and thus are the wrong places to fight: the bedroom and the dining table (or the place where you normally eat your meals). The Christian home should be a center of peace, and the dining table and the bedroom should especially be places of peace. If they have also been places of conflict, they will retain an atmosphere of pain entirely inappropriate to their purpose.

For each married couple the situation will be different, but we should find the right neutral ground for arguments in our home. Then we can match the words *and* the tune. ❦

*T*ODAY'S THOUGHT: *Where is the best place for you to deal with marital conflict?*

You shall have no other gods before me. Exodus 20:3

Over the next ten days, we'll examine the Ten Commandments and what they say to us as Christian married couples and families.

A Gallup survey revealed that 84 percent of Americans believe the Ten Commandments are valid and authoritative today, yet only 42 percent could name as many as four of them! We live in a time when we are looking for standards by which we can hold people accountable, but there is a tendency to shy away from the Ten Commandments as too restrictive and negative. However, they were written to enhance life, not deny it. Through them, God has not restricted our freedom so much as given us guidelines for our own protection.

In the first commandment, God was calling people away from their subjection to the pagan gods to whom, in some instances, children were sacrificed. In the Christian family today, we need to be careful that we are worshiping the Lord, instead of other gods. The pagan gods of old may be things of the past, but "keeping up with the Joneses" certainly isn't. What about the gods of materialism, sex, power, popularity, success, self? Are we worshiping them individually, or as a married couple? Perhaps it's time to examine ourselves. ❦

*T*ODAY'S THOUGHT: *What are your feelings about the Ten Commandments?*

You shall not make for yourself an idol. Exodus 20:4 NIV

There's a difference between materialism and idolatry. *Materialism* is turning things into a god, thereby raising anything less than God to the level of God himself. It violates the first commandment. *Idolatry* is turning God into things, reducing God to anything less than himself. It violates the second commandment.

The idol maker wants a manageable god. In the old days, idols were carved from wood (see Isaiah 44:9-17); the idol maker thus whittled God down to size. In our day, just as the weather bureau might downgrade a hurricane to a tropical storm, there is a tendency to downgrade God from who he is to something we can deal with more comfortably. We deceive ourselves if we don't recognize that society, including many church people, continually downgrades God.

This places a special responsibility on Christian married couples, especially those with children (who are constantly seeing God downgraded in the secular school system and through the media). It is only as we know the God who is, worship him regularly, and grow in our knowledge of him daily that we can avoid falling into the trap of downgrading God. 🦃

*T*ODAY'S THOUGHT: *What are you doing to keep God, and not some mere representation of him, supreme in your household?*

You shall not misuse the name of the Lord your God.
Exodus 20:7 NIV

To the ancient Hebrews, a person's name was of utmost importance. To name something was to capture its essence. Adam was given the privilege of naming the animals (Genesis 2:19), and thereby was a sort of cocreator with God. Throughout the Bible, people's names were changed to reflect changes in their stature: Abram becomes Abraham ("father of a multitude"), Jacob becomes Israel ("he who struggles with God"), and Simon becomes Peter ("the rock"). Biblically, a person's name represented his or her character.

The ancient Jews were so aware of the holiness of the name of God, so anxious not to use it wrongfully, that they never pronounced it. God, when asked his name by Moses on Mount Sinai, said YAHWEH, which means, I AM.

Today, it's easy to get into the habit of using God's name in casual profanity. Some years ago, a friend was in a store where the person waiting on him kept using God's name in that way. Our friend prayed and was led to say to the man, "You certainly have a God-consciousness." The man, a professed lifelong Christian, apologized for the bad habit he had developed that had previously gone unchallenged. As members of a Christian family, we need to uphold the honor of God's name in our own household and beyond. 🍎

*T*ODAY'S THOUGHT: *Are you using the Lord's name wrongfully? If so, in what ways?*

Remember the sabbath day, to keep it holy. Exodus 20:8

When we think that by keeping the Ten Commandments we will be right with God, we have things in reverse order. If we are right with God, we will keep the commandments. The Ten Commandments are not so much a prescription for what we should be doing as they are a description of what we will be doing if we are right with God.

The ancient Jews took the command that the Sabbath be honored so seriously that there were over a thousand things that couldn't be done on the Sabbath. It's easy to fall into the same restrictive view today.

But, in any event, there are at least two things we should be especially conscious of concerning the Sabbath. The first is that we honor it by worship and by using our time on Sundays in God-honoring ways. The second is that we should not, by what we choose to do or not do, impair the ability of our spouse and our children to honor the Sabbath in the way that is most meaningful to them. We may feel, for instance, that Sunday afternoon is an ideal time to spend in the yard. That does not mean, however, we should force family members to do their yard chores on Sunday. Second only to being a day of worship, the Sabbath is to be a day of rest from usual routines. ❧

*J*ODAY'S THOUGHT: *Are you remembering the Sabbath in an appropriate way?*

LOVE

Honor your father and your mother. Exodus 20:12

A friend of ours says he looked forward to the day when his children would "rise up and call him blessed," but instead they call him collect!

We are now at the dividing point within the Ten Commandments. Jesus told us to love God and to love our neighbor (Matthew 22:36-40). The first four commandments have to do with loving God, the last six with loving our neighbor. In many ways, the fifth commandment is transitional, standing between our responsibilities to God and our responsibilities to others. This commandment deals with the most basic human relationship: that of parent and child. Our first impressions of God, for good or for ill, are patterned after our parents.

The way in which we honor our parents models for our own children the relationship between children and parents. There is a great deal that our children learn about their responsibilities to us by seeing the way in which we carry out our responsibilities to our parents. If we want to be the kind of parents whose children find honorable, we should begin by being the sort of children who honor our parents. 🍂

*T*ODAY'S THOUGHT: *In what ways do you honor your parents?*

You shall not kill. Exodus 20:13

The principle behind the sixth commandment is that life is sacred because people are created in the image of God. In the Old Testament, disregarding this principle and murdering another resulted in the perpetrator forfeiting his life. Taking the murderer's life was not considered murder, but justice.

Against this background, Jesus taught us to turn the other cheek (Matthew 5:39), and Paul said we should permit ourselves to be defrauded (1 Corinthians 6:7). These options are open to us as Christians, regardless of what has been done to us. God forgives, and we are called to be forgivers as well.

Jesus said, "You have heard that it was said to the men of old, 'You shall not kill; and whoever kills shall be liable to judgment.' But I say to you that every one who is angry with his brother shall be liable to judgment" (Matthew 5:21-22). We can kill with our attitudes as well as with our actions.

Within the Christian family, we must not kill the incentives of those with whom we live, murder their legitimate dreams and goals in life, or destroy the spirit within them. These are the ways that many of us violate the sixth commandment today. Instead, we must treat all life and relationships — especially those within the family — as sacred. ❦

*T*ODAY'S THOUGHT: *Are you guilty?*

You shall not commit adultery. Exodus 20:14

C. S. Lewis called the seventh commandment the least popular of the Christian virtues. Its New Testament counterpart is, "Shun immorality" (1 Corinthians 6:18). Committing sexual sin is adultery, if you're married, and fornication, if you're not married. The biblical standard is clear: complete sexual faithfulness within marriage, abstinence outside of it.

Some "experts" tell us that the three fears of sexual promiscuity have now been overcome: (1) unwanted pregnancy (overcome by the pill and by abortion); (2) unwanted disease (now that we have penicillin and other wonder drugs); and (3) the stigma attached to it (because there isn't one anymore). Premarital intercourse is even recommended by many today. Anyone who speaks a word in favor of the seventh commandment is often regarded as hopelessly irrelevant and maybe dangerously repressive.

But the Bible doesn't approach the issue of extramarital sex on the bases of unwanted pregnancy, unwanted disease, or the stigma attached. The spiritual teaching is that physical union expresses spiritual union, which expresses commitment to one another. Sex is the sharing of all of life. There is no higher obligation that Christian married couples have to one another than to obey the seventh commandment. Sex is a precious gift from God; we shouldn't settle for less than what God has planned for us. ❦

*T*ODAY'S THOUGHT: *In what ways can you stand up for Christian sexual standards?*

You shall not steal. Exodus 20:15

There are two themes that run throughout Scripture. The first is that God's will for us is good (freedom rather than restriction; life-enhancing, not life-denying). The second is that there is something in us that is not good: sin. The commandments, though they may seem negative, are good for us because it is only when we know we are sick that we'll seek a doctor who can heal us; it is only when we know we fall short of God's best for us that we will seek a Savior.

Who would argue with the eighth commandment? Yet, every time we fudge on our expense account or hide income from the Internal Revenue Service, we violate the commandment just as much as if we robbed a bank. It's particularly easy to fall into the "everybody's doing it" syndrome on this commandment and rationalize our sinfulness.

We build trust in our relationship with our spouse and develop Christian values in our children by being thoroughly honest in matters of money—and by not stealing time, security, and their rights from them. We need to be available, provide for them, and give due consideration to their rights. ❦

*T*ODAY'S THOUGHT: *Are you guilty of any forms of "stealing"?*

LOVE

You shall not bear false witness against your neighbor.
Exodus 20:16

The ninth commandment doesn't say we aren't to lie. It says we shouldn't lie with regard to what someone else has said or done. False witness against our neighbors destroys their reputation and steals their good name. We can learn to keep the ninth commandment by keeping the eighth: Don't steal at all! We fail God when we take his name in vain; we fail our neighbors when we take their names in vain.

In the Epistle of James, we are told, "The tongue is a little member and boasts of great things. How great a forest is set ablaze by a small fire! And the tongue is a fire. . . . staining the whole body, setting on fire the cycle of nature, and set on fire by hell. For every kind of beast and bird, of reptile and sea creature, can be tamed, . . . but no human being can tame the tongue—a restless evil, full of deadly poison" (James 3:5-8). Those of us who have escaped censure in looking at the other commandments may find it difficult to do so when considering the ninth.

As we realize the ease with which we can let our tongues slip into slander against our neighbors, we need to remind ourselves who our closest neighbor is: our spouse. When we have been stung by a disagreement with our loved one, we need to be very careful not to let that cause us to say things about him or her that we will regret. We can choose, instead, to control our tongues. ❦

*T*ODAY'S THOUGHT: *Do you talk about your spouse in ways that could be seen as negative?*

You shall not covet. Exodus 20:17

If we have managed to escape finding ourselves in any of the other commandments, it is difficult indeed to escape the tenth. Until now we have been looking at things we might have done to our neighbor; now we are being told, don't even think about it.

We may be able to fool other people, but we can't fool God. Theologian and writer John Stott has said that the tenth commandment makes the commandments, taken together, not just an outward legal code, but an inward moral standard. Covetousness belongs to our inner life; it lurks in the heart and mind. What lust is to adultery, what temper is to murder, that's what covetousness is to theft. We think, *Just a little more and I will be content.* No, there is no contentment in anything less than Christ himself abiding in us.

Covetousness can be a constant battle in marriage. We can so easily covet what our neighbors have. We can even rationalize it on the basis of the wants and needs of each other or of our children: *I'm not coveting it on my own behalf but because my spouse or my children deserve better.* We deserve nothing. By the grace of God we can have life in Jesus Christ, and that far outshines anything else anyone could have. ❦

*T*ODAY'S THOUGHT: *What covetous thoughts do you need to clean out?*

Until we all attain . . . mature manhood, to the measure of the stature of the fullness of Christ. Ephesians 4:13

There are four stages of development toward Christian maturity: *Jesus loves me.* We certainly want our children to know this, and bedtime is a wonderful time for teaching them about the love of Jesus (especially when they don't want to go to bed!).

Jesus is with me. We learn this as we grow as Christians, by such things as realizing that our prayers are answered.

Jesus is in me. Through the teachings of the church, we learn that Jesus is alive in his people through the Holy Spirit within them. This is how we are able to minister to one another, through the gifts that God gives to each of us in order that we may serve others, especially our spouse and children.

Jesus lives instead of me. This is the ultimate maturity to which we are called as Christians: to realize that it is not us, but Jesus, to whom we have given our lives, who lives to do his work in the world. When we have attained this level of maturity, there is no limit to how God can use us. We truly can be a healing presence to those we love. 🕯

*J*ODAY'S THOUGHT: *At which level are you?*

Unless you turn and become like children, you will never enter the kingdom of heaven. Matthew 18:3

Next we'll spend three days looking at various aspects of change that might be needed within our marriage. The first is a change of attitude.

In Philippians 4:8, Paul wrote: "Finally, brethren, whatever is true, whatever is honorable, whatever is just, whatever is pure, whatever is lovely, whatever is gracious, if there is any excellence, if there is anything worthy of praise, think about these things." Have a positive attitude, Paul is saying. Statistics show that people who have a positive attitude live longer, especially those who are also happily married. And certainly they are happier in the course of their lives here on earth!

Those, on the other hand, who end up divorced have a list of charges (things done wrong) against their spouse that they've been compiling in their mind for years. Paul tells us, instead, to spend our time listing all the good things about the one we love. That is how we build a positive attitude, as we see all we have to be thankful for. ❦

*T*ODAY'S THOUGHT: *What positive attitude changes do you need to make?*

LOVE

Go into all the world and preach the good news to all creation.
Mark 16:15 NIV

We may not only need to change our attitudes, but our actions. We are not simply to think about what God wants us to do, we are to "go."

The Epistle of James says this: "They are like those who look at themselves in a mirror; for they look at themselves and, on going away, immediately forget what they were like. But those who look into the perfect law, the law of liberty, and persevere, being not hearers who forget but doers who act—they will be blessed in their doing" (James 1:23-25, NRSV). James is saying that we not only need to examine ourselves and see the things that need to be changed, we need to do something about them.

In our relationship with our spouse, what bad habits have we adopted? Are there ways we have neglected our spouse and our children? Has work caused us to come home fussy and contentious? Are recreational activities interfering with quality time together? Has our focus been on ourself, what we want and need, rather than on our loved ones?

If the answer to any of these, or similar questions, is yes, God wants us to make an action change, so that we might share good news with those we love. ❧

*T*ODAY'S THOUGHT: *What does the face in the mirror tell you about your attitudes and actions?*

Can the . . . leopard [change] his spots? Jeremiah 13:23

Just because leopards can't change their spots doesn't mean that we can't change. Old dogs *can* learn new tricks. Over the last two days we have examined attitudes and/or actions we may need to change for the benefit of our spouse and children. Today let's think about what we cannot change: our spouse.

We cannot change our loved one by direct action, no matter how much we might like to do so nor how hard we try. We can only change ourselves. It is a fact, however, that as we change constructively, the dynamics of the situation change. If a married couple squabbles, and one changes by not being so contentious anymore, the other is likely to become more agreeable too. When one changes for the better, the other is free to change in response to that action.

The shortened version of the "Serenity Prayer" is helpful in thinking about this subject: "God, grant me the serenity to accept the things I cannot change, the courage to change the things I can, and the wisdom to know the difference." We can't change our spouse. But, with courage, we can change ourselves. The good news is that, by the helpful changes we make within the family environment, we create an atmosphere in which constructive change may indirectly take place for the benefit of all. ❧

*T*ODAY'S THOUGHT: *Copy the words to the "Serenity Prayer" and put them where you will see them each day.*

Be still before the Lord, and wait patiently for him. Psalm 37:7

Our society promotes instant gratification. We service our cars in a jiffy, brew our coffee in an instant, and cook our meals in a microwave second. Our attitude is, Give me what I want and give it to me now. Our natural inclination is to avoid the process that is necessary to reach a conclusion; we want to get to the bottom line as quickly as possible. The destination becomes more important than the journey. We miss the scenery along the road because we are concentrating on what lies ahead. We need to stop and smell the roses.

Often our spiritual lives can follow a similar pattern. We want to be efficient in our time with God. We let him know what our needs are and then get busy doing whatever we think is important to do. Instead of asking, *Lord, what would you have me do?* we say, in essence, *Lord, this is what I'm going to do, so please give it your blessing.* Instead, we need to stop and wait patiently on the Lord.

Our relationship with our spouse can fall into the same routine. We want to have sex, but get it over quickly. We watch television while we eat; there's no need to set the table when we use trays. We don't have time to talk because there's something we have to do. Take time to stop and love your spouse. ❦

*T*ODAY'S THOUGHT: *How can you slow down? Make a list of the ways, and then carry out one of those ways this week.*

LOVE

Weeping may tarry for the night, but joy comes with the morning. Psalm 30:5

The Psalms often express the depths of human despair and anguish. It's important to note that the good news of the gospel doesn't eliminate the weeping. Our lives are filled with bitter disappointments, untimely deaths, and nagging doubts. We, like the psalmists, cry out to God for solace, explanations, and faith. The surrounding darkness of the world sometimes appears impenetrable.

It is significant, however, that despite the grief the psalmists often express, they do not dwell on human suffering. The psalms of lament always end with an affirmation of God's deliverance from the affliction. The light of the good news always breaks through the apparently unbreakable darkness. Indeed, "joy comes with the morning."

One of the special blessings that married life affords is being a comfort to one another in times of sorrow. Because of the intimacy of holy matrimony, both of us suffer when one of us does. Even though the particular weight of sorrow may fall on one of us more than the other, it is nonetheless shared; and a shared burden is much lighter. This is one of the reasons we shouldn't hide our pain and disappointment from our loved one; he or she cannot truly share it with us unless we let our pain be known. ❦

*T*ODAY'S THOUGHT: *What burden are you carrying that your spouse needs to know about?*

Woe to those who call evil good and good evil. Isaiah 5:20

We're all familiar with the episode between Adam, Eve, and the snake in Genesis 3. What the snake was doing was challenging the word of God. "Did God say . . . ?" he asks. When Eve explains that God said they shouldn't eat of the tree that was in the middle of the garden or they would die, the snake then says, "You will not die." He goes on to try to convince Eve that the reason God threatened them was because God didn't want them to become like him. Eve bites.

The apple was good to eat, and it certainly had been beautiful. Eve's choice (and Adam isn't off the hook, because he was right there listening to all of this) was between something that seemed to be very good and the word of God. When society says there shouldn't be moral constraints upon consenting adults engaging in activities that won't hurt anyone else, we're being offered a beautiful and delicious apple. The problem is that the word of God may be that we shouldn't eat that apple.

If Christian married couples do not stand up for the word of God on matters that affect marriage and family values, who will? If we allow others to go unchallenged in calling good evil and evil good, who will do so? ❦

*T*ODAY'S THOUGHT: *Is it time for you to get involved in combating systems or programs that uphold ungodly values?*

LOVE

The husband should give to his wife her conjugal rights, and likewise the wife to her husband. 1 Corinthians 7:3

Friends of ours were involved in a lawsuit some years ago resulting from an injury to the husband. The wife was testifying concerning the extent of the injuries when the attorney began to question her in detail as to the degree that the injury had interfered with her conjugal rights. To her humiliation, she realized she was going to have to discuss her sex life in front of the jury.

Our sexuality is such a private and mysterious thing that we are often reluctant to discuss the subject even within the marriage relationship. Perhaps the only good thing that has come out of the sexual revolution of past years is a greater openness to talk about sexual activity between husband and wife. Our understanding of the subject has perhaps been muddled by the fact that much of our sex education came from the anecdotes and outright exaggerations of our more promiscuous or imaginative friends.

The fact is, however, that sex is a great gift from God, and we should enjoy it thoroughly as Christian married couples. Openness to our sexual desire for one another (our "conjugal rights") can make for good communication on this vital subject. As married people, our bodies are not our own. They are to be shared with our spouse that we may become one flesh. God made us that way, and we should be glad. ❦

*T*ODAY'S THOUGHT: *How open are you to sharing your sexual needs with your spouse?*

Do not deprive each other except by mutual consent and for a time. 1 Corinthians 7:5 NIV

In the next few days, we'll cover more things that affect the quality of our sexual encounters as a married couple.

It has been said that the primary sexual organ is the brain. Our sexual relations are greatly affected by what we carry from the past, the notions we bring into the relationship, and by whatever is going on in our lives today (our fears, hostilities, insecurities). Recognizing this fact and dealing with it can bring breakthroughs in good sex.

Many medications are available today to deal with various ailments. But we need to realize that medications can affect our moods and our desire or proficiency in sexual relations. If we are on medication, it's important to know what we are taking, why, and what the side effects may be.

We shouldn't lay unrealistic expectations on ourselves in regard to our sexual relations. The culture in which we live can leave us so confused about the sex act that it becomes a performance and we, as participants, become like spectators. Rather than concerning ourselves with "how we're doing," we should focus on enjoying the encounter. 🍎

*T*ODAY'S THOUGHT: *How would you rate your sexual encounters with your spouse?*

Your heavenly Father knows that you need them all.
Matthew 6:32

Every married person has two fundamental needs. One is sexual acceptance: to know we are loved. The other is personal, emotional acceptance: to know we are valued for who we are. When either sexual or emotional acceptance is lacking within the relationship, difficulties occur.

Some examples might be helpful. When men don't experience sexual acceptance, they often feel rejected, frustrated, angry, and defeated. This can lead to workaholism, emotional withdrawal, and escapism (sports, going out with the guys, excessive drinking, and even adultery).

When women don't experience emotional acceptance, they often feel rejected, unattractive, taken for granted, fearful, and abandoned. This can lead to manipulation, nagging, tears and tantrums, depression, and escapism (concentrating purely on personal interests and neglecting the home).

The above examples give a glimpse into the kinds of problems that can exist when we don't give each other the sexual and emotional acceptance we need. The answer, of course, is to seek to provide for each other's needs. ❦

*T*ODAY'S THOUGHT: *Do you feel sexually and emotionally accepted by your spouse? How do you show your spouse sexual and emotional acceptance?*

September

Love

For your love is better than wine. Song of Solomon 1:2

Following are some guidelines for good sexual relations:

First, take time for sex. It shouldn't be an afterthought or something we try to accomplish in record time.

Second, make it a priority. Plan for it. Look forward to it just as you would a special occasion of some other kind.

Third, stay emotionally close to one another. If we are in harmony in our feelings toward one another, our sexual relations will be profoundly more satisfying.

Fourth, "stay in touch." Frequently kiss, hug, and otherwise touch one another lovingly.

Fifth, keep the romance alive. Have a date once a week, send flowers, and remember special occasions.

Sixth, protect your relationship. Be cautious of the things that might drive you apart. Give your loved one the priority he or she deserves.

Seventh, don't take sex too seriously. Have fun.

Eighth, surprise your loved one. Don't limit your sexual activities to the same old time and place. Find new ways to enjoy one another sexually.

Ninth, be open. Talk about sex, what it means to you, questions you have, what pleasures you most, whatever.

Good sex makes for good health and good marriages. 🍒

*T*ODAY'S THOUGHT: *What can you do to improve your sexual relations?*

Love

Let all things be done for edification. 1 Corinthians 14:26

How can we learn to affirm rather than criticize one another? First, we must remember that love is a decision, not a feeling. We choose to love our spouse, and affirming is an act of love.

Second, we can try to understand ourselves better. Are we positive in our approach to things, or negative? Why? What can we do to be more positive?

Third, the closer we are to our spouse, the less likely we are to be critical. (We're not talking about physical closeness here; during periods of constant physical closeness, we can get on each other's nerves.) When we are emotionally and spiritually close, we will tend to be more affirming.

Fourth, we can find creative ways to compliment each other and look for the good points of our loved one rather than the things we want changed. We can, in prayer, ask the Lord to show us ways to be more affirming.

Fifth, we can commit to be a more affirming person, because that is what God wants us to do. Finally, we can decide not to be defensive (or offensive!) but to yield to one another in love. ❦

*T*ODAY'S THOUGHT: *What will you do to affirm your spouse?*

Love

They strengthened their hands for the good work. Nehemiah 2:18

Marriage counselors generally agree that there are three fundamentals of successful marriages. Successful married couples understand the importance of: (1) continuing to grow in their relationship; (2) becoming good communicators; and (3) resolving conflicts. Couples who work to master these three fundamentals are strengthening their hands for the good work, and their marriages are prospering as a result.

We have a special responsibility to make the most of our marriage, not only out of an obligation to one another, but also to Christ. Thus, continually working on the fundamentals of success in marriage is a vital portion of our Christian duty.

Because these fundamentals are so important to good marriages, couples need to concentrate on living them out, no matter what stage of married life they're in. Therefore, we'll look more closely at these three fundamentals over the next few days. ❧

*T*ODAY'S THOUGHT: *In which of these areas does your marriage need improvement?*

Love

Commit your way to the Lord; trust in him.   Psalm 37:5

What do we mean by the importance of continuing to grow in our relationship in marriage? To some, that would mean permanence of the marriage and sexual fidelity within the marriage. Although that view is correct, and essential, it doesn't go far enough. If we are simply loyal to one another and physically present, we haven't accomplished much—we could say that of our pet dog!

Our love for one another is to be patterned after Jesus' love for us, and that requires a great deal more than loyalty and presence. We must be willing to give ourselves to the relationship, and that calls for a deep level of personal engagement and self-revealing vulnerability in serving and accommodating one another. More than a commitment not to leave the marriage, we need a commitment to growth.

Some couples do something every year specifically to enrich their marriage, such as attending a couples' retreat, reading and discussing a marriage book, or participating in a couples' group that focuses on marriage improvement. Each of these involves a commitment to relational growth. ❧

*T*ODAY'S THOUGHT: *How deep is your commitment to growth in marriage?*

SEPTEMBER 5

Love

You will know the truth, and the truth will make you free.
John 8:32

Unless we speak the truth in love to one another in marriage, we won't fulfill our responsibility to grow. Many marriages get stuck and stay that way for years because one of us is unwilling to get the other to face up to some serious personal problem such as alcoholism, a violent temper, chronic depression, sexual dysfunction, or an inability or unwillingness to communicate. Ignoring such problems or refusing to deal with them is the opposite of our responsibility to grow in the marriage. Instead, it evidences lack of care for one another and lack of trust in God.

The purpose of our lives is to learn to grow in love, and marriage is the ideal framework within which that can happen. It is in marriage that we begin to develop ourself as the whole person God wants us to be. Our love for one another should, then, manifest itself in concern, not only for our own development, but our spouse's.

If we limit the potential of our marriage by an unwillingness to deal with serious issues, our relationship will always be much less than God wants it to be. It will not grow. On the other hand, we can, by the grace of God, commit ourselves to an ever-deepening bond of love that will keep us not only on the growing edge of marriage, but the growing edge of faith. ❦

*T*ODAY'S THOUGHT: *Is there a problem in your relationship that needs to be dealt with right now?*

Speak tenderly to her. Hosea 2:14

In marriage we give the gift of ourselves to one another, and we cannot do that without communicating. The gift of ourselves is the willingness to open our hearts to one another in vulnerable self-disclosure. It means being willing, not only to say the words and to express the feelings that convey messages to our loved one, but also to receive our spouse's communication intentionally and lovingly.

Communication is risky business—and that's why many of us do not do it often enough or well. The better we know each other, the more we can hurt each other. Through communicating with one another, we may find that there is something about ourself we'll have to change. Some couples never fight because they never talk. They just exist in the same household until something comes along that attracts them more than their spouse, and divorce results.

The problem is not that couples don't care about one another. It's that we're afraid to say the hurtful thing, so we tend to protect one another from painful truths. That may work in superficial relationships, but it doesn't work in marriage. Marriage partners who try to protect one another from the truth, no matter how painful it may be, end up inflicting even greater pain on themselves because the marriage disintegrates. One of the greatest gifts we can give in marriage is open and loving communication. ❦

*T*ODAY'S THOUGHT: *What can you do to improve communication in your marriage?*

Love

Choose this day whom you will serve. Joshua 24:15

We have a choice. We can trust God and communicate effectively with our spouse, but we must intentionally choose to do so. We have to decide that we're going to let our loved one into our life.

There is much more to communication than talking a lot. In addition to the things that are easy enough to share, we must also be willing to tell about our needs, our fears, why we are sad or feel we are failing. In short, we have to let our spouse know what is bothering us. We have to share why we are irritable or withdrawn concerning matters that have nothing to do with our spouse, so he or she won't be worrying about it, thinking he or she did something wrong.

Likewise, as our spouse shares honestly with us, we must be willing to pay attention, to hear what is said by the heart as well as the tongue. We shouldn't judge or prejudge what is being said. Instead, we must encourage our loved one to unwrap for us the gift of communication—and treat it as precious. Sometimes the gift will be marked "fragile," and we have to learn how to handle it with care. ❦

*T*ODAY'S THOUGHT: *Do you need to share your feelings and thoughts more with your spouse?*

Teach me thy way, O Lord. Psalm 27:11

In marriage, we need the right kind of communication. We can say things lovingly or in a way that hurts or produces arguments. We can engage in constructive dialogue or needless fighting. The ideal is telling the truth in love.

What communication skills help in our relationship?

1. Being careful in talking about sensitive matters, proceeding as gently and as tactfully as possible.
2. Sticking to one issue at a time.
3. Being specific so our loved one knows what we're talking about.
4. Being sensitive to the feelings of our loved one as we disclose our feelings.
5. Talking more about ourself than about our spouse.
6. Being open to the possibility that our interpretation of the matter under discussion or our attitude concerning it may need change.

We also don't try to read our loved one's mind, imputing motives or psychoanalyzing him or her. When we become angry, we take time out to cool down rather than lashing out or being sarcastic. When our spouse speaks, we listen intently without interrupting. When we are in doubt about what is being said, we ask for clarification rather than guessing what is meant. 🐛

*T*ODAY'S THOUGHT: *How are your communication skills?*

Love

What causes wars, and what causes fightings among you?
James 4:1

Because we are human beings possessed of our own ideas, opinions, prejudices, preferences, values, needs, and interests, resolving conflicts is also fundamental to success in marriage. As we deal with the issues that inevitably come before us day by day, is it any wonder we disagree?

Conflicts can be approached positively, as opportunities for growth and self-sacrifice for the benefit of our loved one. When we yield a point, or give up a "right" out of sheer love for our spouse, we open the door to a responding gift of love and acceptance. On the other hand, when we are obstinate, we create an atmosphere of ill will that calls for retaliation from our spouse. We have no guarantee that our gift of self-sacrifice will be accepted; we can only hope our generosity will result in a positive response.

Unfortunately, we have all known marriages that were like battlegrounds, with conflicting egos and the slightest of differences blown into full-scale warfare. Conflict management doesn't have to be that way. When we, instead, give the gift of ourselves to one another, both of us win. ❦

TODAY'S THOUGHT: *How do you and your spouse handle conflict?*

SEPTEMBER 10

Love

Not by might, nor by power, but by my Spirit, says the Lord.
Zechariah 4:6

Conflicts within marriage should not be regarded as power struggles or contests between who is right and who is wrong. More likely, it is a case of differences of opinion about what we want, how we should do something, or what is more convenient for one or the other of us. Conflicts arise in dealing with how to decorate a room, maintain the yard, or discipline the children. When conflicts come, it's helpful to talk about feelings rather than rights. It's especially helpful to discuss the feelings that underlie why we have difficulty giving in on a particular point.

If important values are at stake, concession is out of the question. Compromise may be necessary if we are at an impasse. This is a time to consider a range of compromises in hope that we can find one that gives each spouse at least something of what he or she values as essential. This is where skill in resolving conflicts can help.

Skill in communication comes from giving first priority to our love for one another and our commitment to the marriage. Then we can look for common ground rather than accentuating our differences. This creates a spirit of goodwill rather than opposition. When conflict is handled in a way that respects each spouse's needs, it brings us closer together rather than further apart. ❦

*T*ODAY'S THOUGHT: *Have you and your spouse ever compromised on a issue? What was the result?*

SEPTEMBER 11

In thy presence there is fulness of joy. Psalm 16:11

According to author Bruce Larson, the presence of Christ gives grace to marriage. It gives us a blessing and a power beyond the ordinary. It's not a coincidence that marriage is the favorite image the Bible uses for the relationship between God and his people. Jesus spoke of himself as the bridegroom and the church as his bride.

"There is something divine in true marriage," says Larson. "It is like a triangle. It takes three to get married—a man, a woman, and God. Frances de Sales put it this way, 'If the glue is good, two pieces of wood glued together will cleave so fast to each other that they can be more easily broken in any other place than where they were joined. God glues the husband to the wife with his own blood.'"

The result is that every Christian marriage has the miracle of God's presence. However, how conscious we are of God's presence, and how dependent upon him we are, is up to us. As we invite him in, he introduces his reconciling love into our lives. This doesn't mean we ask for a wall of protection from the world as much as for the glue to hold us together from within. This "glue" brings with it love, patience, and understanding by which we can adhere to each other in willing faithfulness. ❦

*T*ODAY'S THOUGHT: *What specific things are you doing within your marriage to recognize God's presence? to invite his reconciling love to glue you even more together?*

Let marriage be held in honor among all. Hebrews 13:4

By listening to how people talk about their courtship and marriage, experts may be able to predict whether a marriage is on track or headed for the divorce court. University of Washington researchers predicted marital breakups within three years with nearly 94 percent accuracy. They did this simply by interviewing married couples and evaluating what was said, as well as attitudes exhibited, by the couples.

Couples who spoke fondly of their courtship, were proud of their struggles to make the marriage work, and showed signs of affection for one another were unlikely to break up. Couples who exhibited a resignation to difficulties rather than a willingness to work to make things better were not likely to last. The researchers said that if, during the interviews, the husband seemed withdrawn, unaffectionate, and critical, the marriage was almost always doomed.

If we hold our marriage in honor, this information can help us assess where we are building a strong foundation and where we might be headed for trouble. Where there is distance between us, whether in lack of affection or in unwillingness to work through the inevitable difficulties we face, we obviously need to close that gap. God wants our marriage to be all that it can be. ❦

*T*ODAY'S THOUGHT: *Are there any "gaps" between you that need to be closed?*

New wine is for fresh skins. Mark 2:22

When Jesus said these words, he had a particular situation in mind. The "new wine" applied to the new life he was bringing, and it was hard for those who were not open to his teachings to accept what he said. They were trapped in old wineskins that had no flexibility to accept new wine, so they'd expand and burst.

If we try to add in something new while still holding on to our old prejudices, attitudes, and illusions, there just isn't room for the new without affecting the old. Something has to give. The new idea must be accepted in its entirety, not just tacked or sewn onto the old point of view.

In the same way, we bring into the marriage something entirely new: our ongoing relationship with one another. Yet we come into this relationship with past baggage: things our parents (by their words and actions) built into our thinking process, thereby shaping our values; things our friends told us about sex (perhaps more often wrong than right); ways in which teachers and friends influenced our understanding of life. Many of these things are good, but now they need to be reshaped in light of our love for one another. We need to be flexible. ❦

*T*ODAY'S THOUGHT: *In what ways has marriage changed your thinking?*

Love

They began to beg Jesus to depart from their neighborhood.
Mark 5:17

Jesus had come into the country of the Gerasenes and had cast many demons out of a tortured soul. The unclean spirit within the man was of such a multiple nature that he called himself "Legion." Jesus sent the spirit into a herd of swine that then ran headlong over a cliff and into the sea.

Faced with the power of God manifested in Jesus, the people wanted him to leave. They were overawed by the healing of the man, familiar to them all, who had seemed so hopeless. But, rather than being grateful for what Jesus had done for the man (and thus, by implication, could do for them), they were either afraid of his power or upset by the loss of the swine.

Jesus can work with great power in our marriage too. But in the process, he will require certain things of us. There will be pigs that need to go over the cliff. Perhaps there are times we would like to be left alone, just like the people who, rather than following Jesus, chose to send him away. We cannot have it both ways. Jesus needs to be central in our marriage, even in times of discomfort over what he would have us do. ❦

*T*ODAY'S THOUGHT: *Is Jesus in the center of your marriage? What evidence is there?*

SEPTEMBER 15

Out of the mouth of babes and sucklings thou hast brought perfect praise. Matthew 21:16

There is a sense in which children begin life in purity and innocence. Nature teaches them certain things about good and bad; if they touch something hot, they learn they will be burned. Parents teach their children to avoid danger, recognize security, and to learn from experience.

Children also learn how to behave from parents, friends, and relatives. Yet, often they see their elders telling them one thing and doing another. No wonder this produces wariness, distrust, and even cynicism.

The Lord provides help to those of us who want to bring our children up in wholeness. Whether we want to be or not, we are transparent to our children. They know our failings. So does God. Thankfully, God will forgive us, and our children will appreciate our vulnerability if we are willing to confess our faults and seek God's forgiveness.

With God's help, we can live a life together that is a positive witness to our children. And, even if we failed to do so, we can show them a new type of love as God continues to work in our lives. It is never too late for God, it is never too late for us, and it is never too late for us to reach our children with God's love. 🌿

*T*ODAY'S THOUGHT: *Where is God in the lives of your children? Where are you?*

But I say to you that hear, Love your enemies. Luke 6:27

Jesus, having named the Twelve, begins a series of teachings that parallel the Sermon on the Mount. He shows his followers how to look at things from God's point of view, which is very different from what they are accustomed to. Jesus' illustrations simply contradict the way things normally work in the world.

Here Jesus is teaching a principle that might be called "love unlimited." As human beings, we tend to express our love in ways that are meaningful to us but may not be to our spouse.

We may like to be told how worthy we are, and so we try to affirm others in this way. Our spouse, however, may think "actions speak louder than words." Love unlimited calls us to understand where our loved one is in his or her need to be loved, and to meet that need as best we can.

Some especially good news is that Luke 6:27-38 ends with, "For the measure you give will be the measure you get back." In a world so desperately in need of love, it's good to know that what we give is what we get. ❦

*T*ODAY'S THOUGHT: *How responsive are you to your spouse's way of needing love?*

Love

Can a blind man lead a blind man? Will they not both fall into a pit? Luke 6:39

Jesus would not have us be like the blind leading the blind. There are things we both need to learn and to put into practice in our day-to-day lives. We should look within every marital challenge we face to find what God wants to teach us rather than concentrating on the faults or failures of our spouse. We can cry, "Lord, Lord," all day long, but if we do not do what God wants us to do, our words are a "noisy gong or a clanging cymbal" (1 Corinthians 13).

As Jesus moves on in Luke 6:39-49, he uses the illustration of fruit bearing. A good tree will produce good fruit; a bad tree will bear bad fruit. What kind of fruit do we want to bear?

Jesus' words could not be clearer. He knows that it is human nature to criticize in others (especially our spouse) those things we cannot see in ourselves. If we hear a sermon or teaching that causes us to think, *I wish my loved one could hear this*, it may be that it applies at least equally to ourselves. We need to discover and deal honestly with our own problems if we want to be the married person God wants us to be, and if we are to be effective instruments of his love in our family. ❦

*T*ODAY'S THOUGHT: *Are there any ways in which you are the blind leading the blind?*

Why do you see the speck that is in your brother's eye, but do not notice the log that is in your own eye? Matthew 7:3

Marriage expert Dennis Rainey tells the story of a man who could spot faults in other people with absolute precision while being totally oblivious to his own shortcomings. Once the man said to Rainey, "My wife is not submissive to me in accordance with Ephesians 5." "Is that so?" responded Rainey. "Let's look at what it says in the Bible." The man immediately turned to Ephesians 5:22 and began to read, "Wives . . ." Rainey cut him off before he could read any more and said, "No, that passage applies to wives; that's not for you. Drop down to verse 25; that's where it talks about husbands."

In order to communicate effectively, we need to deal with the log in our own eye rather than the speck in our spouse's eye. We need to talk about what is going on inside ourselves rather than what we think is going on with our loved one. It's not very constructive to protest "you always have the last word"; or "you are always right."

Instead of accusing our spouses of wasting money, it's much more constructive to say, "I'm having a hard time dealing with the financial situation we are in these days." That doesn't avoid the issue, but it puts it on a nonjudgmental level and lays the foundation for reasonable discussion. Having an argument in which each of us is simply trying to win is different from having a discussion in which each of us is trying to listen for the truth. ❧

*T*ODAY'S THOUGHT: *Do you tend to accuse your spouse when you get into areas of conflict?*

SEPTEMBER 19

I thank my God every time I remember you. Philippians 1:3 NIV

Although it's important to affirm our loved one, we don't, however, have to praise one another as though our spouse were perfect. There's no need to say anything we don't genuinely mean. But because honest praise means much to our loved one, we should be willing to do it at every reasonable opportunity.

There's a lot of room for expressions of appreciation, affirmation, and thanksgiving: "You look great." "Thanks for mopping the kitchen (or taking out the trash)." "You are a really good mother/father." "You've got a tremendous sense of humor." "I don't believe anybody does that as well as you." "Thanks for that really good meal." "Thanks for taking me out." "You're my favorite person in the whole world."

Remarks such as these cost so little but are valued greatly. They don't lay anything on our spouse. They don't sound old or trite, no matter how many times they are said. They put a spark into the life of our loved one, make things easier to bear even on the hard days, and bring us closer together. When we express our love, we are simply reflecting the love that God has for our spouse. 🐦

*T*ODAY'S THOUGHT: *How much do you appreciate the spouse God has given you?*

Refrain from anger, and forsake wrath! Fret not yourself; it tends only to evil. Psalm 37:8

There is a lot of anger today. Even if it doesn't manifest itself between us and our spouse, nonetheless it affects us. We encounter it at work, as we travel to and from work, in our neighborhoods, and even in our churches. Thus, even at the best of times within our marriage, we carry some of the effects of anger with us into the home. For that reason, we'll spend several days learning how to deal constructively with anger.

It often happens that, within a marriage, the spouses encountered anger in very different ways while they were growing up. One spouse will be from a family where anger was quickly, openly, and loudly vented. The other spouse will be from a family where anger was suppressed and only dealt with when it could no longer be contained.

As a result, anger can become a problem in the marriage. One spouse's anger will erupt toward the other as soon as something displeasing happens. The other spouse will become silent and distant. However, if the couple is willing to work together to find effective ways to deal with anger, they can build an extremely healthy marriage. The explosive spouse will learn to curb his emotions somewhat, and the silent spouse will become more aware of her anger and how to express it appropriately. ❦

*T*ODAY'S THOUGHT: *How do you handle anger? How about your spouse?*

Moses' anger burned hot, and he threw the tables out of his hands and broke them at the foot of the mountain. Exodus 32:19

Anger may be the most difficult emotion to deal with in relationships. Perhaps it's helpful to see that our spiritual leaders struggled with anger too. That made them human and lets us know that God can forgive us, as he did them.

Anger is inevitable in close relationships, and marriage should be the closest relationship of all. The very intimacy of marriage reveals our differences, which are frustrating and threatening.

Yet, for all the problems it poses, anger also serves a useful purpose. It provides information: It lets us know how we feel when we're threatened or when a situation has had an unhappy effect on us. It also provides the energy we need to deal with the situation so we can attain a level of comfort once again.

Despite teachings that sometimes seem contrary, there is nothing immoral about anger itself. It's how we deal with it that is moral or immoral. Some of the greatest good for the benefit of mankind has occurred because Christian people became angry with injustices that were being imposed upon others. ❧

*T*ODAY'S THOUGHT: *When did you last get angry? What was it about?*

Love

Who can endure the heat of his anger? His wrath is poured out like fire, and the rocks are broken asunder by him. Nahum 1:6

This verse has to do with the anger of God, a whole different category than human anger. But it's a graphic illustration of anger being vented. Sometimes when we experience the wrath of people who cannot control their anger, it feels just like that! When anger is given full rein, it can manifest itself in shouting, cursing, throwing objects, physical abuse, and even killing.

The person who gives anger full vent can experience exhilaration, a sense of great power, and a deeply satisfying vindication. But people and property are victims of such outbreaks. Relationships cannot handle much anger. It is a symptom of a problem that needs to be dealt with if the marriage is to survive.

When anger burns so hotly that feelings are severely injured, the spouses must deal with these unhappy results. Reconciliation must occur, and the offending spouse must commit to dealing with the symptoms of the disorder. Otherwise, the behavior will ultimately become too heavy a burden for the marriage to carry. We need not let anger control us if we ask God for help. ❦

*T*ODAY'S THOUGHT: *Is anger a problem in your marriage? If so, what will you do about it—together?*

Love

A man's spirit will endure sickness; but a broken spirit who can bear? Proverbs 18:14

Venting anger is not constructive, but neither is suppressing it. Many of us have grown up thinking that anger itself is bad, perhaps never seeing our parents express it. As a result, when we believe we have been wronged, we stuff the feeling down inside us. There it lies, festering and causing all sorts of miserable side effects. Ultimately it manifests itself in withdrawal, silence, avoidance, tears, and sickness.

When anger exists but is suppressed, it can be extremely damaging to our inner life. We often pay the price of depression. The skills needed to cope with suppression of anger are awareness and assertiveness. First, we have to admit that our problem is one of anger before we can gain any relief. If we tend to suppress anger because we think it's improper, a sign of weakness, or sin, we need to deal with those feelings because, although subconscious, they'll mask the anger. Once the anger is admitted, we need to share it with the person we think has wronged us, take some other type of constructive action, or find better ways to care for ourselves so that anger is not a frequent visitor in our lives. ❦

*T*ODAY'S THOUGHT: *Do you suppress anger?*
If so, what steps can you take to get it out in the open
so you can turn it into something constructive?

Love

Acknowledge and take to heart this day that the Lord is God.
Deuteronomy 4:39 NIV

As we continue to look at the issue of anger, note two things. First, even if we don't think we have a problem with anger in our own marriage, we need to recognize it as a major factor in the world, among our friends and neighbors, and perhaps our children. We all need to know more about anger. Second, there are specific ways to deal with it—and that's what we'll be considering over the next eight days.

The first step in dealing with anger is acknowledging it. As painful or as humbling as it might be to admit that we are angry, we need to admit it. Denying or minimizing it won't work; it will still be there, waiting to be dealt with in one way or another. Because of the intimacy of marriage, we owe it to our spouse as well as ourself to acknowledge our anger.

Next, we reflect on the meaning of the anger and decide what to do with it. We might decide that it really is no big deal, or that we were the one at fault rather than our spouse, and we really have no reason to be angry with him or her. If we decide we are angry with our spouse but feel that to express the anger, based on past experience, will really get us nowhere, we need to think through what we *will* do with it. We know we cannot change our spouse, but maybe we can change something about ourself that will keep this kind of anger from injuring our relationship in the future. 🍂

*T*ODAY'S THOUGHT: *Are you harboring any past anger that you need to acknowledge now?*

Love

He confessed, he did not deny. John 1:20

The second step in dealing with our anger is to express it without venting it. Even those of us who tend to have explosive tempers can choose how we will express the anger we feel.

If it has been a pattern for us to blow up with anger toward our spouse and children, we may think we have no choice and that it is just our nature. On reflection, however, we have to acknowledge that we don't express anger in a violent manner toward customers, our supervisor, or others who could hurt us. (If we do, we need psychological help.) We simply have a feeling of power over our loved ones and are powerless against the others, in which case our temper tantrums are evidence of cowardice. We do have a choice; we can control our manner of expressing anger.

Bad habits aren't changed overnight. However, we can make the choice to respect our loved ones and to stop the temper tantrums, the cursing, the verbal and perhaps physical abuse that may have been the way we have released our anger. As we look toward handling anger constructively in the future, we can choose to break the bad habits of the past. ❦

TODAY'S THOUGHT: *To what extent do you think we can choose how we handle anger?*

He feels only the pain of his own body, and he mourns only for himself. Job 14:22

Anger is the result of injury, frustration, or fear; it's a reaction to these painful experiences. Thus, the third step in dealing with our anger is to share those feelings.

The emotion we call *anger* functions to defend us when we're threatened. It's a strong emotion with a great deal of latent power. Now that we've decided not to let that power explode in such a way as to injure our relationship with our spouse, we must decide how to release it.

Because of anger's pain, we are vulnerable, wounded. Sharing that woundedness can be done in a tender way, letting tears flow if they are there. The strength of the emotion can evoke strong feelings of compassion from the other, who knows we're dealing with serious stuff. It's much easier for our spouse to hear and understand our pain when it's shared. And expressing our pain gives our loved one more information about what's really troubling us than would happen in the midst of a storm of anger. Because this method makes us vulnerable, it's difficult to do. But the effort is definitely worth it. ❧

TODAY'S THOUGHT: *How can you share anger more constructively?*

SEPTEMBER 27

Everyone should be quick to listen, slow to speak and slow to become angry. James 1:19 NIV

The fourth step in processing anger deals with how to react when our loved one expresses his or her anger to us. As the Bible verse indicates, we need to be attentive and listen.

There's nothing fun about listening to our spouse's anger, but it lets us know in no uncertain terms that he or she is hurting. Our spouse, most of all, needs to know we care, and we express that care by the manner in which we listen. We shouldn't interrupt, and we certainly shouldn't try to defend ourself. If we do so, we just compound the problem.

Unless our spouse's anger is released, serious inner damage can occur. Thus, whether our loved one is constructively releasing anger or not, we need to give him or her the gift of allowing the release.

If we listen attentively and acknowledge that our loved one has some justification for the anger, it often decreases significantly. Then we will have the opportunity to share our thoughts. ❧

*T*ODAY'S THOUGHT: *Remember that your spouse is always worth listening to.*

Love

The result of righteousness [will be] quietness and trust.
Isaiah 32:17

The fifth step in dealing with anger occurs when things are on the verge of getting out of control. Despite all that's been said about how to process anger properly, times will come when tempers flair and calmly reasoning the matter out is no longer realistic. That's when we must cool down, prayerfully seeking quietness and trust.

When we are both at the boiling point, we should call time-out. It's best to have an understanding in advance that either party may do that when it appears that the anger is likely to cause serious injury to at least one of the spouses. Then the discussion should cease immediately so each spouse can go his or her own way until we can regain control of our tempers.

Prayer should be an essential part of the cooling-down process. God can give us peace and assurance. He can also help us see what the flash point was that sent things spinning out of control. Often God shows us where we have been wrong and brings us to repentance. He inspires us with loving ways to deal with the situation and reestablish intimacy. Following the time-out, we need to get back together and try to bring the matter to a conclusion. ❦

*T*ODAY'S THOUGHT: *Do you and your spouse go to prayer as a first, or last, resort?*

Lo, this we have searched out. Job 5:27

Seeking the underlying causes of our anger and doing something about them is the sixth step in the process of dealing with anger. If we find ourselves trapped in a pattern of anger, we certainly need to know why. If symptoms indicate we have a dreaded disease, we surely would want to get to the bottom of that, and recurring anger is disease enough!

If we have a tendency to lose our temper over trivial matters, there is probably something below the surface that causes our recurring irritability. It may be unhappiness with our job or life in general. Maybe the children aren't turning out the way we thought they would, or perhaps the marriage itself is dissatisfying. It could be burnout from too much hard work without a vacation or some vague sense of pressure we are unable to identify and deal with.

We need to take time to seek out the reasons, to evaluate them and find the proper resolution. Prayer, again, can be a major help. Talking it out with our spouse, a valued adviser, or a professional counselor is worth consideration. Maybe it's time for an annual physical examination; sometimes there are physiological factors underlying our distress. Taking good care of ourselves is at the heart of dealing with life's irritations. ❧

*T*ODAY'S THOUGHT: *Is anything bothering you that needs to be resolved?*

Love

The memory of them is lost. Ecclesiastes 9:5

The seventh step in processing anger has to do with past issues that lurk in our subconscious, causing us to overreact to present situations. We owe it to our spouse and children to resolve these issues so they won't continue to have a negative effect upon us.

When we have angry reactions that are out of proportion to the actual circumstance, there is probably something in our past, perhaps our childhood, that is triggering it. Until we deal with the original event that causes this reaction, we are likely to remain a slave to it.

If it is a serious problem, we may need professional help in uncovering and dealing with it. Prayer, however, is another route available to Christians. If we are willing to take the time, perhaps with fasting, to go back prayerfully into our past, we can often find the culprit, the traumatic thing that happened to us that we have never resolved and that continues to plague us in disguise. Once we discover it and release it to God, its power over us is often dispelled. A trusted Christian spiritual adviser can be a help in this process. ❦

*T*ODAY'S THOUGHT: *Do you have painful memories for which you need healing? If so, what will you do about them?*

October

Why then are you angry over this matter? 2 Samuel 19:42

We have a three-step method we often use in dealing with anger in our marriage. Perhaps it is a fitting close to our exploration of anger.

First, we report the anger. The person who is angry expresses in a calm voice how he or she is feeling. One of us might say to the other, "You need to know that I am feeling angry toward you right now." The other person, then, immediately begins to ask questions to understand the anger. When we take the time to report and try to understand the anger, we can deal with the matter right away, before stronger emotions come into play.

Second, we try to identify the source of the anger. We recognize that very often—probably most of the time—the anger is not directly related to our feelings toward one another. The angry person is really angry with himself or herself or is angry as the result of something someone else has done or said. Once we can understand the source of the anger, we can help each other deal with it.

Third, we clear the air between us. When we feel angry, we need to think about what obstacles our anger may have placed between us. Often we discover that there is at least something secondarily creating the feeling of anger in one of us toward the other. We then work together to process that anger in a positive way. 🍂

*J*ODAY'S THOUGHT: *Next time, try this method and see how it works.*

I tell you, not even in Israel have I found such faith. Luke 7:9

The story of the Roman centurion who sought healing for his servant can teach us many things. This Gentile showed more faith than Jesus found among his own people, the Jews.

First, the centurion cared enough about his slave to humbly ask Jesus for help. Second, he believed Jesus could heal the slave without being physically present. Third, he uses words of true humility—something that must have been rare for a Roman officer—when he says to Jesus, "I am not worthy to have you come under my roof." Fourth, in doing so, he avoids the problem that could have been created for Jesus by going into a Gentile house (especially belonging to a Roman officer).

Humility, faith, and sensitivity lead to healing. Caring about another person enough to be vulnerable brings commendation from Jesus. In this story are the ingredients for effective healing, whether of physical, emotional, or spiritual needs.

We need to have the attitude of the centurion toward one another within our marriage and family. ❦

TODAY'S THOUGHT: *How can you emulate the centurion in caring for your spouse and children?*

Ask, and it will be given you; seek, and you will find; knock, and it will be opened to you. Matthew 7:7

When we pursue God, we should pray persistently. Jesus gives us the action verbs of *ask, seek,* and *knock* and tells us not to be passive. Just as children eagerly ask questions and expect answers, we can have confidence that God will answer us.

Jesus is standing at the door of our heart, waiting for us to take the initiative so he can give us the desires of our heart. But at the same time he wants us to do the asking, seeking, and knocking.

Often people will give up trying to pray after a few weak attempts. If their answer is delayed, they conclude that God is nowhere around. But getting to know God takes effort. We must be diligent in prayer, in searching for truth in Scripture, and in knocking on the door of fellowship within the community of faith.

As a Christian married couple, not only do we have an obligation to grow in our own relationship with God in asking, seeking, and knocking, we are to be an example and encouragement to our loved ones so they also may share fully in the life the Lord has for us all. ❦

*T*ODAY'S THOUGHT: *What are you doing to build faith in your household?*

LOVE

In God I trust; I will not be afraid. Psalm 56:11 NIV

Fear is not to be taken lightly. It manifests itself in many ways. At any given time in the life of the family, there is probably someone who is suffering from fear, perhaps seriously afraid. Yet, "fear not" is one of the primary things we learn from the Bible.

Do we choose to focus on fear or on God? If we choose fear, we know what will happen. Fear robs us of joy. It paralyzes us from taking action. It can cause physical, as well as emotional and spiritual, problems. Fear makes everything dark and leaves us at the mercy of what seem to be insurmountable obstacles.

If we choose to trust in God, on the other hand, fear can be overcome. Trusting God instead of yielding to fear means giving ourselves over to him, trusting him for the results. Knowing that God is now in control can give us faith that he will see us through the situation. Focusing on faith makes us forget our fear.

The key to overcoming fear through trusting God is to put the matter in God's hands as soon as the fear is perceived. That shows where our priorities are and prevents the fear from getting a hold on us and building itself out of proportion. The best defense against fear is taking it into the presence of God and leaving it there, taking him at his word to "not be afraid." ❦

*T*ODAY'S THOUGHT: *How do you deal with fear?*

God was in Christ reconciling the world to himself.
2 Corinthians 5:19

One of the primary things missing in Christian churches today that was a part of early Christianity is "tough love." This kind of confrontation came from a framework of trust between the individuals concerned and usually resulted in reconciliation. Because today's churches are often larger, it's difficult to have that same level of trust.

Therefore, many Christians gather in small Bible study/prayer groups, or other types of commitment groups, in which there can be honest sharing and accountability. Within this kind of relationship, people can more realistically show tough love by holding each other accountable to God, to their commitments to him, and to one another. In such a setting, unresolved conflicts can be brought out into the open and dealt with.

God cannot break through walls of resistance unless and until there is an openness to receive. As long as there are unresolved conflicts in the home, the fullness of Jesus' presence is missing. There is no place for hatred and bitterness between us and our loved ones. Jesus came to teach us about reconciliation and restoration of relationships. If there is something that needs to be done to bring reconciliation in our home, we had better get about the job of doing it. ❦

*T*ODAY'S THOUGHT: *Do you need reconciliation in any area of your home or marriage?*

Therefore you also must be ready; for the Son of man is coming at an hour you do not expect. Matthew 24:44

The day before her husband's death, a friend of ours let her husband's young law partner go into the hospital room to have some time alone with him. He stayed in the room so long that she became anxious and was just about to check on them when the young man came out with a radiant smile on his face. "What a blessing it was," he said, "to spend such precious time talking about faith with a man who will be with God tomorrow!"

Such stories are more rare than they should be. More often we hear of people who have lost a loved one and are burdened with remorse for not having had an opportunity to show their love before he or she was suddenly taken by death.

We must not take one another for granted, especially within the marriage covenant. Death can come unexpectedly to ones we love, regardless of their age. We need to take time today to notice the many little things our spouse does for us, the many things he or she is to us. We need to "get around to" all the loving things we know we should say and do—before we have to be sorry. ❦

*T*ODAY'S THOUGHT: *What words of love and appreciation do you need to speak to your spouse right now?*

LOVE

Give, and it will be given to you. Luke 6:38

There is a lot of reciprocity in marriage. The giving of ourself for the benefit of our spouse can be expected to yield the blessing of our spouse likewise giving to us. It is a joy to give, and there is no one to whom we should enjoy giving more than to our marriage partner. This can apply to our sexual relationship, as to any other act in marriage. The more generous we are in the giving of ourselves, the more likely we are to be rewarded with a generous response.

A woman can feel sexual toward the husband who voluntarily makes up the bed, washes the dishes, and mops the kitchen floor. A man can feel loved when his wife lets him read the newspaper or watch the news or sports on television.

There is an endless variety of things we can do for one another. Unexpected things are best: when we care enough about our loved one to foresee what may be a burden for him or her that is a breeze for us; when we love enough to be willing to do routine things for our spouse that neither of us likes to do; when we remember that special occasion and make plans to celebrate it in an appropriate way. And the bonus is that those things we do for our loved one will be given back to us; we shouldn't expect it (that takes the joy out of the gift), but we should be grateful when it happens. ❦

TODAY'S THOUGHT: *What unexpected gift can you give your spouse?*

LOVE

You are of more value than many sparrows. Luke 12:7

Sometimes we fail to value one another in the marriage covenant. A friend who is a dentist tells how he came to realize this the hard way. He says (we haven't checked this out to see if it's fact, but it's real to him) that, of professional people, dentists are second only to psychiatrists in committing suicide. He thinks there is a reason for it.

People who visit a doctor's office expect to wait; those who go to see their dentist do not, our friend told us. Yet, at any given moment, there may be several procedures going on at the same time in the dentist's office, and unexpected situations do occur. The result is constant pressure, which is managed successfully only by the dentist being in complete command of his staff. When he says to do something, he expects his assistants to respond immediately and appropriately.

What happens, then, when the dentist comes home from his stress-filled day? He has been in command all day. Therefore, he expects to be treated with utmost consideration on the one hand and to be obeyed immediately on the other. A spouse having to put up with that sort of treatment from her dentist husband every day can understandably feel undervalued and perhaps explode, as happened in the case of our friend. No matter how stressful our work, our marriage should always come first. 🐝

*T*ODAY'S THOUGHT: *Do you adequately value your spouse? How do you show it?*

LOVE

Husbands, love your wives, as Christ loved the church and gave himself up for her. Ephesians 5:25

Despite the fact that so many women work, statistics show that the husband, in the vast majority of cases, continues to be the breadwinner (the one providing most of the household income). Thus, even in situations where the wife works, the husband is expected to provide the bulk of the financial support. Women, by nature, need the sense of security that comes from knowing that bills can be paid, that the family is financially OK. Thus, one of the ways the husband can demonstrate he loves his wife is to provide her with the financial security she needs.

In Christian marriages, security comes from a different source. The husband who prays daily with his wife and acts as spiritual leader in the home provides much more security to the wife than one making a lot of money. Within the framework of the Christian home, real security is in Christ rather than in possessions.

How does the Christian husband act as spiritual leader? By living as a godly man. That certainly involves prayer, Bible study, and regular worship of God within the fellowship of the church. But it manifests itself more powerfully in gentle and tender acts of love that reflect to his wife and children that he knows Christ and walks with him. ❧

*T*ODAY'S THOUGHT: *Is your home secure?*

Let us run with perseverance the race that is set before us.
Hebrews 12:1

For people who are in Twelve Step programs, the key slogan is "one day at a time." It means that the program is not for sprinters but for long-distance runners. The sprinter doesn't have to worry about pacing himself: a short burst of speed, and it is all over. To the long-distance runner, pace is every-thing. He has to gain strength along the way and get a "second wind" to ultimately carry him over the finish line.

Marriage is for the long-distance runner. We are to run with perseverance the race that is set before us. Short bursts of speed just cause trouble. We have a lifetime together; there is a lot of growing God wants us to do. Things that grow slowly and steadily have a good root system and stability. Things that grow rapidly have no substance and no staying power.

"One day at a time" is a good motto for marriage. God would have us make the most of our marriage today, but not by sprinting around trying to accomplish too much and flaming out. If we expect too much of one another too soon, we will only be disappointed. If we proceed like the long-distance runner, we'll be able to overcome any disappoint-ments and build on the positive attributes of one another. These will provide the "second wind" to carry us into a more mature and wholesome relationship. ❦

*T*ODAY'S THOUGHT: *How can you become a*
more effective long-distance runner?

LOVE

Let the wise listen and add to their learning. Proverbs 1:5 NIV

A Sunday school teacher wanted to "break the ice" with her class, to get them talking and listening to one another. So she began the class by asking them a question. "Who can tell me what is small and gray and eats nuts?" No answer. She tried again, "Well, it also has a long, bushy tail and climbs trees." Finally, a small boy's hand went up tentatively. "Teacher," he said, "the answer must be Jesus, but it sounds like a squirrel to me."

How often do we fall into the same trap? We think we know what our loved one has on his or her mind, so we immediately jump to conclusions. But that isn't wise listening, and it isn't very helpful in leading to understanding.

Wise listening that leads to understanding is patient listening, not thwarted by preconceived notions. We love our spouse enough to be willing to hear what he or she has to say, to provide time for it to be said, and to listen with an openness and a loving acceptance that allows us truly to hear. When these factors are present, our response is much more likely to be appropriate. 🍂

*T*ODAY'S THOUGHT: *How can you avoid jumping to conclusions when you talk with your spouse?*

Be subject to one another out of reverence for Christ.
Ephesians 5:21

Sexual intimacy represents only one aspect of marriage, but certainly a significant one. It reflects the strengths and weaknesses of the total marriage relationship. If things are not right between us in other areas of our married life, something will be lacking in our sexual encounters. Problems in sex often indicate there are other issues that need to be dealt with.

The husband may, for instance, feel his wife isn't interested in his work and this bruises his ego. The wife, on the other hand, may carry the load of a full-time job, feeding the family, and taking care of the children. The husband, who has been relaxing while the meal was being fixed, the dishes washed, and the children put to bed, is in an amorous mood. The wife is exhausted, resentful, and angry. The deepening of sexual intimacy depends on discovering ways to be more understanding of one another, improving communication, and showing mutual respect.

The extent of sexual intimacy between a husband and wife is also affected by the warmth we show toward one another in all aspects of our life together. The way we touch, how often we hug and kiss, the tender words that pass between us, attentive listening, showing our appreciation — in these and so many other ways we communicate our love and improve our sexual relations. ❦

*T*ODAY'S THOUGHT: *Is there room for improvement in your marriage? What needs to be done?*

I came that they may have life, and have it abundantly.
John 10:10

God wants us to enjoy one another in marriage. He wants abundant life for us, and we can do a great deal to make life abundant for one another. He particularly wants us to keep the romance of our marriage alive, no matter how old we are or how long we have been married.

There's a pattern that works against romance in marriage. When we're young and newly married, there is an excitement about belonging to one another in this new way. We are very conscious of our love, frequently showing affection, and we're together as often as we can be. Then children come along, and our vocations become more demanding. There seems to be less time to be together, and there are so many other things to think about. The romance begins to die.

It need not be so. There are so many little things we can do for one another to keep the spark alive, if we're willing to take the time and effort (and it's worth it!). We can make time to be alone together, having a date at least once a week. We can surprise one another in a multitude of ways: a gift, a card, a love letter. Having fun together, breaking routines, and going on new adventures that allow us to forget our troubles for a while all help to bring romance back into the marriage and keep the spark alive. ❦

*T*ODAY'S THOUGHT: *What do you need to do to kindle the spark of romance in your marriage?*

Contribute to the needs of the saints, practice hospitality.
Romans 12:13

Instinctively, we know our homes should be models of Christian hospitality. But what, really, is Christian hospitality?

By worldly standards, hospitality is entertaining others, and the focus is on the host and hostess. Their home is clean, the food is special and abundant, all has been well planned and prepared in advance. The host and hostess are smiling, and seem to have everything in order. Their guests enjoy the evening, and will soon reciprocate.

By contrast, Christian hospitality focuses on the guests. They are not ones to whom we are obligated because "they have had us over." They are saints of God, struggling Christians just as we are, who have a need. The first priority is meeting that need, which might be a place to stay, a listening ear, or just fellowship. If food is to be served, the quality and quantity of it are not important. The house doesn't have to be spotless but can look as though someone lives there.

It is the atmosphere that counts. Is this a home where love abounds? Is this a place where Jesus is Lord? Is this somewhere that needs can be met, where saints will feel at home? We never know when we may be entertaining an angel unaware (Hebrews 13:2). ❧

*T*ODAY'S THOUGHT: *To what extent is your home open to the saints?*

No one after lighting a lamp covers it with a vessel, or puts it under a bed, but puts it on a stand, that those who enter may see the light. Luke 8:16

A favorite song of youngsters in Sunday school classes begins with the words, "This little light of mine, I'm gonna let it shine." The children learn that Jesus is the light that illuminates our hearts. As adults, we learn that Jesus sees into the very center of our heart. He is the light that makes all things visible, including our thoughts and motives.

When we clean out a closet, we need to put some light on the subject. We find hidden objects, remove debris, straighten things up. We feel better when the closet is clean. Likewise, the light of Jesus penetrates the dark closet of our heart. We can't deceive him about our hidden sins. He is waiting to clean our spiritual closets, and all we have to do is ask him to do it. As long as our spiritual closets remain unclean, our home and our marriage cannot accommodate the light of Christ.

When we ask the penetrating light of Jesus into the dark corners of our hearts, he sweeps away the debris of our foolishness, forgives our sins, puts things in order, and floods our soul with the light of his love. When we live for Christ, he makes our lives much brighter. Then we can shine for him! ❦

*T*ODAY'S THOUGHT: *Do you need to do any spiritual housecleaning?*

OCTOBER *16*

LOVE

What therefore God has joined together, let no man put asunder.
Matthew 19:6

Some friends of ours run a retreat center for married couples. Theirs is a type of marriage-enrichment program that
caters to people who are having marital problems as well as
those who simply want to improve an already good marriage. It's not unusual for there to be a couple in which either
or both of the partners have been married before.

Because of that, our friends needed guidance in how to
talk about divorce. When they began to face the issue head-
on, they discovered that couples who were in their second
marriages didn't want them in any way to water down how
God feels about divorce. As one of them put it, "Divorce isn't
an unpardonable sin, but it isn't like the TV shows portray
it, either."

Divorce is not like changing clothes. It's powerful and it
hurts. Many divorced people will say things like, "I could
handle this much better if my former wife were dead; she's
not, so there is no resolution to the pain. Still hanging out
there is what we once meant to each other and what we did
to each other; it doesn't matter that we both have remarried,
the hurt is still there." In other words, despite the divorce,
many couples are still not completely asunder. It is good for
us to remember such things in case our marriage ever gets
on rocky ground. 🍂

*T*ODAY'S THOUGHT: *How do you feel about
divorce?*

Whatever you loose on earth shall be loosed in heaven.
Matthew 16:19

One of the most significant symbols in the church takes place during the marriage ceremony. The man takes the woman's hand as they begin to exchange vows. But, after declaring his promises, the man must release her, before the woman takes the man's hand in hers. The power in this custom is profound. It demonstrates the freedom of choice in the joining of the two lives. There is nothing forced here. Each freely chooses, releases, and then allows the other to choose.

This custom also represents what married life is like: joining and loosing, embracing and releasing. We are bound together in a most powerful way, yet we must continually release one another, so that each of us may grow into the person God intends us to be. Because we love one another, the grasping is much easier than the letting go. But because we love one another, we must also be willing to release each other.

There is comfort in the releasing of our loved one; we know that Jesus is always waiting with open arms to enfold, lead, comfort, and encourage our spouse. We are not releasing him or her to something totally unknown, because our loved one is in Christ, who wants the best for him or her. ❧

*T*ODAY'S THOUGHT: *Do you release your spouse to be the person God wants him or her to be?*

A prophet is not without honor, except in his own country, and among his own kin, and in his own house. Mark 6:4

The problem is often referred to as "familiarity breeds contempt." More often it is not contempt as much as just taking for granted those whom we know intimately. We have seen their humanness, and we are skeptical when they are elevated to some position that seems to us to be above their worth or ability. Jesus had been a carpenter, raised among the people who now judged him (as they ate off the dining table he may have crafted).

From time to time, we undertake a thorough cleaning and rearranging of our study. Papers, books, and other assorted items have accumulated. At first, we are very careful about what we place where in the realignment process. But, before the day is over, we are mainly trashing and stuffing.

This parallels what can happen in marriage. In the early days of our life together, in the freshness of young love, we are very attentive to one another. As the years go by, however, we can begin to take each other for granted. Our relationship should never be taken for granted. It should always be handled with loving care, not with trashing and stuffing. ❦

*T*ODAY'S THOUGHT: *Are you, in any way, taking your spouse for granted?*

I have said this to you, that in me you may have peace.
John 16:33

A clergy friend prepared a popular tract entitled "Why pray when you can worry?" A sign on a bank said, "Worry is interest paid on trouble before it falls due." Another friend says, "Worry is like a rocking chair; it gives you something to do, but it doesn't get you anywhere."

Too often, it is just at the time that we need to stop, clear our heads, and think through some crisis that is facing us in the home that, instead, we are paralyzed with worry. At such times, we need to seek the peace of God, not just to relieve us of our worry, but to allow us to deal with the crisis in a godly way. Before taking hasty action we may regret later, we need to "stop, look, and listen." This allows us to break free from the bonds of worry so we can think and pray, assess the situation, and seek guidance.

We Christians must never forget that, in the covenant of marriage, we have a third party: God. In the moment of quietness we take when in crisis, he can guide us, comfort us, clear our heads, and help us see the way. ❦

*T*ODAY'S THOUGHT: *Do you give God time to help you in crisis?*

Even in laughter the heart is sad, and the end of joy is grief.
Proverbs 14:13

We will all experience grief. Likely, we'll outlive our parents
and many other relatives and loved ones. Our children will
suffer disappointments and illnesses, as will we. The more
seriously we take our faith, the more concerned we will be
about other people, and that may also lead to grief. Jesus
never promised us escape from reality—only some ways to
cope with it.

In the process of dealing with grief, we may well find that
our spouse has a different style of grieving than we do. The
form our grief takes and how long the process lasts can vary
greatly between us. One may cry openly, while the other
finds some other release for the pain. One may need intimate
comfort, the other may need to be left alone. One may
experience the grief deeply, yet be over it quickly, while with
the other the pain seeps in gradually and lasts for a long
time.

The important thing is to understand our differences and
respect them. Each person's grief is unique. Many factors
affect the way each of us will react, including our relationship
with the person for whom we grieve and our own emotional
makeup. Out of love and respect for one another, let's try to
be as helpful as we can to our loved one without questioning
how or why we process grief in the way we do. ❦

*T*ODAY'S THOUGHT: *What differences exist
in the way you and your spouse process grief?*

Let brotherly love continue. Do not neglect to show hospitality to strangers. . . . Let marriage be held in honor among all, and let the marriage bed be undefiled. . . . Keep your life free from love of money, and be content with what you have. Hebrews 13:1-5

These are what might be called "household rules"—challenging us to live in harmony with every member of our family and, in turn, with the members of our Christian family and then with the world.

There are many opportunities to celebrate life within the walls of our own home. A friend of ours had a childhood tradition—the family "loving cup." When the family gathered for a special occasion, the cup was filled and passed around for a series of toasts appropriate for the occasion. One toast was: "To keep a marriage brimming full as the loving cup, when you are wrong, admit it, and when you're right, shut up."

That toast is a good household rule itself, reminding us of the importance of living together in peace and harmony. It's good to have an honest and open relationship in the marriage and in the home, but we don't need to waste our time arguing about who is right and who is wrong. 🍎

*T*ODAY'S THOUGHT: *What are some of your household rules?*

LOVE

But as for me and my house, we will serve the Lord.
Joshua 24:15

One of Aesop's fables tells about a bat that was involved in a war between the beasts and the birds. The bat tried to belong to both parties. Whenever the birds won a battle, the bat would fly around announcing he was a bird. But when the beasts won a fight, he would assure everyone he belonged to the beasts. Soon both sides discovered his hypocrisy and rejected him. As a result, said Aesop, the bat flies openly only at night.

The theme of Joshua's final sermon is "Choose this day whom you will serve." In chapter 24, Joshua bids farewell to the people he has led so long and so successfully. He foresees, however, their temptation to follow other gods than the one true God. He knows that many will, like the bat, want to be both bird and beast. Thus, he persuades them to pledge their loyalty to God.

It is a choice we all have to make. We make it once and for all, but we also have to make it again and again, day by day. As a Christian married couple, we want to serve the Lord, and we want all of our household to do so. It is as we demonstrate our faithfulness to God before one another (by all that we are, say, and do) that we strengthen and reinforce the commitment to him that is at the heart of our covenant. ❦

*T*ODAY'S THOUGHT: *To what extent do you and your house serve the Lord?*

As one whom his mother comforts, so I will comfort you.
Isaiah 66:13

Most of the lessons we have covered have had to do almost exclusively with the husband and the wife, and that has been intentional. That is where the primary obligation between human beings exists. But when a married couple has children, they are not only a blessing, but a responsibility we must assume with the utmost care.

Archbishop Michael Ramsey said, "We who are Christians believe that the family is a part of God's scheme of things. When men and women take part in the procreation of children they have the wonderful privilege of sharing in God's creation of human life, and they are called to do this in God's way. And God's way means that procreation takes place by a man and a woman who are joined together in a lifelong union, a union in which they give themselves to one another until death parts them. That is the atmosphere of love and stability into which, in God's design, children are born."

We have talked about how the covenant of marriage is a three-party arrangement because God is a partner along with us. When there are children, they also become a part of the arrangement, and our responsibility to them requires faithfulness to one another. ❧

*T*ODAY'S THOUGHT: *Are your children given their proper place in your circle of love?*

And in the morning, a great while before day, he rose and went out to a lonely place, and there he prayed. Mark 1:35

We have individually, and together, led many workshops, conferences, seminars, and retreats on prayer over the years, yet we find there is always more to learn about prayer. We have also found that as our children have grown, left home, and begun families of their own, the need to pray for them doesn't cease—it becomes greater.

In trying to find a more effective way to pray for our loved ones, we've found that as we take the matter we're praying about more seriously, we sense more of God's purpose. Here is a nine-step method of praying that might work for you.

We come to God in *humility,* recognizing we can't do it, but he can. We pray *honestly,* from the bottom of our hearts, letting the tears flow when our hearts are especially sad or joyful. We *have faith* that God can handle the situation and *confidence* that he will. We pray *in Jesus' name* and, to the best of our ability, *in accordance with God's will.* We *persist* in our prayer, and we pledge ourselves *to do anything* in connection with the prayer that he might ask of us. Finally, we *thank him* for caring more about the person and/or situation than we do. ❧

TODAY'S THOUGHT: *Is this a method of prayer you are willing to try?*

Jesus said to him, "Have you believed because you have seen me? Blessed are those who have not seen and yet believe."
John 20:29

Because we live in a world that is largely unchristian and, in many cases, hostile to any real showing of faith, we have to have a lot of faith as married couples. Faith in God must be at the center of the Christian home.

Father Andrew, an Anglican monk, said this, "We have to remember that we will never have this life again. In this life we have a unique opportunity of serving God and our neighbor in a particular way, and that will never come to us again. It is well for us to remember that we have our opportunity here and now to witness to God in this world and to do our part as well as we can while there is time. This life is the opportunity of faith. When we can see God, we shall be able to give him our worship and our love, but we shall no longer be able to give him our faith. That belongs to our period here."

Faith is following our Lord when we cannot actually see him or know beyond doubt that he is there. Father Andrew also said, "Great faith is not the faith that walks always in the light and knows no darkness, but the faith that perseveres in spite of God's seeming silences, and that faith will most certainly and surely get its true reward." ❧

*T*ODAY'S THOUGHT: *When was your faith last tested?*

You shall tithe all the yield of your seed, which comes forth from the field year by year. Deuteronomy 14:22

When we were a newly married couple and were first asked to consider pledging a certain amount to the church, the one who called on us certainly used the soft-sell approach. He was a banker with whom we had a loan on our new house. He saw we were enthusiastic about our faith and that we were glad to have the opportunity to pledge. This made him a little anxious, and he went out of his way to assure us we shouldn't pledge too much: "You're just getting started. It will be awhile before you are able to earn a comfortable salary," he said. "After all, the church is getting along all right on its present income." He never even mentioned tithing.

As a result, we pledged a nominal amount. It was a decision we regretted when we later learned about tithing. Once we began to give God 10 percent of our income, our joy of participating in the life of the church and the service of God became infinitely greater.

It's difficult to give away 10 percent of your income when you are young and struggling, but it only becomes more difficult later. As a couple becomes accustomed to living on more than 90 percent, decisions concerning expenses lock us into a lifestyle that is not the one God wants for us. Giving the first 10 percent to God gets our priorities in order at the beginning of our life together. ❦

*T*ODAY'S THOUGHT: *Where are you and your spouse on the matter of tithing?*

For where your treasure is, there will your heart be also.
Luke 12:34

The passage of Scripture that concludes with this verse (Luke 12:22-34) has to do with priorities. Jesus is teaching his followers not to be anxious.

A young wife had come to pastor Larry Christenson for advice about the couple's future needs. She was thinking of going to work despite having two small children at home. The husband needed some additional education, and getting that education would reduce the family income for a time. After he had heard the woman out, Christenson concluded that the children needed the mother at home more than the couple needed the added income.

When the husband came home that evening he said he had come to the same conclusion. It wasn't the right time for the wife to go to work; they would just have to manage things some other way. They decided to stop worrying and trust God. A few days later, a young widow came to see Pastor Christenson about a problem she had: finding someone to care for her little boy during the day while she worked. Immediately Christenson thought of the other young woman, got the two of them together, and both found the solution to their problems. The widow would leave her boy with the woman and could pay her a reasonable sum for keeping him. The mother was able to stay home with her children and take care of the other boy as well. ❧

*T*ODAY'S THOUGHT: *When has trust in God brought an unexpected solution to your problem?*

LOVE

The body is not meant for immorality, but for the Lord.
1 Corinthians 6:13

It's easy to get trapped into the world's way of looking at things, especially when it comes to matters of personal morality. Sometimes it's hard to see that God's rules are for our benefit and help us in the long run, whereas ignoring them or disobeying them can get us into serious trouble. We want to adopt a "live and let live" attitude that goes along with the current cultural norms rather than strict obedience to Scripture.

Fortunately for us, early in our married life we were in an adult Sunday school class that studied William Law's classic, *A Serious Call to a Devout and Holy Life.* We learned in that class about how practical the Bible is in dealing with issues of morality. For one thing, we learned that in addition to "fleeing fornication," it's a good idea to stay away from books, movies, and magazines that stimulate sexual desires.

There's no doubt that much of what we are is shaped by media and the conversations to which we expose ourselves. We seldom give the Bible credit for being a practical guidebook, but God's reasons for sexual purity are found in the words of many verses of Scripture. The Bible, rather than the trash that the world makes available to us, reveals depths of meaning and principles by which we can live. ❦

*T*ODAY'S THOUGHT: *How much time do you spend in the Bible versus exposure to less healthy influences?*

LOVE

If any one thirst, let him come to me and drink. John 7:37

In these verses, Jesus is talking about the "living water" that he makes available to us. It is the power and love of God that can be in us, overflowing for the benefit of others.

Author John Sanford learned a truth about "living water" when he was a boy visiting his family's summer place in New Hampshire. It was a 150-year-old farmhouse without modern conveniences. The water supply came from an old well that stood just outside the front door. The water was especially cold and pure, and the well never ran dry.

Later the Sanfords were able to improve the place, adding modern plumbing. The old well was sealed over. One day, out of curiosity, Sanford uncovered the old well to see how it was doing. To his surprise, it had gone bone dry! Why? Because the little rivulets of water that feed a well like that close up when the steady flow of water through them comes to an end. The well went dry because it hadn't been used.

As long as our love flows, as married couples, it is always fresh and pure. When we neglect one another, the wellspring of love begins to dry up. But Jesus gives us "living water" so we can provide "loving water" to one another. ❦

*T*ODAY'S THOUGHT: *Are you keeping the water flowing in your marriage?*

But God said to him, "Fool! This night your soul is required of you." Luke 12:20

The rich fool had more possessions than he knew what to do with, so he decided to build bigger barns to hold all that he had.

The wife burying herself in her children in order to fight loneliness or the husband fighting his loneliness by worka-holism are both making the same mistake. In their book *Your Money or Your Life*, Joe Dominguez and Vicki Robin say, "Our jobs are also called upon to provide the exhilaration of romance and the depths of love. It's as though we believed that there is a Job Charming out there—like the Prince Charming in fairy tales—that will fill our needs and inspire us to greatness. We've come to believe that, through this job, we would somehow have it all: status, meaning, adventure, travel, luxury, respect, power, tough challenges, and fantastic rewards. All we need is to find Mr. or Ms. Right Job. Perhaps what keeps some of us stuck in the home/free-way/office loop is this very Job Charming illusion. We're like the princess who keeps kissing toads, hoping one day to find herself hugging a handsome prince. Our jobs are our toads."

Under God, husband and wife are to put each other first, before work and other activities, even before our children. It's easy to get off track. We need regularly to remind ourselves of our priorities. ❦

*T*ODAY'S THOUGHT: *How recently have you examined your priorities?*

Turn thou to me, and be gracious to me; for I am lonely.
Psalm 25:16

Companionship is certainly one of the primary motivations for marriage. Deep within, we have a sense of loneliness that cannot be met as fully as through a happy marriage. For both husband and wife, entrance into marriage should mean the desire to meet each other's need for companionship.

Love focuses on giving one's spouse the companionship and intimacy he or she needs to eliminate loneliness. Marriage means being willing to be God's instrument for healing this loneliness or incompleteness in our spouse because God made us incomplete without each other.

Marriage is a covenanted arrangement between two people to become each other's companion for life. In marriage we covenant to keep each other from being lonely as long as we both shall live. This is the plan ordained by God.

God made us incomplete so we will seek out and find in each other that which will lead us to wholeness. It is a lifelong process. It can be a great joy. 🐦

*T*ODAY'S THOUGHT: *To what extent is your spouse your companion?*

November

NOVEMBER 1

LOVE

And they become one flesh. Genesis 2:24

In marriage each partner brings unique qualities representative of his or her gender, and special to his or her personality. Each has the potential to complete or fill out the other's life. The wife can bring completeness to the husband by bringing into his frame of reference a new feminine dimension. The husband brings to the wife a masculine perspective that enlarges her life.

To some extent, each person, whether male or female, has characteristics of the other. A very masculine man can have a tender side; a very feminine woman can possess masculine competitiveness. Those who have analyzed Jesus' personality have concluded that he had the ideal balance of the masculine and the feminine personality.

If we want to be more complete, we find that completeness by sharing life with our spouse. Each of us will still retain our distinct character, but we'll grow more whole by living with and learning from one another. Thereby we are molded more into the image of Christ. 🐦

*T*ODAY'S THOUGHT: *Can you see evidence of this type of growth in your marriage?*

NOVEMBER 2 *L*OVE

But you shall receive power when the Holy Spirit has come upon you; and you shall be my witnesses. Acts 1:8

God takes what otherwise might seem routine — a man and a woman joined in holy matrimony — and makes it divine. That is God's plan for marriage.

By the grace of God, the Christian marriage becomes the gospel in the flesh, our sermon to the world. It is a direct call by God to a lifestyle in accord with his intent and purpose.

Simply put, our marriage should model what it means to follow and be joined to Jesus. The love, faithfulness, dedication, and intimacy in our marriage should model our love, faithfulness, dedication, and intimacy in our relationship with Jesus. Our relationship with our spouse gives tangible evidence of God's love to the world.

God has empowered his people — Christians — to be witnesses to all the world. But, as married couples, we are more. There are many practical reasons for staying together in marriage: survival, companionship, economics. The truth is, however, that marital indissolubility can be pushed to a higher level: being a witness of the spiritual things of life. ❦

*T*ODAY'S THOUGHT: *How high a view do you have of Christian marriage?*

*L*OVE

But grow in the grace and knowledge of our Lord and Savior Jesus Christ. 2 Peter 3:18

If we were asked to name the primary vehicles of God's grace and presence in our lives, we might list Scripture, worship, prayer, etc. How many of us would immediately think of our spouse? We often forget the primary role our loved one plays in God's work of salvation in our lives.

As part of God's plan for marriage, we are meant to experience, through our spouse, the dynamics of God's salvation brought to us in Jesus Christ. Our loved one's touch is evidence of Jesus' unmerited and gracious gift of himself.

We are to experience more deeply God's forgiveness of our sins through the experience of our spouse's forgiveness of the wrongs we commit against him or her. We experience our need for repentance and integrity in our relationship with Jesus through our need for repentance and integrity in our relationship with our spouse.

As we grow in marriage, we grow in the grace and knowledge of our Lord Jesus Christ. 🍎

*T*ODAY'S THOUGHT: *In what ways do you see Jesus in your spouse?*

*L*OVE

Consider the lilies of the field, how they grow; they neither toil nor spin; yet I tell you, even Solomon in all his glory was not arrayed like one of these. Matthew 6:28-29

A local man has developed quite a bit of knowledge about, and relationship with, butterflies. As a result, many residents (including us) are beginning to have a new appreciation for these beautiful insects. Flowers for the yard are chosen on the basis of whether they will attract butterflies.

Some would consider such behavior excessive. Most people don't get excited about butterflies. Many of us seem to take God's beauty for granted. In our hurried and harried world there seems to be little time to "stop and smell the roses." Yet beauty is one of God's great gifts to us, to inspire us and fill us with wonder and joy. Many believe that earthly beauty is a foretaste of heaven.

We owe it to our loved ones to slow down and enjoy the beauty of life. We are models for our children, just as the "butterfly man" is to a whole community. In marriage, we are models for one another, letting each other know what we really value—our spouse more than anything. It's important to share the beauty of the world with our loved ones. ❦

*T*ODAY'S THOUGHT: *In what ways do you share the beauty of nature with your spouse?*

*L*OVE

He who has ears to hear, let him hear. Mark 4:9

A man who was running late in getting to the airport decided the only way to make his flight in time was by a shortcut through the countryside, a route he had never tried before. He was doing fairly well until he came to a fork in the road and had no idea which way to go. He rolled down his car window and hollered to a farmer, "Does it matter which way I go in order to get to the airport?" The farmer replied, "Not to me, it don't."

We must be careful how we word our questions or statements, particularly as we communicate with our spouse. It's important for us to understand one another. Serious disputes can erupt if we don't. Something that needs to be done can be missed. Feelings can be hurt because a statement is misinterpreted. There really is no need for this when we love one another. Surely we can take the time and effort to be more careful what we say so we are sure the communication has been clearly given and properly received. ❧

*T*ODAY'S THOUGHT: *Have you and your spouse miscommunicated recently? How did it happen? How could it have been avoided?*

For everything there is a season and a time for every matter under heaven. Ecclesiastes 3:1

Just as there are life stages, there are marriage stages. The courtship stage is when we realize we've "fallen in love" and we begin to think about the possibility of a life together as husband and wife. Following the wedding are the early married years when we are getting adjusted to one another; there is still the freshness of "young love" but also some disappointment with one another for which adjustment is needed. This period is normally followed by a time during which success in the work environment is important at the same time children have arrived on the scene. Prioritizing our time can be vital during this period.

A settling-down time comes next; we have the home we've always wanted, our niche in the workplace, and the children are growing up. Crises can soon appear on the scene, however: problems with the children, the death of relatives, illnesses. In love, and by the grace of God, we cope.

The later part of our life together begins with the empty-nest syndrome, when the children leave home. We have more time together, but we soon realize we are slowing down, not able to do as much as we used to. Ultimately we move into retirement stage, and then death. Fortunately, for Christians this "final stage" is just the threshold to a new beginning, life with Christ eternally, for which marriage can prepare us as nothing else can. ❦

*T*ODAY'S THOUGHT: *What stage are you in? How are you handling it?*

LOVE

If we say we have fellowship with him while we walk in darkness, we lie and do not live according to the truth.
1 John 1:6

Having reflected yesterday on the stages of marriage, today we face a critical issue head-on. Married couples who are serious about their faith are not immune from the possibility of adultery. As a matter of fact, if we believe in the influence of Satan in the world today, perhaps we can accept the fact that Christian couples are targeted for adultery. Satanists pray for the destruction of the Christian home.

Each of us has a responsibility to decide how we will handle tempting persons or situations before they occur. We need to have an "I'm not available" sign stamped on our heart, and the conviction to speak those words to anyone who would try to lead us astray. Otherwise, we can get blindsided at a point of spiritual, emotional, or psychological weakness and do something we will later deeply regret.

Marriage is a covenant with our spouse and God. There will be times when we're angry with or hurt by our spouse (almost to the point of wanting to get even) and God doesn't seem present to us. At those times, we will be vulnerable to sexual temptation. But that is no excuse. As Christian married people, we are fully responsible for our moral choices. ❦

*T*ODAY'S THOUGHT: *How well prepared are you to deal with an adulterous threat to your marriage?*

LOVE

It happened, late one afternoon, when David arose from his couch and was walking upon the roof of the king's house, that he saw from the roof a woman bathing; and the woman was very beautiful. 2 Samuel 11:2

King David is an example of the fact that success can lead to adultery. Success can lead to arrogance. We know how good we are in what we do, we're impressed with the power we have, we think we're invulnerable. Unfortunately, the pride that makes us think we're invulnerable is the very thing that makes us extremely vulnerable. Pride gives Satan a highway into our heart. Here's what can happen.

Our success and the pride with which we display it causes us to rise above everyone else (even our spouse). Suddenly, we are alone. The isolation we have created for ourselves leads to fear, insecurity, and denial. Typically, a person caught in this cycle will look for some method of escape from himself or herself, some new challenge.

Because the challenge is not the answer to the predicament, greater and more daring challenges will be sought. There will be an insatiable appetite for adventure. In such situations, adultery is just around the corner.

"Pride goes before destruction" (Proverbs 16:18). If we aren't realistic about who we are before God (which is what real humility is), we are on a dangerous road. Our marriage deserves better than that. ❦

TODAY'S THOUGHT: *How realistic are you about yourself?*

*L*OVE

The faithfulness of the Lord endures for ever. Psalm 117:2

The Lord is faithful to us in all ways. We can be faithful to him by being faithful to our spouse. Here are some of the things God tells us through Scripture:

"Rejoice in the wife of your youth, a lovely hind, a graceful doe. Let her affection fill you at all times with delight, be infatuated always with her love. Why should you be infatuated, my son, with a loose woman and embrace the bosom of an adventuress? For a man's ways are before the eyes of the Lord, and he watches all his paths" (Proverbs 5:18-21).

"The commandment is a lamp and the teaching a light, and the reproofs of discipline are the way of life, to preserve you from the evil woman, from the smooth tongue of the adventuress. Do not desire her beauty in your heart, and do not let her capture you with her eyelashes; for . . . an adulteress stalks a man's very life" (Proverbs 6:23-26).

"The Lord . . . no longer regards the offering or accepts it with favor at your hand. You ask, 'Why does he not?' Because the Lord was witness to the covenant between you and the wife of your youth, to whom you have been faithless, though she is your companion and your wife by covenant" (Malachi 2:13-14).

God is a God of faithfulness. We need to be faithful as well. ❦

*T*ODAY'S THOUGHT: *Even joking about adultery and sexual matters can open the door a crack, leading to speculation and vulnerability.*

*L*OVE

The Lord preserves the faithful, but abundantly requites him who acts haughtily. Psalm 31:23

How can we be faithful to our spouse? First, by a commitment of the will. In the marriage service, we said, "I will." It is an act of the will to love. Feelings come and go.

Second, marriage is a relationship of wholeness. We give the whole of ourselves to the whole of our spouse. It's not a partial gift; thus, there is nothing left to give to anyone other than our spouse.

Third, we recognize that marriage is a growing relationship. It takes time for us to become everything to one another that God wants us to be. Patience, honesty, and total devotedness are needed.

Fourth, marriage is a relationship entered into between us and Jesus Christ. We are not alone in the covenant. Our union is a sacrament of the church.

Finally, we learn to forgive. It has been said that one good marriage takes two good forgivers. These are steps to faithfulness in marriage that apply to us all. ❧

*T*ODAY'S THOUGHT: *Are all these steps to faithfulness meaningful to you? Why or why not?*

God is faithful, by whom you were called into the fellowship of his Son, Jesus Christ our Lord.   1 Corinthians 1:9

Having looked at the theological steps to faithfulness, let's now consider some practical steps to insure faithfulness in marriage.

The first has to do with schedule, priorities. We are asked to do all sorts of things; there is always someone wanting us to be somewhere, to do something. Our time with our spouse should be our top priority. Therefore, we need to be sure that we have put our special times with our loved one on the calendar so we can honestly say, "I already have an engagement."

The second faithfulness builder is good communication. Are we sharing with our spouse what is going on in our life, and are we listening attentively to what is going on in his or hers? Are we making plans together?

The third is caring enough to make life as joyful as possible for our spouse. Flowers, gifts, dates, cards: Are we remembering the special occasions, and making special occasions out of ordinary days? Do we help with household chores? Do we run errands our spouse can't do because of a work schedule? Do we let our spouse know how special he or she is? ❦

*T*ODAY'S THOUGHT: *If you were arrested for loving your spouse, could it be proved in court?*

*L*OVE

Let what you say be simply "Yes" or "No"; anything more than this comes from evil. Matthew 5:37

Accident reports are filled with interesting stories concocted by people who undoubtedly are concerned about financial liability for what has happened and are feeling guilty for violating traffic laws.

Some examples can be quite amusing. "As I approached the intersection, a stop sign suddenly appeared where no stop sign had ever appeared before. I was unable to stop and had an accident." "I pulled away from the side of the road, glanced at my mother-in-law, and headed over the embankment." "I had been driving for forty years, when I fell asleep at the wheel and had an accident."

These poor attempts at communication cause us to laugh, but they make an extremely important point. Good, clear communication is important in life—and essential in marriage. ❦

*T*ODAY'S THOUGHT: *How is your communication as a couple?*

Even though you do not believe me, believe the works.   John 10:38

People who have been involved in Twelve Step programs are familiar with the expression, "Act yourself into a new way of living instead of trying to live yourself into a new way of acting." This is sometimes abbreviated to "fake it until you can make it."

Sometimes we need to demonstrate our love for our spouse even when we don't feel like it. A major way to break negative feelings toward one another is to put love into action for the benefit of our spouse. If we do so, our spouse will probably begin to return love to us.

Jesus told those who would not believe his words to look at what he was doing. When things are going the wrong way in our marriage, rather than trying to talk our way out of it we can simply do the loving thing. Often that action will get things back on the right track. ❧

*T*ODAY'S THOUGHT: *What do you need to do to let your spouse know of your love?*

LOVE

And forgive us our debts, as we also have forgiven our debtors.
Matthew 6:12

Many of us are offended by the proliferation of four-letter words today. In the verse from the Gospel of Matthew, Jesus gives us a two-letter word that can be even more offensive: *as*. We get what we give; we don't get what we are unwilling to give. If we won't forgive the other person, we cannot expect God to forgive us.

Many of Jesus' teachings are similarly tough. If we're going to be his people in the world today, there are certain expectations of us. If we're going to represent Jesus, we have to be like Jesus.

There is no better training ground for forgiveness than in the home. The importance of our relationship, the constancy of it, the intimacy and vulnerability all work together to make it likely we'll often fail to live up to each other's expectations. But marriage gives us many opportunities to seek and grant forgiveness when we fail. The well-rounded Christian home is not a place free from offenses; it is a place where offenses are forgiven. ❦

*T*ODAY'S THOUGHT: *Is there something your spouse has said or done that you have never forgiven? What will you do about it?*

NOVEMBER 15 LOVE

Be merciful, even as your Father is merciful. Luke 6:36

When we do offend our spouse and there is pain in the relationship, we need to be merciful to one another. Where there is no mercy, there can be no intimacy.

People cope with relational pain in one of three ways. The first is *withdrawal.* We've been hurt; the pain is so great we don't even want to talk about it. Maybe we feel we've been through this one before; our spouse failed us then and has done it again. What's the good of talking about it? We'll just fight. We hope the pain will go away if we're alone. But it doesn't.

A second way of coping is to *attack.* We think, *If I let my spouse get by with this, it'll just happen again. Enough is enough! It's time to remind him/her of all the things he/she has done to me. I'll get even.* This coping mechanism doesn't work either.

The third way is *forgiveness.* It's the most creative way to deal with the pain, and it's the one that will lead back to intimacy. After all, we love this person more than anyone in the world. Isn't he or she worth a little forgiveness? ❦

*T*ODAY'S THOUGHT: *Have you had relational pain in your marriage? If so, how do you deal with it?*

NOVEMBER 16 LOVE

If you bite and devour one another take heed that you are not consumed by one another. Galatians 5:15

An English vicar's wife was having a yard party. She invited everyone in the parish; but, by some mistake, one of the oldest, most devoted, and least forgiving of the parishioners failed to receive her invitation. The woman was furious. And she let everyone in the community (except the vicar's wife, of course), know of her fury.

The day of the party, the vicar got wind of the uproar and told his wife what had happened. Being the considerate person she was, she immediately dropped the preparations for the party and went to the woman's home to apologize. "We're so sorry you failed to get an invitation," she told the woman. "Of course we want you to come." "It's too late," the woman replied. "I've already prayed for rain."

Overlooking slights like failing to get invited to the party almost cheapens the significance of real forgiveness. Author Lewis Smedes has said, "Real forgiveness is love's toughest work and love's biggest risk." Real forgiveness comes when we deal with heartfelt pain we don't deserve; things like betrayal, disloyalty, and even infidelity. Forgiveness is the only thing that can heal pain of that magnitude. The gospel is rooted in forgiveness. It's the reason Jesus died for us. 🍂

*T*ODAY'S THOUGHT: *Have you ever had to deal with "real forgiveness"?*

17

All have sinned and fall short of the glory of God. Romans 3:23

There are four stages to forgiveness. The first stage is *crisis:* the moment we become aware the offense has occurred. Our reactions can lead us from shock to disbelief, to painful reality, and back to shock again. There is real pain and sometimes guilt or shame *(maybe I'm the one who's at fault)*.

The second stage is *anger.* Some Christians think they're not supposed to get angry. However, angry *feelings* are not sinful; angry *actions* are. This stage is crucial. We have to acknowledge the anger in order ultimately to experience healing. We must be honest about what has happened and how we feel, but we must also renounce revenge, consider what our part may have been, and remind ourselves of the consequences of unforgiveness.

The third stage is *healing.* We ask God to help us see the person who wronged us as God sees him or her. It's also helpful to be able to differentiate between what the person did and who he or she is.

The fourth stage is *coming together again.* We invite the offender back into our life. Life together can become more satisfying and joyful than it was before. ❦

*T*ODAY'S THOUGHT: *Do you need to forgive your spouse for anything? If so, consider using the above stages as steps toward reconciliation.*

I want to test the sincerity of your love by comparing it with the earnestness of others. 2 Corinthians 8:8 NIV

Do your outside activities contribute to a balanced life, or do they leave little time or energy for your spouse and the things you could do together? The following exercise tests the genuineness of your love for your spouse by helping you evaluate your activities through four questions.

First, does the activity bring you together, or drive you apart? Does this activity support mutual interests, or is it something that only benefits you?

Second, does the activity build you up, or tear you down as a couple? Is it constructive to your marriage, or destructive?

Third, does the activity express your love and loyalty toward your spouse, or reveal self-centered individualism or personal ambition?

Fourth, does the activity require sacrifice on your part, your spouse's part, or in the marriage relationship? And, if it does, is God asking you to make that sacrifice? ❦

*T*ODAY'S THOUGHT: *Set aside time to do the above exercise together.*

We all, with unveiled face, beholding the glory of the Lord, are being changed into his likeness from one degree of glory to another; for this comes from the Lord who is the Spirit.
2 Corinthians 3:18

As married Christians, we learn that our relationship with Jesus is a normal, continuous process of new beginnings, just as our relationship with our spouse is.

We are meant to encounter and be transformed by the humility that comes from being accepted —without merit— by our spouse. Our spouse's godly example helps us to become more like Jesus, as we strive for purity and holiness.

As we are loved, unconditionally, we no longer fear giving of ourselves. Giving becomes a greater desire. In the process, we move from knowing Jesus as Savior to freely and unconditionally giving ourselves to him as Lord —to be the ruler of our lives. ❦

*T*ODAY'S THOUGHT: *How are you being transformed by the grace of God as reflected through your spouse?*

LOVE

In the world you have tribulation; but be of good cheer, I have overcome the world. John 16:33

The world advertises complete fulfillment *now*. However, this is false advertising because the world can never deliver on its promise. Only after this life, in paradise with Jesus, can we enter into complete fulfillment.

Jesus promised paradise to only one person: a thief dying on a cross. He told the rest of us that we'd have trouble in this world. But he followed that statement up by saying we can be confident because he has overcome the world. The truth is, we'll not be complete in this imperfect world; because something is wrong with the world, we'll hurt.

In this life, our marriage relationship is God's best vehicle to attain the most fulfillment. There's no question it'll be imperfect; we'll experience pain, but there is nothing better. There are many ways we can pursue life. We can place our primary attention on our work, on our children, on our ministries; but nothing will bring us the fulfillment marriage can bring. That is God's plan, and we can be grateful to be a part of that plan. ❦

*T*ODAY'S THOUGHT: *In what specific ways does marriage prepare you for paradise?*

NOVEMBER 21 LOVE

I am sure that he who began a good work in you will bring it to completion at the day of Jesus Christ. Philippians 1:6

People cannot find ultimate fulfillment in a purely horizontal relationship. Marriage is meant to be the greatest experience in this life that grounds us, teaches us, and points us to our eternal relationship with Jesus. Though we can experience some of that relationship with Jesus now, its fullness is in the age to come.

God takes what we would call a normal relationship and raises it to the level of the divine. He can do this because our marriage is a covenant, a relationship in which he is a partner. He can empower this relationship to give us a foretaste of the heavenly banquet he has prepared for us.

Our marriage, though inherently imperfect, offers the best possible opportunity for satisfying life in this transient world. In addition to pledging our lives to the Lord, marriage is the best investment we can make in this lifetime. ❦

*T*ODAY'S THOUGHT: *What investment are you making in your marriage?*

NOVEMBER 22 *LOVE*

But they who wait for the Lord shall renew their strength, they shall mount up with wings like eagles. Isaiah 40:31

In the movie *Hook*, the central character, a grown-up Peter Pan, needed to learn three things: that his work shouldn't be an all-consuming passion that alienated him from his wife and children; that there has to be joy in life, even frivolous joy; and that he had to have his "happy thought"—the realization that finding what he truly valued in life would allow him to soar like an eagle.

That's a worthwhile formula for us all! The pressures of our vocation, particularly if both of us are working outside the home, can become all-consuming, to the detriment of our loved ones. This is true whether we like our job or not. Coming home with nothing but work on our mind can cast a pall over our loved ones.

The solution is balance, and balance comes from being in a right relationship with God. The Christian's happy thought is accepting Jesus Christ as Lord and Savior. Following him and his way for us can put everything else, including our vocation, into perspective. If he is our priority, our family life automatically comes next, and our lives become balanced. That balance produces joy, and we can soar like an eagle. ❦

*T*ODAY'S THOUGHT: *Are you "soaring like an eagle"? If not, what primary thing keeps you from soaring?*

LOVE

Have mercy on me, O God, according to thy steadfast love.
Psalm 51:1

How many times have we said something and immediately wished we could take it back? We wish what had happened had been on a movie set, and rather than spoiling the movie with the inappropriate line, the director could holler, "Cut!" and we could do a second take.

The above psalm was David's desire for a second take. He had committed adultery with Bathsheba and plotted the death of her husband so he could have her for his own. When confronted with his sin by the prophet Nathan, David was deeply repentant. But what had happened could not be taken back.

Although the things we have said and done that we wish we could take back may not be as grievous as David's sin, it is right for us to be repentant. We need to ask the forgiveness of our spouse. We also need to pray, with David, that God will "set a guard over my mouth" and "keep watch over the door of my lips" (Psalm 141:3), to help prevent our saying or doing the wrong thing when we know we may be in danger of doing so. If we approach critical moments with both a prayer that God will guard our words and an attitude of repentance concerning those things we may say that are unloving and unkind, we can vastly improve our communication. Then we'll seldom need a second take. ❧

*T*ODAY'S THOUGHT: *Have you ever wished for a second take? What can you do when a similar situation arises?*

NOVEMBER 24 LOVE

Martha, Martha, you are anxious and troubled about many things. Luke 10:41

Friends of ours, who run a retreat center for married couples, tell about the problems that occur when husbands and wives undertake an activity for which they have different expectations. For instance, both want "a night out"—but the wife wants a nice supper and the husband, a humorous movie.

Because these expectations were not shared in advance, the husband was not concerned about when and what they ate; so, when they found themselves running late, his solution was to go to the movie first and then grab a hamburger at McDonald's when it was over. Although capitulating to her husband's desire, the wife seethed with resentment because she had missed the romantic, leisurely dinner she had in mind and hated the silly movie. The predictable explosion followed.

The story of Martha and Mary is the Bible's example of mixed expectations. Martha thought she was doing just the right thing to take care of Jesus and his friends, while Mary lazily sat around listening to what Jesus had to teach. What a shock to Martha to find out that, from Jesus' point of view, it was Mary who was doing the "right thing"!

The answer: We need to share our expectations in advance of undertaking a particular activity, to make sure we understand and are sensitive to the needs of our spouse. ❧

*T*ODAY'S THOUGHT: *When have you and your spouse had different expectations?*

LOVE

He went up into the hills by himself to pray. Matthew 14:23

There are times when we need to be alone. Jesus needed to be alone with his heavenly Father in prayer. We also need times of retreat, when we can be alone with God in prayer, or just away from the hustle and bustle of everyday living. Sometimes we even need to be away from our spouse.

There is, however, an aloneness that can damage our marriage—when we keep to ourselves the things that are troubling us because we don't want to weigh our spouse down. But whether we want them to be or not, our problems *are* our spouse's problems. When we avoid our loved one, or are distracted by our own concerns, the natural tendency is for our spouse to assume he or she is the problem. If our relationship with one another is what it should be, we sense our spouse's troubled times, and we worry without knowing what to do.

In the covenant of marriage, we are to help and comfort one another in prosperity and adversity. We're bound to one another in a way that no other relationship equals. There's no room for the aloneness that excludes our spouse from our life issues. God means for us to share them—and lighten each other's load. 🍂

*T*ODAY'S THOUGHT: *Do you need to share a burden with your spouse? to lighten your spouse's load?*

For I the Lord your God am a jealous God, visiting the iniquity of the fathers upon the children to the third and fourth generation of those who hate me. Deuteronomy 5:9

God is not being wrathful just for the sake of being wrathful. He is simply pointing out a principle of life. Those compulsive, ungodly things we do have a tendency to repeat themselves from generation to generation. Where there is child abuse or alcoholism in a parent, statistics show that the condition is often repeated in the children until the pattern is broken.

This says at least two important things to us as Christians. First, we need to discover our compulsions that are adversely affecting our spouse, our children, perhaps even our grandchildren. When we discover what they are, we need to repent and bring them to a screeching halt. If we cannot do that on our own, we need to get help.

Second, because we are Christians, we can break negative patterns that may already exist in our family system, whether they are our fault or someone else's. Jesus said, "Whatever you bind on earth shall be bound in heaven, and whatever you loose on earth shall be loosed in heaven" (Matthew 18:18). That is serious business! Again, we may need help to break the bonds that hold our family hostage. But Jesus assures us they can be broken. ❦

*T*ODAY'S THOUGHT: *Are there any destructive patterns in your family that need to be stopped?*

LOVE

None of us lives to himself, and none of us dies to himself.
Romans 14:7

A common problem occurs when one of us is enamored of a time-consuming activity, such as golf. More often than not, it is the husband who is the golfer, so that's the illustration we will use, although the same principle would apply regardless of the activity and which spouse is involved in it.

The wife of the golfer loves her husband and simply wants more time with him, but she wants him to be the one who notices that he is paying too much attention to golf and too little to her. When he doesn't, she explodes with, "Your golf is ruining our lives; you have no time for me." The husband immediately becomes defensive and says something like, "What do you mean? I've done everything around the house you've asked me to do!" Argument leads to argument, and the situation deteriorates.

How different the results would be if the husband realized he was neglecting his wife and raised the question himself. Being realistic enough to admit that will probably not happen, the wife has the alternative of raising the issue in a more positive way that reflects how she really feels: "Honey, I love you, and I need to be with you more. How can we work that out?" 🌾

*T*ODAY'S THOUGHT: *Are you engaged in any activity that may be hurting your marriage?*

NOVEMBER 28 LOVE

Pray then like this: Our Father who art in heaven, hallowed be thy name. Matthew 6:9

In our pluralistic society, our family name doesn't seem as important as it once was. That's a shame.

Author Peter E. Gillquist said, "Many of us were raised by concerned parents who understood the value of an honorable family name. Being identified with that name, and with the parents who gave it to us, we behaved in a manner which honored it. I have a friend who often asks his children what their last name is as they go out of the door on their way to some special event. His children have been taught that whatever they do reflects on the family's name, either for the better or for the worse. It is their name, individually and collectively, and they are expected to use the honor of that name as a reference point for their conduct, wherever they are."

That's not a bad practice, even in our own day. And it's important to remember that, as Christians, we bear two names, because we are also of the family of God. ❦

TODAY'S THOUGHT: *Does your family name have a good reputation in your community? Why or why not?*

Make me to know thy ways, O Lord; teach me thy paths.
Psalm 25:4

In our church, there are two vocational ministries: ordination and holy matrimony. Approximately 1 percent of the members of the church become ordained, while 90+ percent become married. Most denominations require three years of intensive training in preparation for ordained ministry, and little more than three hours of instruction in preparation for marriage!

What can we do about that? Two things immediately come to mind. First, we can encourage the church to take preparation for marriage more seriously. Intensive premarital instruction can give couples at least a glimpse of the commitment they'll be making through holy matrimony.

But marriage is a lifelong vocation, and we need more help than premarital instruction, no matter how good it is. Thus, we can encourage our church to provide other resources for healthy marriage, such as marriage-enrichment programs and counseling.

What we ask the church to do is only one answer, however. The second thing we can do to improve instruction in the vocation of marriage is to work at it ourselves. ❦

*T*ODAY'S THOUGHT: *In what ways are you working on your marriage?*

NOVEMBER 30 LOVE

What therefore God has joined together, let not man put asunder.
Mark 10:9

In his book *The Closing of the American Mind*, Alan Bloom says that, among the many items on the agenda of those concerned about America's moral regeneration, "I never find marriage and divorce." Faced with an increasing divorce rate, people living together rather than getting married, and the increasing deterioration of the American family (once the backbone of our society), there is still a great deal of apathy.

Does the old adage, "The family that prays together, stays together," even ring true today? Although divorce rates among Christian couples are generally lower than those among non-Christians, there is little to brag about.

Whenever a marriage breaks down within our fellowship of faith, the loss and pain is not limited to the couple alone. As members of the body of Christ, we all are affected; we all lose.

We all face a challenge. Not only do we need to do all in our power to make our own marriage the best it can be, but we need to be sensitive to the marriages of our brothers and sisters in Christ. When trouble brews, we should be available to help in any way we can. ❧

TODAY'S THOUGHT: *What can you do to strengthen Christian marriages?*

December

LOVE

DECEMBER 1

Refrain from anger, and forsake wrath! Fret not yourself; it tends only to evil. Psalm 37:8

In Alcoholics Anonymous, the buzzword *HALT* stands for hungry, angry, lonely, and tired. When introduced into a discussion, it is for the purpose of reminding alcoholics that they should never make a major decision when they are experiencing one of those debilitating conditions. People whose emotions are being controlled—or, at least, unduly influenced—by hunger, anger, loneliness, or weariness cannot make objective decisions. They are likely to lash out at others and to act irresponsibly.

This principle applies especially to marriage. Because our spouse is the person closest to us, we need to protect our relationship with the greatest care. If we see that an argument is brewing, or that we are about to launch into a discussion or action we aren't prepared to handle properly because of a HALT condition, we need to say so. It is far better to admit our vulnerability, momentary though it may be, and avoid the inevitable, senseless dispute. 🍎

TODAY'S THOUGHT: *Have you failed to HALT? What were the results?*

LOVE

So faith, hope, love abide, these three; but the greatest of these is love. 1 Corinthians 13:13

One of the great Christian writers of our day told of an incident that happened when his children were young. During that time, knowing the stress that raising small children placed upon his wife and the resulting tensions in the home, he would bring her a present from time to time. But, even if the surprise were an especially good one, his wife always somehow seemed disappointed. The gift was never enough to offset the situation that had caused it to be given.

Then, one snowy and wind-howling night, he and his family were gathered around a fire. His wife was knitting and he was reading. The children were crawling all over him. At one point, he stopped his reading and began unselfconsciously to play with the children, wrestling with them good-naturedly and bringing forth squeals and giggles. Through the scramble of little bodies, he looked across the room and saw tears of joy streaming down the face of his wife.

We are most winsome in our intimate relationships when we simply love others rather than trying to manipulate and change them. Spontaneous love paints a much more beautiful picture than those things we intentionally do in order to effect some result of our own choosing. ❧

*T*ODAY'S THOUGHT: *How spontaneously affectionate are you?*

Lord, teach us to pray. Luke 11:1

As the number of Christian divorces increases, the old saying, "The family that prays together stays together," is being questioned. However, a study done to analyze church attendance, prayer, and marriage stability produced interesting results.

Although the divorce rate in the United States is high, researchers found that, among couples married in the church and who continue to attend church regularly, the incidence of divorce drops to one in fifty. And, for such couples who also have a prayer life at home, the divorce rate drops to one in 1,105!

The point is that, for Christian marriages to work, there is much more involved than just a perfunctory commitment to prayer, such as asking a blessing at the evening meal. If we are truly serious about our faith, a regular participator in our community of faith, and have a real prayer life at home, we can "beat the odds." The best kind of prayer life is for husband and wife to pray together daily, and to take time for individual, personal prayer as well. Prayer needs to be informed by Bible study, as we increasingly come to know our Lord. It's a package deal: As we learn to avail ourselves of the resources God provides, we'll grow in our relationship with him and with each other. 🍎

*T*ODAY'S THOUGHT: *What steps can you take to improve your attendance and participation in the life of your church? your prayer life at home?*

Your wife will be like a fruitful vine within your house.
Psalm 128:3

As women have entered the work world to a greater extent in recent years, some have attempted to minimize the innate differences between men and women. But as Christians, we should seek to understand and honor these differences.

Studies show that women have a more profound interest in people and feelings, and in building relationships. Men tend to be interested in practical solutions reached through deductive reasoning. Men are more inclined toward competition and "winning" than women, as reflected in their interest in contact sports. Women are inclined to find their identity through close relationships, while men gain their identity through their vocation.

These differences play themselves out in our married life and can lead to serious conflicts in the togetherness of any married couple. A classic example is the husband who has received a wonderful promotion that will necessitate his family moving to an entirely new area of the country. While he feels rewarded and challenged, his wife feels disoriented and threatened.

It's important that we recognize that differences exist, that they are normal, and that they are due adequate consideration. God made us different so we can learn from one another. ❧

ʃODAY'S THOUGHT: Are you and your spouse able to recognize and honor your differences as man and woman?

He who is greatest among you shall be your servant.
Matthew 23:11

One of the most consistent differences between men and women is manifested when they drive together on a business trip or family vacation. The man is typically interested in getting where he's going and thinks nothing of driving five hundred miles each day. The woman, on the other hand, is relational and wants time to stop for coffee, relax, and smell the roses. This attitude is extremely frustrating to the man who sees stopping frequently as a waste of time and a threat to his goal of getting to his destination.

What does the Bible tell us? We are to lay down our lives for one another, and that is especially true in the marriage relationship. Instead of solely seeking our own goals, we are to find healthy ways to serve one another.

In the trip scenario, the husband can help by setting goals that take his wife into consideration. Must he really drive five hundred miles every day? The wife can accommodate her husband's need to accomplish by finding ways to build relatedness into the trip without having to stop every few hours. She packs a thermos with coffee and nibbles, perhaps a picnic lunch; and she brings with her stimulating conversation concerning matters of mutual interest. ❦

*T*ODAY'S THOUGHT: *How can you make your next trip more enjoyable by finding ways to meet your differing needs?*

Love does not insist on its own way. 1 Corinthians 13:5

Men and women also differ sexually. While a man needs little or no time in preparation for sexual intercourse, a woman does. Women are stimulated by touch and romantic words, by the personality of the man, while men are visually stimulated.

Therefore, men who hurry into and through the sex act cheat their wives because they rob them of the fulfillment they need and deserve. The husband can also be insensitive to the effect that conflict between him and his wife can have on their sexual intimacy. A wife who feels she's emotionally trampled on won't be ready for sexual intercourse and can even feel prostituted when psychologically forced to have relations with her husband in such a state of mind.

Many men enter marriage thinking they know everything about sex but actually knowing very little about how to express unselfish love. Women want to be more than an expert sexual companion; they want to be lover, home-maker, best friend, and respected partner in the marriage covenant. If men would spend as much time thinking about how to nurture the love relationship, in all of its aspects, as they spend in thinking about sex, marriages today would have a much greater record of success. ❦

*T*ODAY'S THOUGHT: *Are you able to talk frankly about your sexual expectations? Why or why not?*

You shall love the Lord your God. . . . You shall love your neighbor as yourself. Matthew 22:37, 39

In *If Only He Knew,* Gary Smalley asks, "As a husband, do you realize that your wife's natural ability for developing relationships can actually help you fulfill the two greatest commandments taught by Christ—loving God and others (Matthew 22:36-40)? Jesus said that if we obey these two commandments, we are fulfilling all the commandments. Think of it! Your wife has the God-given drive and ability to help you build meaningful relationships in both these areas."

Cecil Osborne, in *The Art of Understanding Your Mate,* says that women tend to become an intimate part of the people they know and the things that surround them. The children, and even the home, become a natural extension of the wife; when either is criticized, it is as though she is being criticized herself. Therefore, when a father yells at the children, his words can cut deeply into the heart of his wife.

Just as the husband is a gift to the wife as provider and authority figure, the wife is a gift to the husband as the nurturer of relationships. If men allow their wives to be an example to them, they can learn much about how to relate to others and to God. ❦

*T*ODAY'S THOUGHT: *What have you learned from each other about loving God and others?*

LOVE

So each of us shall give account of himself to God. Romans 14:12

The kind of accountability that existed in the early days of the faith seems lacking among many Christians today. That band of people who first brought the gospel to the world apparently lived in intimate relationship with God and with each other. They lived in the church and went to the world; today, we tend to live in the world and go to church.

Many Christians would probably be offended if a Christian friend confronted them about words spoken or actions taken that were inappropriate to the faith. They don't feel that others have a right to judge or to interfere. Yet, if we are accountable only to God, we can convince ourselves that what we did was really not that bad and that we have an all-forgiving God. It is only when we are willing to share our Christian responsibilities and our failures to live up to them with another human being who has the right to confront us with our self-deception that we are truly being accountable to God.

This principle applies with at least equal force to our marriage. If we want our marriage to be all it should be, we should be willing to be accountable to at least one other human being (other than our spouse) for loving our spouse and children. This should be someone who is free to ask us how we are doing as a couple and as a family, to confront us when we need to be, and to regularly hold us up in prayer. ❦

*T*ODAY'S THOUGHT: *To whom (other than your spouse) are you accountable for your marriage relationship?*

His enemy came and sowed weeds among the wheat.
Matthew 13:25

Following devastating floods, a former missionary traveled to a remote part of Argentina to find out what his people needed. He crossed an area of mud slides, arriving covered with slime from his knees down. There, waiting for him, were two women who had lost everything in the flood, but had a bowl and enough fresh water to wash his feet and legs.

What lessons we can learn from Christians in Third World countries! Those two women, who had lost everything, were willing to give the only thing they had. On the other hand, many of us, in the Western world, live in relative luxury and resent inconveniences. Yet, learning to live with inconveniences is one of our primary tests as Christians, as human beings, and certainly as married couples. It has been said that contentment is not getting what you want but enjoying what you have.

We have a choice. We can resent things that interfere with our own selfish desires and can be bitter about them, or we can see them as challenges God has placed before us to help us grow. If we become bitter, the result will be bitter fruit for our spouse and family. If we only do the best we can, and then leave the results to God, our lives will be more grace filled, and our family life much more pleasant. ❦

TODAY'S THOUGHT: *How do you regard inconveniences?*

Let your light so shine before men, that they may see your good works and give glory to your Father who is in heaven.
Matthew 5:16

There is so much to do today! There never seems to be time enough for each other, for our children, for the things that need to be done around the house.

How many of us arrive home at night in a state of total frustration? So much to do, so little time to do it in, and there we were—stuck in traffic, held up at work by our supervisor, or running errands on the way home!

With all these demands and frustrations, there is certainly no time for God. Right?

Wrong. The busier we are, the more we need God. We simply have to be more creative in finding time. Being stuck in traffic is a wonderful time to pray. Riding on a commuter train is time to pray for the people around us, if we are left standing; if seated, there is time for Bible study and devotional reading.

The crucial thing is to arrive home with our "light shining" for the benefit of our spouse and family. That can happen only if we are in relationship with God and with one another. 🍎

*T*ODAY'S THOUGHT: *What image do you reflect when you come home? How can it become the light of Christ?*

I praise you because I am fearfully and wonderfully made.
Psalm 139:14 NIV

Our relationship with one another in marriage is enhanced by a realistic understanding of ourselves. We are truly fearfully and wonderfully made, but self-awareness and self-examination are things we tend to avoid. As someone once said, "If I got rid of my defects of character, I might find that I have no character at all!"

It isn't easy for any of us to admit our defects. It hurts to realize we aren't all we should be, especially to admit that we continue to do compulsive things we really don't want to do. But it's even harder to see our strengths. Because of the low self-image so many people have, they can come up with a list of defects twice as long as their list of strengths.

An accurate and balanced inventory is necessary if we are to be in a right relationship with ourselves, God, and our spouse. The key to inner health is in trusting God. He has made us as we are; we truly are fearfully and wonderfully made. We should rejoice in our gifts and seek the grace of God to deal with our weaknesses. If we are truly willing to release them to him, he can bring us to wholeness. ❧

*T*ODAY'S THOUGHT: *How honest are you in examining yourself? What do you find?*

Put on the whole armor of God, that you may be able to stand against the wiles of the devil. Ephesians 6:11

For the benefit of our spouse and family, as well as ourself, it is wise to begin each day by committing it and our loved ones into the hands of God. Many people accompany this commitment by "putting on the whole armor of God," as spelled out in Ephesians 6:10-17.

That's not a bad idea. We need all the protection we can get in these troubled times. The characteristics Paul lists in the Ephesians passage (which we'll be examining over the next several days) are characteristics of Jesus. As Christ's people in the world today, we should want to be clothed in the attributes of Christ. As we take these unto ourselves, we are mentally and spiritually equipped to be Christ to the world around us. Perhaps even more so, we are thereby protected from the wiles of Satan.

As a Christian, what is our obligation to spouse and children? It isn't to be the best looking, nor the smartest, wealthiest, or most successful. It is to be the best we can be from God's point of view. That means committing each day into God's hands and equipping ourselves as best we can to do his will and be his person all the day long. ❦

*T*ODAY'S THOUGHT: *How do you feel about "putting on the whole armor of God"?*

DECEMBER 13

And take the helmet of salvation. Ephesians 6:17

If we start at the top in getting dressed with the whole armor of God, we begin with the helmet of salvation. In theological terms, *salvation* means at least two things. The one that immediately comes to mind is that, because of Christ, we have been saved from eternal doom and given eternal life in him. That is no small salvation!

The other aspect of salvation is that it means wholeness for those who accept Jesus Christ as Savior and follow him as Lord. God did not come into the world in human form just to get us to heaven. We Christians are not to deny life, be miserable and downtrodden here on earth, just because there is a better place to which we will go. God wants us to grow in wholeness here on earth, and that is part of what Paul promises in the helmet of salvation.

Worship should enhance us spiritually, uplift us in joy. Prayer should be real contact with God, who loves us and wants to be in relationship with us. Bible study should guide us into God's abundant life. Fellowship should give us strength and courage as we share with others, giving and receiving the precious love of God. These are just some of the ways in which God and his church bring us into wholeness. As they become real in our lives, we can convey that reality to our loved ones.

TODAY'S THOUGHT: *In what ways do you manifest growth toward wholeness to your spouse and family?*

LOVE

Put on the breastplate of righteousness. Ephesians 6:14

As we continue to "put on the whole armor of God," the next piece of equipment is the breastplate of righteousness. Plato, when accused of certain crimes, was quoted as saying, "Well then, we must live in such a way as to prove the accusations a lie." In that sense, righteousness truly becomes a protective covering. Our reputation is a defense against false accusations. If we are living a righteous life, that life speaks for itself.

The Bible has a great deal to say about righteousness. The prophets of the Old Testament demanded right action and fair dealing between people. But, in its broader sense, righteousness has to do with being in a right relationship with God and with our fellow human beings. Righteousness is conforming to the will of God.

To some extent, our righteousness as spouse and parent acts as an umbrella over the rest of our family. Our being in a right relationship with God and with one another provides a protective shield against evil. Unfortunately, the reverse is true; if we are not living holy lives, if we are engaging in ungodly activities, we have a "leaky umbrella," leaving our loved ones defenseless. We must continually ask ourselves, *Which type of umbrella do I want to be?* ❦

*T*ODAY'S THOUGHT: *In what ways are you truly putting on the breastplate of righteousness?*

Having girded your loins with truth. Ephesians 6:14

This part of the "whole armor of God" is usually referred to as either the girdle or belt of truth. As someone once remarked, "When you are having a problem with overweight, 'the belt of truth' takes on a whole new meaning!"

Truth really has to do with openness and honesty in our relationships. As our primary relationship, our marriage covenant needs especially to be centered in truth. There can be no room for deception. Deceit leads to cover-up, which leads to guilt, which leads to shame, which leads to self-justification and rationalization, which can lead to treachery, which can lead to destruction. Each step is a step away from our relationship of togetherness.

Often we don't want to face the truth. Pontius Pilate asked Jesus what truth was; but instead of waiting for an answer, he went out and tried to work out a compromise with the crowd (John 18:38-40). Too frequently we are tempted to compromise the truth rather than being entirely honest and open in our covenant relationship with our spouse. Instead, Scripture tells us to put on the belt of truth. ❦

*T*ODAY'S THOUGHT: *Are you being truthful with your spouse? Why or why not?*

Having shod your feet with the equipment of the gospel of peace.
Ephesians 6:15

There are at least two ways of looking at the shoes of the "gospel of peace." One is that we are to put on our shoes of the gospel to carry the good news of Jesus Christ to others, the work of evangelism. It is, of course, something that all of us, based on our particular gifts and opportunities, should do. This way of looking at the verse of Scripture puts the emphasis on the gospel aspect of it.

However, as married couples, we need to specifically consider another word in the verse: *peace.* Our homes should be centers of peace. When we arrive home at night, we should sense we are coming into a safe harbor, a haven of love and peace. We have faced the stress of the work world all day, and we need peace.

Peace can rest on the home only if it dwells in the hearts of the couple who live there. Here peace does not simply mean absence of conflict, but a deep and abiding relationship with God and with each other. It comes from caring enough about God and our spouse to give quality time to the effort. ❦

*T*ODAY'S THOUGHT: *To what extent is your home a center of peace? What can you do to make it more so?*

Taking the shield of faith, with which you can quench all the flaming darts of the evil one. Ephesians 6:16

We need a big shield of faith! It's what holds all the rest of our "whole armor of God" in safety. If we didn't have faith, there would be little sense in the rest of the equipment, and we would be spiritually naked and unprotected. We would be Adam and Eve after the apple incident.

Faith, of course, grows through regular worship of God, Bible study, prayer, and other spiritual disciplines. It also grows through support of one another. Especially within the covenant of marriage, it's important for us to affirm each other's experiences of Christ. We need to "talk God" to one another so we come to see God in the everyday occurrences and are increasingly aware of his watchful protection of us. We also need to share and experience this in the fellowship of other Christians. One of the most profound aspects of evangelism in our day is sharing with one another the power of God in our lives.

Temptation is the enemy of our faith in Christ, and it can be extremely detrimental to our marriage. Therefore, when Paul spoke of the shield of faith, he had in mind a particular kind of shield. It was made with two sections of wood glued together so that fiery darts, dipped in pitch and set aflame, would sink into the shield, killing the flame. Faith can deal with the darts of temptation; it can quench them as nothing else can. ❦

*T*ODAY'S THOUGHT: *What can you do together to build faith within your family?*

And take . . . the sword of the Spirit, which is the word of God.
Ephesians 6:17

Next to the shield of faith, the sword of the Spirit—the Bible—is perhaps the most important ingredient in the "whole armor of God." Without faith, we are naked. Without Scripture, we are ignorant.

We feed our children the food they need to grow into strong and healthy human beings. We seldom neglect our own physical nourishment. But what about our spiritual nourishment? Isn't it at least as important for us to be growing in the knowledge and love of the Lord as to be growing physically?

The Bible is God's story. It's the best way we can come to know about him. If we have a method of studying Scripture that allows us to absorb a little bit of understanding each day, we are sure to grow spiritually. Over a period of time we become increasingly better at knowing what God's will is for our lives. It's an ongoing process, and the richest and most rewarding way we can spend our time. ❦

*T*ODAY'S THOUGHT: *What method of Bible study works for you? Is it enough?*

Do not be anxious about tomorrow, for tomorrow will be anxious for itself. Let the day's own trouble be sufficient for the day. Matthew 6:34

Chronic anxiety is an affliction, and sometimes it's catching. When we're caught up in tomorrow's (or next year's) problems, we cannot see the beauties or joys of the day at hand. It's bad enough for us to miss God's glory for today, but often we rob our spouse of that special gift also by wearing a worried, down-in-the-mouth attitude that can spoil the day for him or her as well.

To heal the affliction of anxiety, a large dose of prayer is recommended, followed by a period of listening for God's answer. We can then either act on the guidance received or leave the problem with God to deal with in his own way. Only then are we free to enjoy the serendipities in, and to "celebrate the temporary" of, the only day we can live right now. Yesterday is gone, tomorrow may not come. The problem may still be unresolved, but if we have left it with God, worrying about it is an admission that we think him incapable of dealing with it properly! 🌿

*T*ODAY'S THOUGHT: *What problem do you need to deal with today? If you analyze it prayerfully, point by point, perhaps it won't seem so overwhelming.*

When I heard these words I sat down and wept, and mourned for days; and I continued fasting and praying before the God of heaven. Nehemiah 1:4

Decisions, decisions—especially with Christmas only a few days away! Many times a day we make big and little decisions. But we can have the benefit of God's guidance, if we will but ask him.

What color should we paint the living room? Get out the color charts, but also say a prayer, asking God for guidance. Too unimportant to bother almighty God? Not at all. In the first place, the color of our living room affects our whole attitude toward life; it can be restful or brash. In the second place, what is unimportant before God? Do not we parents hear the inconsequential as well as the vital requests of our children?

Someone once asked a priest who heard confessions in a convent what it was like, and he replied that it was rather like being stoned with popcorn. But he was faithful in dealing with each penitent with his full attention.

Are you in the process of buying something—a new rug, automobile, house, stock? Be sure to ask your spouse to join you in your prayer quest. ❦

*T*ODAY'S THOUGHT: *To what extent do you involve God, through prayer, in your decisions?*

Judge not. . . . The measure you give will be the measure you get.
Matthew 7:1-2

Christmas should be an especially joyous time of the year, but often it's not. Even Christians seem to get caught up in the commercial side of Christmas; we wear ourselves out with celebrations, parties, the hassle of shopping, and so much more. Perhaps we shouldn't be surprised that during this season psychological problems come to the fore, and the number of suicides increases.

With that in mind, many would be surprised to learn that "what goes around comes around" is just another way of saying the above quoted verses. Hasty words, spoken in anger, have a way of becoming a boomerang. The first thing we know, they smack us in the face. But loving, forgiving words return to bless us.

"Judge not, condemn not; forgive and give" is a brief rule of thumb for happy marriage. We often hear that marriage has to be a 50-50 proposition, but the truth is that it should be 100-100. If both parties are willing to give and forgive 100 percent of the time, then at least 50 percent of the time we will be on the receiving end. That's a pretty good return according to any measure! ❦

*T*ODAY'S THOUGHT: *What can you do to relieve the pressure in the home that results from the approach of Christmas?*

Pay all of them their dues. Romans 13:7

Some friends recently celebrated their fiftieth wedding anniversary. They have learned many important things about married lives, including how to handle finances. They say this: "Our policy about money has proven itself. We divide the income and we divide the bills between us. That way both of us know when it is an especially tight month. And, from time to time, one of us 'borrows' from the other because of an unusually heavy load. We have preserved a complete openness in financial matters, and it has paid off.

"Along the way, we have found that praying about major expenditures pays off as well. We have some investments, and we pray for guidance concerning them. When it's time for a new car, we are in prayer about the make and model. The same goes, of course, for the times we have had to make decisions about a new house. This openness to God and with each other is the very foundation of the Christian married life. It has helped us to make real our prayer that God will 'give us this day our daily bread.' And it has helped us see money as a means to an end, not an end in itself." ❧

TODAY'S THOUGHT: *God gave you people to love and things to use.*

LOVE

Behold, I am doing a new thing; now it springs forth, do you not perceive it? Isaiah 43:19

The beginning of a marriage is exciting—learning to know each other, making a home together, planning for the future. Things seem perfect, and the world is rosy.

Then reality sets in. If great care is not taken to deal with problems, they can soon throw a monkey wrench into the smooth machinery of the marriage. One of us feels worn out from overwork; the other feels neglected. There comes a time of sameness, things are taken for granted, the excitement is gone. There are grinding daily chores. Meeting the needs of the children becomes paramount, and adult needs are shoved aside.

This can be a deadly trap. But, behold, God is always doing a new thing. He gives us a new and wonderful day every twenty-four hours. How we regard each day has to do with our state of mind. A great Christian leader used to say, "It's either 'Good morning, God,' or 'Good God, morning!'" We can either rejoice in the sunrise or grumble about having to get up so early. We can exercise because our bodies are temples of the Holy Spirit, or we can indulge ourselves and become overweight and unhealthy. We can meet our problems head-on, or let them control our lives. Behold, God is doing a new thing every day in our marriage. Together, we can reach out and accept the lovely gift he has for us. ❧

*T*ODAY'S THOUGHT: *Is your marriage cup half empty, half full, or running over?*

DECEMBER 24

LOVE

The Lord waits to be gracious to you. . . . Blessed are all those who wait for him. Isaiah 30:18

At what should be the holiest times of the year, such as Christmas Eve, we often get out of our devotional routines. There are so many last-minute things to be done, we just can't get around to having quiet time with the Lord. Pressure builds, calamity strikes.

It's not that married couples can't find strength in the Lord when calamity strikes; often the high drama of calamity causes us to rise above our usual faith to build strength upon strength. Instead, it's the nitty-gritty that breaks our back: the little irritations that build, minor frustrations, unthoughtful remarks, slights by our loved ones. Problems mount up until we reach the breaking point.

For these reasons, it's especially important for us to have quiet time with the Lord in times of pressure. God wants us, as a married couple, to "be there" for each other—something we can truly do only if we are in a right relationship with the Lord. If we are to manifest to our loved one the "peace that passes understanding" just when our spouse needs to sense that peace, it has to be peace that has been gained from our reliance on, and time spent with, God in prayer, worship, and Bible study. ❧

TODAY'S THOUGHT: *What are you doing to spend time with God?*

Every good endowment and every perfect gift is from above, coming down from the Father of lights. James 1:17

"Oh no, you shouldn't have." How often do we respond to a gift in this manner? We seem to take the position, at least ostensibly, that the gift is undeserved, or is too much, or is beyond the ordinary means of the giver. With God as the giver, however, our attitude tends to change. We don't often greet some undeserved blessing with a prayer that begins, "Oh, Father, you shouldn't have."

God is the unlimited giver. Although we frequently treat his blessings as good luck or coincidence, instinctively we know his unequaled capacity to give. Why not be bold enough to ask God to give us those things that will make us a better spouse and parent, a better person? We can't earn those qualities, but God can certainly give them to us, if we are receptive.

The best and most perfect gift God gives us is our spouse. We don't deserve him or her; it's only by God's grace we have him or her. As we celebrate this Christmas day, let's thank God for the spouse he's given us. Let's be bold in our prayer by asking God to make our marriage everything he wants it to be. ❦

*T*ODAY'S THOUGHT: *What are you most grateful for this Christmas?*

In peace I will both lie down and sleep; for thou alone, O Lord, makest me dwell in safety. Psalm 4:8

When a friend was at the beach surfcasting one day, his mother-in-law came down and said, "Hurry up and fish; we need to go to Miami." (He said he wished she had told the fish to hurry up instead of him.) That expression, "hurry up and fish," became a byword in his family.

When we lie awake at night, needing to go to sleep, we may well think, *I've got to hurry up and go to sleep.* This is particularly a problem when there has been excitement in the family (such as Christmas), and there are a million thoughts running around in our heads. We owe it to our spouse (particularly if we are sleeping in a double bed!) to be able to get a good night's rest so we'll be cheerful and energized for the day ahead, rather than tossing and turning and keeping our spouse awake, as well as ourselves.

But "hurry up and go to sleep because tomorrow is a big day" just assures us of not being able to sleep. If we, instead, commit tomorrow to the Lord and begin to praise him for loving us and caring for us, before we know it we are waking up to a bright and beautiful new day. The Lord allows us to lie down in peace and to dwell in safety. ❦

*T*ODAY'S THOUGHT: *How do you deal with insomnia?*

But God shows his love for us in that while we were yet sinners Christ died for us. Romans 5:8

It is when we are most unlovable that we most need to be loved. While we were still sinners, Christ was willing to die for us; and that principle is one we need to take seriously in marriage.

When our loved one is cross, uncommunicative, offended by everything we say and do, and totally miserable to be around, he or she needs to be loved. When our spouse rejects us, blames us for whatever is going on in the family or in life, it is often because he or she is feeling rejected and/or rejectable, blamed or blameworthy. Instead of retaliating, we need to take Christ as our example and show acceptance, understanding, and love.

In diagnosing the situation as one in which our loved one is really not angry with us but with himself or herself, we also don't need to tell our spouse not to feel that way. That won't help. What will help is a lot of patience, and time. In a real sense, we have to "die" for our loved one. We have to be willing to give totally of ourself for our spouse to understand how totally he or she is loved. In the process, we might remember that there are times when we are the one feeling unlovable and yet needing desperately to be loved. ❧

*T*ODAY'S THOUGHT: *When your spouse feels unlovable or unloved, what can you do to show your love?*

Trust in the Lord, and do good; so you will dwell in the land, and enjoy security. Psalm 37:3

When we're newly married, struggling to make enough money to live on and thinking about how to afford beginning to have children, salary is important. We compare our meager remuneration with what others are receiving, and it may not seem fair. We see other couples who have advantages we didn't have, such as inherited money, the benefit of a better education, "connections," and frankly, we're envious.

In middle age, as we try to pay for our children's education and maintain a household that's comfortable to us and appropriate for our age and status in life, we may wonder why others are doing much better financially.

As we approach and move into retirement, we wonder whether there will be enough to cover medical expenses and provide a place for us and our spouse that will allow for quality of life. Others don't seem to have to worry; yet we too have worked hard, have served the Lord, have been wise in our stewardship.

In all these situations, God asks us not to compare ourself with others, but to trust him. ❧

TODAY'S THOUGHT: *When it comes to finances and security, how much do you trust the Lord?*

He determines the number of the stars, he gives to all of them their names. Psalm 147:4

As we stand, hand in hand, looking up at the stars on a cloudless night, we can be aware of the expanse of God's kingdom, and the beauty and glory of what he has created. To see such a sight is to marvel at the God who can create and sustain all this magnitude of being. We can also picture ourselves as children, secure in his loving arms, trusting in one who can deal with our petty problems with the pointing of a finger.

When, on the other hand, pollution fills the air, or the rainy season is on us and the sun, moon, and stars seem to have disappeared from the sky, it's easy for us to be overwhelmed and discouraged. As a friend from Canada once summarized her winters: "First the sky becomes gray, then the ground becomes gray, then the people become gray."

As married couples, we must cope with life on the dank, dreary days as well as the clear, crisp ones. Choices under stress are as unclear as the cloudy sky. But faith tells us that there are still stars in the sky, shining as brightly as we have ever seen them, above the overcast. Faith tells us that God is in his heaven and all is right with his world. He can pierce the darkness and give us the guidance we need. ❦

*T*ODAY'S THOUGHT: *How do you call God's goodness to mind in times of trial?*

For where your treasure is, there will your heart be also.
Matthew 6:21

If our spouse doesn't win first place (after God) in our heart, we lose!

If you began this series of studies on January 1, over the past year you've had an opportunity daily to think about and work on some aspect of your coupleness. You've been given tools to make your marriage covenant work. It was just a start but, we trust, truly a start.

Where do you go from here? There are more possible answers to that question than there is space to provide them. Perhaps you can go back to the front of the book and start over again. Each day you'll gain new insights into your relationship that you didn't see the first time around.

Additionally, there are many good Christian books on how to have an effective marriage and improve communication. Daily Bible study certainly is encouraged, and there are plentiful resources available for that good work.

But what else? Here's a suggestion. Sit down together at least weekly, at a set time when you can have both quantity and quality time, and answer these questions:

1. What especially deepened your love for each other this week?
2. What was the nicest thing you did for each other?
3. What made your marriage stronger this week?
4. What specific thing can you do this coming week to make your marriage even better? ❦

*T*ODAY'S THOUGHT: *What can you do to nourish your love for one another?*

LOVE

I am the light of the world; he who follows me will not walk in darkness, but will have the light of life. John 8:12

Most of us are familiar with the famous painting of Jesus standing at a door and knocking, with a lantern in his hand. There is a sense in which he is always standing at each person's door, patiently waiting to be invited in. When he is, he brings the light of life with him.

Likewise, Jesus calls us to be light (Matthew 5:14). Ours may be only reflected light, as we let the light of Christ shine through us, but that may be the only light another person will see today. God wants us to be the light for someone who is in darkness, to be his light to this broken and sinful world. As Christian married couples, we need to reflect the light of our covenant to other couples who may not be as fortunate as we.

As we reach the end of one year and stand in anticipation of another that is about to begin, we need time to reflect. This past year may have been an especially light-filled one for us, or maybe one that has brought pain and darkness. Most likely, it's been some combination of the two. Yet, even in our pain, the light of Christ was available to comfort us and show us the way. Let's carry that light in our lives, in our marriage, in our family, and into this new year! ❦

*T*ODAY'S THOUGHT: *What special "light" do you, as a couple, carry into the new year?*

original Document

original Document

original Document

original Document

original Document

original Document

original Document

original Document

original Document

original Document

X

original Document

ENDORSE HERE

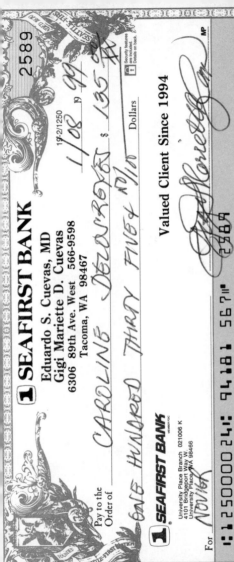